ROUTLEDGE LIBRARY EDITIONS:
ECONOMICS AND SOCIETY

Volume 18

INDUSTRIAL TRADE ASSOCIATIONS

INDUSTRIAL TRADE ASSOCIATIONS

Activities and Organisation

Routledge
Taylor & Francis Group
LONDON AND NEW YORK

First published in 1957 by George Allen & Unwin Ltd.

This edition first published in 2026
by Routledge
4 Park Square, Milton Park, Abingdon, Oxon OX14 4RN

and by Routledge
605 Third Avenue, New York, NY 10158

Routledge is an imprint of the Taylor & Francis Group, an informa business

British Library Cataloguing in Publication Data
A catalogue record for this book is available from the British Library

ISBN: 978-1-032-97576-4 (Set)
ISBN: 978-1-041-13647-7 (Volume 18) (hbk)
ISBN: 978-1-041-13648-4 (Volume 18) (pbk)
ISBN: 978-1-003-67082-7 (Volume 18) (ebk)

DOI: 10.4324/9781003670827

Publisher's Note
The publisher has gone to great lengths to ensure the quality of this reprint but points out that some imperfections in the original copies may be apparent.

Disclaimer
The publisher has made every effort to trace copyright holders and would welcome correspondence from those they have been unable to trace.

INDUSTRIAL TRADE ASSOCIATIONS

Activities and Organisation

1957

LONDON:
POLITICAL AND ECONOMIC PLANNING
16 QUEEN ANNE'S GATE

GEORGE ALLEN AND UNWIN LTD
40 MUSEUM STREET

Made and printed in England by
STAPLES PRINTERS LIMITED
at their Rochester, Kent, establishment

CONTENTS

ACKNOWLEDGMENTS

THIS report is the result of an inquiry carried out by PEP over a period of two and a half years, with the guidance of an Advisory Group drawn from industry, trade associations, the professions and the universities.

As is apparent from the text of the report, P E P has received a great deal of co-operation in this research. P E P is much indebted to the Federation of British Industries, to the National Union of Manufacturers, and to a large number of industrial trade associations; to many firms of all sizes; to several government departments; to the Registrar of Companies and the Registrar of Friendly Societies; to the Institute of Public Supplies Officers; to various local authorities and hospital groups; to several public corporations; to the Co-operative Wholesale Society Ltd., and to the Scottish Co-operative Wholesale Society and to many individuals. The survey on which the data in Chapter 8 is based was carried out for P E P by the Social Survey of the Central Office of Information.

The Group wish to thank the Senior Research Officer in charge of the research, Mr. George McRobie, and his colleagues, for the hard work they have put into the report.

INTRODUCTION

THIS report is concerned with associations found in manufacturing industry. During the past ten years much has been heard of the restrictive activities of trade associations. Apart from this, comparatively little was known about them, especially of the very large number outside the investigations of the Monopolies Commission. By contrast with the extensive literature on trade unions, there were no studies of the trade association as an industrial institution.

The inquiry which is the subject of this report was prompted by the results of a small sample survey of trade associations made by P E P in 1944 and published as a broadsheet.* That investigation aroused considerable interest in business and academic circles, and showed conclusively that associations had become a permanent and important feature of industrial life, and, as such, warranted more detailed and comprehensive study. To this end, the present report contributes the results of two and a half years' investigation into the structure, activities and organisation of national associations in manufacturing industry. This inquiry was made possible by a grant under the Conditional Aid Scheme for the use of Counterpart Funds derived from the United States Economic Aid.

Method of inquiry

The inquiry, which was started in October 1953, was carried out under the guidance of a P E P Group, whose members were drawn from industry, trade associations, the professions and the universities.

The material for the report was compiled from three principal sources: trade associations themselves; other organised bodies, including government departments; and individual firms. With the help of a large number of trade associations, detailed case studies were prepared of their histories, their scope and activities, and their organisation and administration. Some forty national

* *British Trade Associations*, PLANNING No. 221, 12 May 1944 (out of print). P E P has published two other broadsheets on this subject, *Government and Trade Associations*, PLANNING No. 240, 5 October 1945 (out of print), and *Industrial Trade Associations*, PLANNING No. 383, 25 July 1955. A section of the P E P report on *Government and Industry*, February 1952, was devoted to the consultative side of trade association activity.

associations, each representing a major industry, and about twenty smaller associations co-operated in this part of the inquiry. Additional information was drawn from the Registry of Companies and the Registry of Friendly Societies. Secondly, in order to establish the impact and effectiveness of the activities of a broad cross-section of associations and to discover how they set about the work of representing their members' interests, the co-operation of government departments, public corporations and local authorities was sought, and detailed studies were made of their experiences of associations. The third main source of material was individual firms, both large and small. About fifty large firms, including some of the largest concerns in the country, and over six hundred small firms were interviewed to find out what associations mean to them in their day-to-day conduct of business.

Combining the material from these sources, it was possible to build up some account of the development, influence and organisation of manufacturers' associations, which, although not exhaustive, at least provides much of the information necessary for a proper appreciation of their place in industrial organisation and their present and potential contribution to industrial efficiency.

All this information relating to the current activities and organisation of associations refers to conditions as they were during the course of the inquiry. There was no fully effective method of keeping up to date, and apologies must be made for any details which events have superseded by the time of publication. The Register at the end of the report, listing the names and location of some 1,300 national associations of manufacturers, refers to those which (so far as could be ascertained) were in existence in 1955.

Definition of "industrial trade association"

In carrying out this study it was necessary to adopt a workable definition of what constitutes an industrial association and to adhere to it strictly. Since the inquiry was concerned with extractive and manufacturing industry, associations of wholesale and retail distributors, merchants and importers were excluded from the outset. Organisations such as trade unions and professional institutions, whose members are individuals, not firms, were also excluded.

The basic definition of an industrial trade association used in the report was "a voluntary non-profitmaking body formed by independent firms of manufacturers to protect and advance certain interests common to all". But in order to restrict the research to manageable proportions, its scope had to be narrowed still further. In the first place, since associations covering an industry or a product were the main object of interest, all geographically-based associations (principally Chambers of Commerce) were excluded. Organisations which exist for certain limited, defined purposes were also left out; among these were research associations, employers' associations concerned primarily with labour matters, and export groups. This still left a large field to be covered, and eventually it was decided to concentrate on national associations. Local or regional associations were taken into account only where they were in fact representative of an industry concentrated in a particular part of the country.

This definition, with the severe restrictions mentioned, therefore indicates the full scope of the report. Attention has been concentrated on what is generally understood by the term "manufacturing" industries. This has meant that although they are included in all statistics and appear in the Register, quarrying, baking, newspaper, film and publishing associations have not been closely investigated.

The general aim of the inquiry and the report has been to present, within the limits of the foregoing definition, a balanced and comprehensive account of all aspects of industrial trade associations, rather than to give emphasis to any particular type of activity, form of organisation, or sector of industry. By this means it is hoped to show trade associations in proper perspective as industrial institutions.

PART I

History and Structure

CHAPTER I

GROWTH OF ASSOCIATIONS

THE first estimate of the number of manufacturers' associations in British industry was made in 1919 by Professor John Hilton, in a memorandum prepared for the Committee on Trusts.* In this he suggested that there were considerably more than five hundred associations of manufacturers then in existence. The committee's report itself listed thirty-five associations in the iron and steel industry—"not at all exhaustive"—and ninety others encountered by the Ministry of Munitions during World War I. What evidence there is suggests that the majority of associations at that time existed in the iron and steel, non-ferrous metals, building materials and fittings, and branches of the electrical and textile industries.

Since then numerous government reports have cited associations concerned with specific products or practices, but nothing in the way of a general picture appeared until 1944, when a sample inquiry by P E P† indicated that there were then about 2,500 trade associations of all kinds. This figure referred to associations of wholesalers and retailers as well as manufacturers, and included both regional and national bodies.

The inquiry on which the present report is based, as explained in the Introduction, has been concerned only with manufacturers' associations (or those which have manufacturer members) and, for most purposes, only with national associations. In the course of compiling this report it has been possible to give a more accurate figure of the number of associations in manufacturing industry. Excluding—with a few exceptions—local or regional associations, there appear to be about 1,300 associations of manufacturers at

* Appointed by the Minister of Reconstruction in 1918. "In view of the probable extension of trade organisations and combinations, to consider and report what action, if any, may be necessary to safeguard the public interest."

† *British Trade Associations*, PLANNING No. 221, 12 May 1944 (out of print).

the present time. Their names and location are listed at the end of this report, classified according to the Standard Industrial Classification.*

A rough map of the distribution of associations among industries can be made by grouping associations under the main headings of the Classification. There is a certain amount of overlapping, where associations are concerned with the products of a number of separate industries, but most manufacturers' associations cover products or groups of products which can be fairly readily identified with the standard classification of industries and their various sub-groups.

A distribution of associations under the fifteen main sections of the classification shows that the engineering, shipbuilding and electrical group of industries accounts for 180 associations, and the textile group for 170. There are between 120 and 140 associations in each of the three groups covering metal manufacture, metal goods, and food, drink and tobacco; and between 60 and 100 in each of the six groups covering chemicals and allied trades, non-metalliferous mining products, paper and printing, manufactures of wood and cork, clothing, and other manufacturing industries (a wide heading which includes rubber, toys, plastic goods, stationery, etc.). Mining and quarrying, vehicles, precision instruments and jewellery, and leather and leather goods each account for fewer than 50 associations.

This rough picture of numerical distribution (which is elaborated in Chapter 2) reveals little beyond the fact that there is a large number of manufacturers' associations. For within the industry groupings, and trade sub-divisions of them, there is a remarkable diversity of sizes and types of association. In terms of membership and representation alone, at one end of the scale there are associations such as the Society of British Aircraft Constructors, the Society of Motor Manufacturers and Traders and the British Electrical and Allied Manufacturers Association, each representing a major industry; at the other end are associations representing manufacturers of shoe rivets, corsets, umbrella ferrules, coffin furniture and specific types of cheese. They present an equally

* In the U.S.A. the *Department of Commerce Directory* gives the total number of associations in business as about 2,500. This figure, however, is acknowledged to include professional groups and others that are not strictly trade associations. The number of manufacturers' associations is estimated at about eight hundred.

wide variety in terms of their activities and their influence, their inter-relationships and their organisation.

What can account for this abundance of associations in every branch of manufacture? Part of the answer must lie in the external forces which persuade autonomous concerns to act together, and it seems possible to trace at least the chief influences which have fostered this co-operation. Analysis would have been simplified if the various possible motives for association had operated independently and at different times, making it possible to attribute clear-cut motives to different periods of association growth during the past seventy or eighty years. This is not so; but it does seem possible to discern the influences predominant at different times—each usually reinforcing rather than supplanting earlier reasons for co-operation.

A general indication of the chief circumstances under which associations multiply is provided by the numbers of associations registering as companies and as trade unions at different times. The legal forms open to associations are described later in this report. For present purposes it is sufficient to note that while the great majority are unincorporated and have no public record of their existence, some which are eligible to register as companies have done so, and some which are in law trade unions have so registered or taken certificates to this effect.

Of the 1,300 or so manufacturers' associations known to exist at present, some two hundred are registered companies and about fifty are registered or certificated trade unions. The rest, about 1,050, are unincorporated. The dates of registration or certification of these 250 associations, which are set out chronologically in the Appendices (pp. 318–324), give some indication of the most rapid periods of growth and hence suggest reasons for their growth.*

There is a marked tendency for these dates of registration to group themselves round the two world wars. From 1881, when the first association was registered as a company, to 1913, 30 were registered as companies and 3 as trade unions. From 1913 to 1919, 31 were registered as companies and 12 registered or certified as trade unions. From then up to 1939, 53 were registered as companies, 23 as unions (with a noticeable increase in the numbers taking trade union status from 1931 onwards). Between 1940 and

* This is on the assumption that there is at least a rough correspondence in the increase in number of registered and non-registered associations.

1947 there is another marked concentration, 55 having been registered as companies, 12 as unions, and from then up to 1955, 22 as companies, 4 as unions.

Given this pointer to the periods of most rapid growth, it is now intended to look in more detail at the reasons why associations emerged when they did.

Factors affecting growth

The movement towards the formation of manufacturers' associations in their present form developed during the last quarter of the nineteenth century. Before then there were undoubtedly many local associations, and in a few instances national (in addition to, or superseding, local) associations were in existence before the 1880s. The present British Paper and Board Makers Association, for example, can trace its ancestry back to 1799, the soap industry was early in the field with an association formed in 1867, and one or two others, for instance in milling, and brass and copper manufacture, date from the 1870s. But it was not until the last twenty years of the century that associations began to appear in any number and to make their existence known. Until the third quarter of the century there had not been much need for co-operative action, except on the labour front. From the 1870s conditions changed rapidly in the field of international competition, while labour organisations were stimulated by the Trade Union Act, 1871.

The initial forces behind this movement seem to lie in changes in the structure of industry and the growth of internal and international competition. Improvements in transport were widening markets, simultaneously extending areas of competition and making large-scale production worth while; and it was being made possible by advances in metallurgy and engineering. The necessary concentrations of capital were readily effected through joint-stock organisation, limited liability, the growth of a capital market and an efficient banking system. As the scale of enterprise grew and production tended to become not only more specialised—a fact which encourages association between firms using the same machinery and processes—but also concentrated in relatively larger firms, control over prices or output, or both, became possible by agreement between independent concerns. Firms whose high fixed costs made them susceptible to trade depressions, between whom competition was becoming a costly struggle among equals, rather than a simple elimination of the inefficient, clearly saw the necessity for such control.

The changing structure of industry thus provided the conditions, and the process of competition itself an initial motive, for co-operation. Taken together with the depressed and unstable conditions of industry after the boom of 1870–75, the growth of international competition, and the rise of a more powerfully organised labour force at home, these factors provided the initial reasons for association.

ASSOCIATIONS UP TO 1914

Control of competition, collective negotiation with labour, and problems arising out of international trade appear to be the principal motives for association up to World War I. So far as commercial regulation by associations is concerned, the movement towards industrial combination, both of permanent combinations and temporary associations, was attracting considerable attention in the early years of this century. In 1906 one observer of the industrial scene named over fifty associations which had been formed in the previous twenty years and were concerned with price or output control. These were chiefly in the iron and steel and the metal-working industries; strong associations existed in pig iron, malleable iron, rails, plates, galvanised iron, tubes, and a variety of small metal trades. Other industries which had by that time developed associations concerned, in one way or another, with the control of competition included milling, branches of chemicals and textiles, cables, rubber and photographic equipment. A number of resale price maintenance associations, including both manufacturers and distributors, were also active by the early 1900s.

Reasons given by manufacturers for the growth of associations concerned with price, output or other forms of limitation on competition were quoted in the Report of the Committee on Trusts,* and suggest that most associations of this character were formed under the pressure of competition both at home and from overseas, especially when markets were depressed. For instance,

* Memorandum by John Hilton in the *Report of the Committee on Trusts*, Cmd. 9236, (H.M.S.O.), 1919, p. 16.

> Co-operation began among the manufacturers only after a period of severe depression and acute competition. . . .
>
> The industry had been very unremunerative for many years and had stood in danger of being crushed out of existence by foreign competition and by too much competition among manufacturers at home, and it was realised that if the industry was to be saved at all the manufacturers would have to come together and form an association. . . .
>
> Its immediate object was the removal of price-cutting which rendered unprofitable practically the entire industry. . . .

One technique of control deserves special mention. This was the form adopted by the Birmingham Alliances, which were started by a bedstead manufacturer, E. J. Smith, in Birmingham in 1891, and spread to spring mattresses, metal and cased tubes, spun brass mounts and ornaments, rope and twine, metal rolling, fenders, china door furniture, china electrical fittings, iron plateware, coffin furniture, pins, marl, jet, and Rockingham ware—trades occupying, in all, some 500 employers and 20,000 workmen. In 1895 Mr Smith published a booklet advocating his method and describing it in some detail.* Each association issued minimum price lists based on average cost plus a percentage profit. The observance of these prices was ensured by an alliance with the trade unions, which, in return for a closed shop agreement and permanent provision for conciliation, undertook to work only for association members, and to call out on strike the employees of any offending employer, the strike being financed by levies on other employers. This method had considerable success for some years, but by 1899 the increase in the number of bedstead makers brought trouble, and over the next few years the alliances, both in this and in the other trades concerned, gradually broke up.

Many of these associations had brief and intermittent lives. That price agreement was not always easily reached, or adhered to, is evident in the course of an interesting account of the United Kingdom Soap Makers Association up to 1906, in *The History of Unilever.*† In the 1850s there had been a temporary price-fixing

* *The New Trades Combination Movement, Its Principles and Methods (as explained by E. J. Smith in a series of articles recently published in the* Birmingham Daily Post). Birmingham, 1895.

† Charles E. Wilson, *The History of Unilever* (Cassell), 1954, Vol. 1, Chapter V.

association of Northern Soap Makers, but it was not until 1867, "when the business world was shaken to its foundations by the fall of the old banking house of Overend Gurney, that the idea of association was revived again in the soap industry".

The association was certainly not at first concerned with price fixing in the full sense of the phrase. The first secretary

> was careful to stress the voluntary nature of the new association and to avoid any suggestion of interference with the free working of economic forces. Truth to tell, the scope of the Soap Makers Association was never easy to define and probably even its members were far from clear as to what it really was. It proceeded to deal on behalf of the trade with difficulties in the Russian tallow market, it prepared statistics of raw materials and it argued with public authorities about transport charges and Parliamentary legislation.

Frequent attempts were made up to 1900 to get agreement on prices and to limit advertising expenditure, but without success. "The history of our association", pronounced the chairman of 1893, "is a history of exploded agreements." In 1901 the association was recast; five regional associations, each with its own members, secretary and price agreements, were formed, and the central association supervised general policy. This worked successfully until 1906 brought crisis; the association appears to have languished, and combination began to replace voluntary agreement.

Although at that time—and indeed up to the present—published references to associations were concerned almost exclusively with restraints on competition, there are occasional references to other motives. For instance to

> the ever-spreading knowledge and recognition of common interests within a trade leading to common action locally and nationally for the improvement of trade processes, the furtherance of general commercial purposes, and the defence of all against intervention by Parliament, aggression by workpeople, or exploitation by the railways.*

Beyond a recognition of the existence of non-restrictive associations, however, there is scant information about them. What

* H. W. Macrosty, *The Trust Movement in British Industry* (Longmans, Green & Co.), 1907, p. 4.

follows is based largely on information provided by associations now in existence.

In some industries employers first came together to negotiate with labour; these associations later extended their activities, separate bodies sometimes being formed to deal with matters concerning their members in their capacity as manufacturers rather than as employers of labour. The present associations in shipbuilding, cotton spinning, clothing and boot and shoe manufacture developed out of employers' associations in this way. To glance at these in turn, the Shipbuilding Conference grew out of the Shipbuilding Employers Federation, which had existed from about 1900 with two secretariats in separate offices. In 1917 these employers' associations, of the Clyde and the Tyne, came together under one secretariat in London. The federation dealt primarily with labour matters but soon found itself faced with many industrial and commercial problems. Accordingly a separate body unencumbered with labour questions—the Conference—was formed in 1928 to cope with all commercial matters, leaving the Federation to deal exclusively with labour.

The Federation of Master Cotton Spinners Associations was formed in 1900, when it united a number of local associations of employers. There were two main reasons for its formation. The first was, broadly, the growing interest of Government in international trade with the growth of protectionist ideas—at that time the campaign against free trade was gathering momentum—and the second was the consolidation of trade union bargaining strength arising from unification among the unions. The federation defined its aims in these early days as: first, to remove difficulties which stand in the way of the smooth functioning of the industry, which may be due to government interference, international trade barriers, shortage of materials, etc.; secondly, to maintain satisfactory labour relations by collective bargaining, and thirdly to indemnify members against claims for compensation from workers in respect of accidents. The federation continues to negotiate with labour, but has greatly widened its field of activities in other directions.

The Wholesale Clothing Manufacturers Federation goes back to 1910, when employers in the heavy clothing industry associated to form the employers' side of a trade board; wages remained the chief concern of the federation for some years.

In boot and shoe manufacture, local associations had been formed as early as 1859 in Northampton, in Leicester and London in 1871 and 1882, and subsequently in other centres. These associations were created to combat what was regarded as the aggressive policies of the unions of boot and shoe operatives (formed into a national union in 1875), and in 1895 the local employers' associations, by that time nine in number, combined in a federal body. In 1898 this assumed its present name of the Incorporated Federated Associations of Boot and Shoe Manufacturers of Great Britain and Ireland. Like the Federation of Master Cotton Spinners, the Boot and Shoe Manufacturers have since extended their activities considerably while continuing to represent employers on the labour front.

Problems arising from overseas trade provided the chief stimulus to association in a number of cases. Alarm at the increasing imports of foreign flour was one of the chief reasons for the formation of the National Association of British and Irish Millers in 1878. The British Engineers Association was founded in 1912 on the initiative of some twenty prominent engineering firms, its chief purpose being to promote and protect the interests of British engineers abroad, especially in China, where the founding members believed that British interests were being neglected to the comfort of competitors. One of the first moves of the association was to set up an office in Peking; and to this day the association's telegraphic address in London is "Yincochi"—Chinese for "Buy British". Another association originally formed to cope with an international trade problem is the Cocoa, Chocolate and Confectionery Alliance, which was founded in 1901 as the Manufacturing Confectioners Alliance. Its chief object at the time was to oppose the Brussels Convention of 1902, which condemned bounties to sugar-beet growers, and the increase in the sugar tax in the Budget of 1901. Sugar remained the chief interest of the alliance until after World War I. In this case labour interests followed later—the establishment of a trade board in 1913 being largely responsible for the formation of an employers' federation, which shared offices with the Alliance until 1939.

In the case of the British Electrical and Allied Manufacturers Association, which was formed as the National Electrical Manufacturers Association in 1902 and took its present name in 1911, the motives for formation were more mixed, but could broadly be grouped under combating restrictive legislation which hindered the development of the industry, onerous conditions of contract and foreign competition in the home market.

Although commercial regulation, labour negotiation and international trade problems were the chief reasons for the growth of associations before World War I, various other reasons are also apparent. The Society of Motor Manufacturers and Traders, for example, was formed with the principal object of bringing order into the industry's exhibitions, the first official S.M.M.T. exhibition being held at the Crystal Palace in 1903, though it also turned its attention at an early stage to legislation affecting its members. Similarly the present Machine Tool Trades Association, which was formed in 1910 as the Machine Tool and Engineering Association, appears to have had its origin in the desire of members not to be exploited by the numerous exhibition promoters who were operating at that time. The immediate cause of formation of the Society of British Gas Industries was the gas exhibition of 1904, though the need for a central body probably stems from the fact that manufacturers were faced with a relatively small number of big buyers, many of whom were closely in touch with each other.

An interesting example of the growth of a smaller, more specific product association, is provided by the Gunmakers Association. This was formed in 1912 as an amalgamation of the Gunmakers Association, representing London makers, and the Birmingham and Provincial Gunmakers Association, and it includes wholesaler and retailer members. Among the objects for which it was formed were combating fraudulent markings of foreign-made goods as British, and promotion of the sale of British-made goods in preference to foreign ones. The association was empowered to register trade marks under the powers given by the Trade Marks Act, 1905. Government and public contracts, and regulations made by public health, building, gas and water authorities and others are also specifically mentioned as interests of the association.

WORLD WAR I

World War I brought a new set of influences to bear on association development. Existing associations extended their scope and influence, and many new associations were created.

From that time onwards, too, Government has had a more or less continuous interest in associations, although its attitude towards them has varied according to prevailing economic conditions.

Wartime shortages, production problems and controls brought many associations into close contact with Government for the first time, especially towards the end of the war when shortages brought stricter government control over industry. This process was not merely encouraged by Government but in several instances associations were established at government instigation. An article in the *National Food Journal* in 1919* shows how this came about in distribution:

> In the case of every controlled commodity it becomes necessary that the Controller should have the advice of somebody able to speak with full knowledge and authority for the traders directly concerned, and in some instances this body must be capable of supervising individual traders or of acting as actual agents for the Ministry of Food. For a great majority of the commodities controlled traders have been represented at headquarters by an advisory committee with no executive powers whatever. In these cases reversion to pre-war conditions is comparatively simple.
>
> The supply and distribution of meat, oils and fats, however, have raised many extraordinarily complicated issues which have made a closer organisation of the trades necessary if the interests of the trades themselves and of the community at large were to be secured. Where this has been the case the traders concerned have been formed into associations, whose business it is to arrange a proper allocation among their members and a just, fair and rapid distribution to the consumer. Their articles give the Ministry of Food power to withhold approval of the membership of the Council and of the Executive of the Association, to control and direct the acts of the body, and to dissolve it if necessary.

Nevertheless this policy had aroused some misgivings:

> The policy to be adopted in future by the State towards these food associations which have grown up under government auspices, and as a direct result of the necessities of the war period, is a matter of great difficulty. The problem can hardly be considered apart from the general question of the attitude of the State towards trade combinations as a whole which have received so tremendous a stimulus during the war.

* *National Food Journal*, 26 March 1919, Vol. II, p. 359.

Much will clearly depend upon the price policy of the associations in question. If the general consumer is to be exploited and all external competition ruthlessly crushed, it will assuredly be necessary for the State, which is the guardian of the interests of the whole community, to intervene.

A year earlier, with reconstruction in the offing, a departmental committee reporting on the textile trades after the war was clearly influenced by the wartime growth and activities of associations in industry:*

We think it would be of great advantage if each of the textile trades, great and small, had a joint association representative of all its component parts for the purpose of consulting upon all matters of common interest, which at present are often nobody's business and end by being neglected, as was the case, for instance, with synthetic dyes and knitting needles. Whenever such associations were formed the government departments should regard them as the authoritative and accredited medium of communication upon all questions connected with the industry.

The experience of the war has shown the great inconvenience and, indeed, loss arising out of the absence of accredited representatives of the great manufacturing industries. The equipment of troops would have been greatly facilitated if such associations had existed before the war, and the Government had recognised and consulted them. Moreover, when it was found necessary to commandeer raw materials and to control industries, to prohibit exports except under licence, and to bring trade generally under war conditions, there would have been available advisory bodies, and possibly even the machinery, for doing what was necessary with the minimum of injury to normal industrial interests.

When we return to peace conditions these associations, if formed, might be able to assist in restoring industries to normal conditions, for we strongly recommend that government restrictions upon, and interference with, industry, which have been recognised and accepted as necessary during the war, should be brought to an end as speedily as possible, having regard to the circumstances of each particular case.

The records of the National Paint Federation of this period show that not only did it have its own committees to consider post-war problems as early as 1916–17, but also that it was closely

* *Report of the Departmental Committee appointed by the Board of Trade to Consider the Position of the Textile Trades after the War*, Cmd. 9070, 1918, p. 113.

in touch with Government on matters of detail. The history of the soap industry provides an example of Government's wartime use of associations. In 1917,

> a really thorough scheme for the control of oils and fats took shape. Like other schemes in other industries it was to be worked largely by members of the trades concerned. A joint trades committee was formed under the presidency of Sir William Lever; it included representatives of the soap and candle trades, the margarine makers, the oleaginous seed and nut crushers, and the feeding stuffs makers.

Dealings in oils and fats were prohibited except under licence, and in 1918,

> impelled by a mixture of motives, strategic, economic and political, the Government proceeded towards the logical completion of their policy. They set up the Soap Makers Federation, which though in form a voluntary association of manufacturers, was in fact an engine of official compulsion. Its contemplated activities included the distribution of raw material, the fixing of prices, and the "rationalisation" of productive capacity. It was hardly born before the Armistice brought about its premature death, but its very inception demonstrated the change brought about by four years of war in Englishmen's notions of the functions proper to their Government.*

Among the thirty or so manufacturers' associations registered as companies during the war years are found two of the major industry associations now in existence, the Society of British Aircraft Constructors and the Association of British Chemical Manufacturers, together with many more specific associations, especially in the fields of textiles and trades concerned with wartime production such as laboratory equipment, scientific instruments, chemical ware and so on.

A development of considerable importance occurred during the war with the formation of inter-industry organisations capable of representing industry as a whole and taking action on matters affecting more than one industry or section of it. The Federation of British Industries was formed in 1916, its antecedents having been the Employers Parliamentary Association, formed in 1898, and the British Manufacturers Association. At the first general meeting of the F.B.I., held in March 1917, the president announced

* Charles E. Wilson, *The History of Unilever* (Cassell), Vol. I, pp. 221–222.

that membership then included fifty associations*; by the time the F.B.I. was a year old it had seventy-eight members, and by 1918, one hundred and twenty-nine. Before the first general meeting, arrangements had been made with the Employers Parliamentary Association by which the various district branches of that association became branches of the federation. In a pamphlet issued early in the 1920s, when its member associations totalled one hundred and seventy, the F.B.I. stated that

> For many years past the manufacturers in many of the leading industries of the country have experienced the advantages to be gained by co-operation and association for the protection of their common interests in organisations devoted to their particular trades. ... Every industry and the majority of trades within each industry now have associations to assist and to foster the manufacture of British goods.

The origin of the other general national organisation, the National Union of Manufacturers, was in the formation of the British Manufacturers Association in 1915. Though there appears to have been some brief connection between the British Manufacturers Association and the F.B.I. during 1917,† the former body became the National Union of Manufacturers later in 1917 and has since continued as an independent body.

Meanwhile the Committee of Trusts had issued its report in 1919, a year after its appointment by the Minister of Reconstruction. The report began:

> We find that there is at the present time in every important branch of industry in the United Kingdom, an increasing tendency to the formation of trade associations and combinations, having for their purpose the restriction of competition and the control of prices.
>
> Many of the organisations which have been brought to our notice have been created in the last few years and by far the greater part of them appear to have come into existence since the end of the nineteenth century. ... There has been a great increase in the creation of trade associations during the period of the war.

Later in the report the committee stated that it had been furnished with details of the Ministry of Munitions' experience in dealing with associations, principally of manufacturers.

* Reported in *The Economist*, 10 March 1917, pp. 479–480.
† *Ibid.*

> To a very considerable extent these experiences appear to have been of a character satisfactory to the Government. Considerable advantages were recognised in dealing with combinations and associations for war purposes. It was found that the larger-minded and more moderate men had a beneficial effect upon the attitude of the trade as a whole, that the best technical advice was more easily available, and that on the whole the trade associations, and especially trade committees created for war purposes, were of the greatest possible assistance to the Ministry.

It was recognised that many of the associations then in existence—bodies such as the Society of Motor Manufacturers and Traders, the Machine Tool Trades Association, the Federation of Master Cotton Spinners Associations, the British Electrical and Allied Manufacturers Association and others—did not include economic regulation among their activities. The committee recommended that the Board of Trade should collect information about those that did and report annually to Parliament, if necessary through a tribunal with compulsory powers of investigation, and recommend appropriate State action.

BETWEEN THE WARS

The report of the Committee on Trusts marks an important stage in the development of trade associations, since from then up to the present time Government has faced the problem of distinguishing where some of their activities stand in relation to the public interest. The report is also important from the standpoint of the present survey in that it listed nearly one hundred associations—over thirty in the iron and steel industry and ninety encountered by the Ministry of Munitions. This makes it possible, before turning to developments in trade associations between the wars, to get some idea of the extent to which associations have changed, either in name or scope, or both, between 1918 and the present time. Of the ninety associations listed by the Committee on Trusts, sixty-seven were manufacturers' associations within the definition used in this report. The others were mostly regional associations, and although today most of them are included in some national body (and some may well have been so even then) they are excluded for the purposes of comparison.

A comparison with the names of associations concerned with

the same products today shows that a third of the associations in the 1918 list have kept their original names. This group includes both large industry associations, such as the Association of British Chemical Manufacturers, the British Electrical and Allied Manufacturers Association, the Society of British Aircraft Constructors, and the National Paint Federation, and smaller product associations, such as the British Laboratory Ware Manufacturers Association, the Collapsible Tube Association, the Brass Wire Association, the White Lead Convention and the British Chemical Ware Manufacturers Association. A further twenty associations have altered their names very slightly, for example from the Balata Belting Manufacturers Association to the British Association of Balata Belting Manufacturers, from the Keg and Drum Association to the British Keg and Drum Manufacturers Federation. Though in some instances the change suggests a slightly more comprehensive membership, they are virtually the same as now. Eight of the associations have disappeared without any obvious successor; they include the Cotton Duck Association, the Fuse Makers and Tinfoil Paper Associations. Of the remaining seventeen, a few have amalgamated (e.g. the Carbon and Tungsten Lamp Associations) but the majority have developed into a number of separate associations. For instance, the committee listed eleven associations concerned with brass and copper manufactures, and three with tubes. There are now some twenty associations concerned with brass and copper, and about twelve with different types of tubes.

It does not, of course, automatically follow that an association which has retained the same name has retained the same membership, and this is also true of its activities. But the comparison gives some indication of continuity of existence, and at the same time provides evidence of their increase in number during the past thirty years.

Government attitudes

Before World War I associations grew spontaneously in the sense that Government neither encouraged their growth nor attempted to influence their activities. By the end of the war this was no longer true; and since then government attention has been occupied more or less continuously with questions of industrial organisation which involve trade associations to some degree. A brief account of government attitudes to associations, and the economic conditions that inspired them, is essential for an understanding of association development from 1919 onwards. This is followed by a description of association growth between the wars.

Following the report of the Committee on Trusts the Government introduced, in the summer of 1919, a Bill to deal with profiteering. This gave the Board of Trade power to investigate costs, profits, and prices; to require persons to appear, furnish information and documents; to receive and investigate complaints; to declare what would be a reasonable price; and to require sellers to reimburse a complainant. The board was to have powers to take proceedings, if necessary, before a court of summary jurisdiction, and it was to have power to order local authorities to establish committees to deal with minor complaints. In its passage through the House of Commons the Bill was amended to make possible the investigation of trusts and restrictive practices.

There followed a series of thirty reports by committees appointed by the Board of Trade to investigate various trades. In many of these, trade associations were active—notably in bricks, cement, explosives, salt, soap, light castings, iron pipes and castings, electric lamps and glassware. In many of the reports the committees recommended action to check abuses, and some idea of their general attitude towards the activities of associations and the type of remedy suggested can be gained from the following summaries.

Brick trade. The committee found that there were many associations—"in fact every district has its own, whose boundaries are determined by the similarity of clay and the method of manufacture". However, they had no evidence that the fixation of prices by associations was detrimental to the interests of the consumer, though it limited the profits of builders' merchants. Danger would arise if the associations co-operated, but the committee could find no case where they had done so. No action was proposed.

Cement and mortar. The Cement Makers Federation was inaugurated in 1918, and the members of it controlled ninety per cent of the cement produced in the country. It fixed the minimum delivered prices of all cement sold in this country by its members, and determined the rebate allowed to the merchants and their terms of resale. This system the committee found desirable during a period of shortage of supplies; but "when the present abnormal conditions no longer obtain, some permanent supervision such as that recommended by the Committee on Trusts . . . will ensure . . . that the operations of the Cement Makers Federation will contrive to act in a manner not injurious to the public interest".

Aspirin. The trade was largely dominated by the Proprietary Articles Trade Association, of which 310 firms owning proprietary articles were members. The committee considered 10d. for twenty-five tablets of aspirin a reasonable maximum price if the Board of Trade should choose to fix one, though higher prices were being charged for the products of many firms.

Electric lamps. The Tungsten Lamp Association was formed in 1913 and became the Electric Lamp Manufacturers Association Ltd. in 1919. This association fixed a common retail price for lamps and an agreed rate of discount to factors and retailers who handled the lamps. Thus they controlled the prices of over ninety per cent of the home supply of lamps. They could also close the normal channels of distribution to the non-association manufacturer. The committee recommended that the proposals of the Committee on Trusts should be given statutory form, in order that the E.L.M.A. might be subjected to public supervision and control.

Oils, fats and margarine. The committee found that competition between groups of manufacturers continued in these trades; it recommended that if the danger of monopoly should arise, a committee of traders and government officials should fix a maximum remuneration on turnover, any surplus made by a trader being paid over to the Government.

Salt. The Salt Manufacturers Association was formed in 1915, and was dominated by the Salt Union, which was responsible for sixty per cent of the salt produced in the country. Prices were fixed to cover the costs of this company, which were the highest in the industry; and in addition it now made a large profit. The committee recommended that no further increase in salt prices was justifiable.

In general, wherever action was thought necessary, price-fixing, by the Board of Trade or the machinery previously proposed by the Committee on Trusts, found favour with the investigating committees. There was no suggestion that any attempt ought to be made to break up the associations; indeed, they were often commended for improving the efficiency of the industry. Protection of the public interest in the matter of prices was much more the concern of these investigations than any suggestion of "trust-busting" in the American sense.

The post-war boom which had made high prices and profiteering possible collapsed, however, and the need for the Profiteering Act diminished. The Government allowed the Act to lapse in May 1921. On the Board of Trade Vote on 9 March 1921, Sir Philip Lloyd-Greame* (Parliamentary Secretary to the Board of Trade) commended the work of the trust-investigating committees, "not because (they) disclosed that the country is in grave jeopardy because of these combinations, but because it has disclosed the fact that these combinations in the great majority of cases are not abusing the position they have got". He went on to assure the House that it was the intention of the Government to pass legislation enabling it to deal effectively with trusts. But the Lloyd George Coalition Government fell in October 1922 before any action could be taken.

In the 1920s two attempts were made by private members to introduce legislation on the subject of monopoly. Both Bills were clearly based on the proposals of the 1919 Committee on Trusts and the principles of the Board of Trade inquiry. The first, introduced by Captain Wedgwood Benn† in the spring of 1923, dealt only with the building industry, and only received a First Reading. The other, wider in scope, had a brief Second Reading debate in June 1925, but was talked out.

Activities of associations in particular industries continued to be investigated from time to time, as in the reports of the Inter-Departmental Committee on Prices of Building Materials (1923) and the Royal Commission on Food Prices (1925), but, in general, official circles were tending to look at this time at other aspects of trade associations and at their potentialities as means of industrial reorganisation. Depression and the growth of foreign competition emphasised the inadequacies of British industry, and "rationalisation" and modernisation were advocated as remedies. Accordingly it became necessary for technical advances to be widely

* Later changed name to Cunliffe-Lister; now Earl of Swinton.

† Now Viscount Stansgate.

encouraged and for inefficient high-cost firms to be eliminated. The trade association was a means of doing this, and began to be officially encouraged on these grounds. Roughly from 1926 onwards, rationalisation began to engage the attention of industry and of Government.

In 1926 a report on the co-operative selling of coal* argued in favour of organised marketing and amalgamation of coal mines. But it was in the report of the Balfour Committee on Industry and Trade, which was appointed in 1924 and issued its final report in 1929, that the change in attitude was most apparent.

In its final report the committee considered the pros and cons of industrial combination and agreement. It considered that, in general, economic efficiency, and, in particular, the process of rationalisation, could often benefit by consolidation and amalgamation in industry; but it was divided on the question of what should be done to control or supervise the monopolistic power embodied in large-scale enterprise. On the whole it felt that

> in the circumstances of the present industrial situation the case for immediate legislation for the restraint of such abuses as may result from combinations cannot be said to be an urgent one. . . .
>
> We think, however, that the Board of Trade should include among its general duties the watching of the movement towards consolidation and agreement in industry, and the continuous collection of data with regard to various forms of combination.

At the same time the committee pointed out that, under its own recommendations, trade associations would be called upon to undertake a great variety of duties:

> . . . to act as organs for the actual carrying out of our recommendations, or as the authoritative mouthpieces of industrial and commercial opinion with reference to matters arising thereunder, or as the authorised means of negotiating with public authorities on behalf of special trade interests, or as the medium through which the industrial and commercial community may be systematically kept abreast of the latest results of research and inquiry and encouraged to take practical advantage thereof.

Consequently it was disturbed at the inefficiency of many associations:

* *Reports of the Departmental Committee on the Co-operative Selling in the Coal Mining Industry*, Cmd. 2770, 1926, p. 23.

> ... well-equipped associations are, we fear, only a minority, and the able trade representatives who gave evidence before us would be the first to admit that the financial strength of their organisations, and the support they receive from the trade, and even from their own members, are often very much below what is needed for the efficient carrying out of their present duties, to say nothing of any new responsibilities.

In the debate on the Board of Trade Vote in the Commons Committee of Supply on 6 May 1929 Sir Philip Cunliffe-Lister, then President of the Board of Trade, referred to the Balfour Report:

> Their attitude towards combinations and trusts is particularly interesting. It endorses entirely the policy and practice which I have on many occasions commended to the House, whether dealing with trusts generally or in special cases....
>
> ... We must have rationalisation. It is necessary for efficiency and it inevitably involves the creation of larger units and the making of agreements. Hon. Members must make up their minds which horse they are going to ride. You cannot in one speech lecture industry and say: "It is your duty to rationalise and reorganise and enter into these agreements and combine yourselves in the most efficient units", and proceed in the very next speech you make to attack people or cast aspersions on them for doing exactly what you invited them to do.

The Report of the Greene Committee on Restraint of Trade, which was published by the Stationery Office in 1931, is concerned exclusively with distributive practices—resale price maintenance and the restriction of the number of retailers. It reflects the prevailing tolerance of monopolistic practices and emphasises that the "ordinary right of freedom to contract ought not to be withdrawn without some compelling reason".

The great depression of 1931 meant that the incentives towards association became sharper, as industry saw the need to restrict competition and to erect safeguards against price-cutting become more urgent. An even more direct incentive was provided by the tariff system created in 1932, for it was then necessary for traders to unite to seek protection against imports, and the Government could make reorganisation a condition of tariff protection, and so promote the rationalisation it thought desirable. The concentration of industry was often impelled by the Import Duties Advisory Committee:

> But whatever the nature of the industry or the measure of success which accompanied these reformist measures, the very fact that I.D.A.C. was obliged to negotiate with industries on the subject of tariffs tended to stimulate the growth of some sort of national organisation. The Government could not negotiate on these matters with individual firms, but only with the leaders of industry as elected through trade associations. These associations, therefore, became less and less debating societies of minor importance and acquired a dignity and sense of responsibility which went a long way towards preparing for industrial self-discipline and self-government.*

During the 1930s the Import Duties Advisory Committee issued a report on the Present Position and Future Development of the Iron and Steel Industry. This gave an account of the existing structure whereby the British Iron and Steel Federation, established in 1934, organised co-ordination through its twenty-seven affiliated associations:

> Until reorganisation, the federation had no jurisdiction over the trade associations in regard to prices, but within the last fifteen months it has secured the assent of the affiliated associations to a more direct interest in this matter and they have now undertaken not to increase prices without prior consultation with the federation.

In its recommendations for the future of the industry the committee said:

> An essential condition for the wise planning of the iron and steel industry is the existence of comprehensive and well-organised associations for all its various sections and their affiliation to a central body with a view to the co-ordination of their activities and collective effort towards the attainment of a common objective.

On the understanding that the Import Duties Advisory Committee would exercise general supervision over the activities of the industry's associations, it argued in favour of the pig-iron industry's affiliation to the federation, and also that of the iron-founders' association, which was just being formed. Though many of the major tube manufacturers were members of the federation, there was no association specifically representative of that industry, and it suggested that one should be formed. It was not enough for a central body to comprise all associations:

* J. Hurstfield, *The Control of Raw Materials* (History of the Second World War, H.M.S.O.), p. 25.

> But we recognise that such associations to be of use must be in their turn as comprehensive as possible, and that their objects must not be limited to price regulation but should extend to all matters affecting both the internal conduct of the particular section which each represents and its relations to other sections and to the industry as a whole.

The approach of World War II meant that the function of trade associations in the war effort had to be considered. This question had been reviewed in 1925 by the Principal Supply Officers Committee, which noted that many trade associations did not cover the whole of their industries, and that they might be criticised politically and administratively. These considerations were, however, dismissed with the comment that "the main function, even of those sufficiently developed and organised, would be advisory". The report added:

> But we believe that the stronger and more representative these associations become, the more valuable they are likely to be in war, and we hope that every opportunity will be taken to foster their growth on the principle that they should be the general headquarters of their particular trade.*

It therefore commended the work of the Board of Trade in assisting the setting up of these associations.

During the 1930s negotiations had been carried on between the Board of Trade Supply Organisation and these associations in preparation for wartime control. By 1938 the "advisory" view of their role had been abandoned, the organisation declaring:

> It has been found in general that the control of a particular material could best be worked through the trade association or other body particularly concerned with it, that body becoming in effect a sub-department of the Ministry of Supply.†

On this basis various shadow controls were created. Some difficulty was experienced in persuading firms or sections of industry who had stood out from an association to accept it as the central authority. For example, the foundry and forge pig-iron and other groups were reluctant to join with the British Iron and Steel Federation in an Iron and Steel Control.‡

* J. Hurstfield, op. cit., p. 67. † Ibid., p. 68. ‡ Ibid., p. 68.

On the outbreak of war there were still misgivings about the employment of associations for some purposes, such as import control:

> Some use might, it was thought, be made of trade associations, but there were doubts as to how far these associations could be relied upon to administer such restrictions (on imports) impartially and efficiently.*

They turned out to be indispensable, however, because they possessed "the technical knowledge without which the licensing of non-standardised commodities could not be efficiently administered."† And for the second time in twenty-five years associations were brought into close liaison with Government on many fronts.

Associations 1919–1939

The attitudes of Government, as suggested above, weighed heavily in favour of autonomous regulation in industry as a means of reorganisation; it was not government policy to intervene. Official support for schemes of rationalisation, and the introduction of tariffs, were the chief contributions of the inter-war years towards the development of associations. The brief survey of events in the trade association world which follows is intended to indicate the part played by associations and how they developed under these conditions. It would, however, be misleading to suggest that all industries solidly closed their ranks in the face of economic depression. In many branches of textiles, for instance, attempts at voluntary control were conspicuous failures, and in many other trades repeated attempts were made without much success to weather periods of depression by means of voluntary price or output agreements.

The number of associations registered as companies increased fairly evenly between 1920 and 1939: about twenty-eight associations were registered in each of the two decades. There is, however, a noticeable concentration of associations taking trade union status between 1931 and 1939—nineteen out of a total of twenty-six for the whole period.

* Hargreaves and Gowing, *Civil Industry and Trade* (History of the Second World War, H.M.S.O.), p. 22.

† Ibid., p. 25.

Many associations appear to have collapsed during the slump which ended in 1922, and although they revived fairly quickly, depressed markets and overseas competition left them unstable for some years.* In the rationalisation movement which followed, towards the late 1920s, existing associations played a considerable part, notably in the iron and steel, shipbuilding, milling and woolcombing industries. Elsewhere legislation, in the form of the Coal Mines, Sugar Industry, Agricultural Marketing and Transport Acts, and in restrictions on competition in the cotton industry, culminating in the Cotton Industry (Reorganisation) Act, 1939, took the place of voluntary agreement.

The first of these voluntary reorganisations occurred in the flour milling industry. The National Association of British and Irish Millers, which was formed in 1878 and incorporated in 1917, appointed a committee in 1924 to report on the state of the industry. After a certain amount of capacity had been bought up the Millers Mutual Association was formed, in 1929, to regulate output (but not prices, which were already fixed by local associations), purchase redundant mills, and reduce costs of manufacture and distribution. The industry was one of the few which did not suffer unduly in the slump of the 1930s.

In shipbuilding, which was particularly hard hit between the wars—capacity was increased by 1 million gross tons during World War I to a total of 4 million, while from 1921 to 1939 launchings never exceeded 1.7 million and were usually far less—the Shipbuilding Conference founded National Shipbuilders Security Ltd. to buy up redundant and obsolete yards as they came on the market. In this way, capacity was reduced by about a third by 1939.† The Conference itself had been formed in 1928 in order to cope with the mounting economic problems of the industry.

On much the same lines the Woolcombing Employers Federation formed the Woolcombers Mutual Association in 1933, to purchase redundant or obsolete mills, plant and machinery.

The reorganisation of the iron and steel industry followed the recommendation of an import duty by the Import Duties

* P. Fitzgerald, *Industrial Combination in England* (Pitman), 1925.

† Some of the yards were put on a "care and maintenance" basis against possible future need, and were reopened during World War II. They were closed again after the end of the war and their equipment transferred to other yards.

Advisory Committee. This resulted in a strong central organisation, the federation, and considerably strengthened sectional associations co-ordinated from the centre. The federation was formed in 1934, replacing the National Association of Iron and Steel Manufacturers, an earlier and more limited association dating from 1920. The Government of the day nominated the independent chairman, and charged the new federation with the task of reorganising the industry in its recovery from the slump of the early 1930s. The pricing and commercial policies of the federation were under the general supervision of the Import Duties Advisory Committee. A separate body, the British Iron and Steel Corporation Ltd., was formed under the British Iron and Steel Federation to engage in commercial activities such as importing and distributing steel scrap and other materials.

The influence of the tariff system, and the effect of the Import Duties Advisory Committee in promoting unity within industries, described in the review of government attitudes above, was perhaps an even greater encouragement to the formation of new, or the strengthening of existing, associations. Between 1932 and 1939, when it was wound up, the Import Duties Advisory Committee dealt with nearly 340 applications for additions to the free list, and about 420 applications for tariff increases. The majority, if not all, of them were made by trade associations.

Once again these were not the only reasons, although they were undoubtedly the principal ones. This mixture of motives can be illustrated by a few examples drawn chiefly from associations which brought together a number of existing product groups.

The central organisation of the wool industry, the Wool Textile Delegation, was set up in 1921 after some two years of negotiation. In its first few years it was largely concerned with tariff matters and legislation. Representation of the industry's views to Government and the formulation of the industry's major policies continues to be one of the delegation's principal functions. The Typewriter Trades Federation was formed in 1923 by fifty London retailers. Its activities were mainly social at first, but soon after its formation manufacturers were enlisted and the federation was making arrangements to regulate competition to some extent. The Federation of British Manufacturers of Sports and Games was founded in 1926, a forerunner having been set up in 1919 with the chief aim of canalising the distribution of sports goods through specialist dealers. As other problems arose the functions of the federation expanded, until in 1926 it assumed its present constitution. The Glass Manufacturers Federation was also formed in 1926, by nine manufacturers of glass containers in London, the North and Scotland. Its principal object on formation was to oppose certain proposals made at the International Labour Conference at Geneva. Representation to Government followed, and more recently there has been a very considerable expansion in its activities.

Two interesting examples of association growth in rapidly developing industries are provided by the British Chemical Plant Manufacturers Association and the British Plastics Federation. The suggestion that the plastics industry was sufficiently clearly defined to form an association was made in a trade journal, *British Plastics*, and as a result the Moulding Traders Association was set up in 1929. It was reformed four years later as the more broadly based British Plastics Federation, whose first activities were those of an information centre for members and customers—a service which is continued today, among many others.

The British Chemical Plant Manufacturers Association was started in 1920 as the Association of British Chemical Plant Manufacturers. It was formed at the suggestion of the Association of British Chemical Manufacturers, the association which represents its members' principal customers and to which it became, and is still, affiliated. During its first years it was principally concerned with standardisation, chemical engineering education, publicity and acting as a clearing centre for plant inquiries; a wide range of activities developed later.

The National Federation of Clay Industries was incorporated under the Companies Act in 1928 by a merger of the Employers National Council for the Clay Industries and the National Building and Engineering Brick Federation of England. The E.N.C.C.I. itself had been formed in 1917 primarily to negotiate on wages and conditions of employment with the numerous trade unions which existed separately at that time. As time went on the E.N.C.C.I. assumed other duties of a common service character. In 1921 certain sections of the E.N.C.C.I. broke away and formed the National Building and Engineering Brick Federation of England. The merger into the National Federation of Clay Industries in 1928 was effected to obviate duplication and overlapping of function by the two separate organisations. The principal objects of the N.F.C.I. were and continue to be to promote and protect the interests of all trades comprised in or connected with the heavy clay industries, particularly building and engineering bricks, roofing and flooring tiles, fireclay and silica refractories, sanitary pipes and fittings, terracotta ware, sanitary fireclay goods and the like.

Moves towards self-government

From the later 1920s up to World War II the attention of Government and of many industries was increasingly turning to the need for industrial organisation to meet the market conditions of the times. The return to protection provided both a general background and, through the Import Duties Advisory Committee, some direct incentive to reorganisation. Agriculture had its parallel protection in the Agricultural Marketing Acts.

Statutory machinery for reorganisation was provided where voluntary arrangements were not made. In shipbuilding, milling and woolcombing extensive measures were taken by the industries concerned; in iron and steel the various associations co-operated under the general supervision of the Import Duties Advisory Committee. In coal, cotton and agriculture, where voluntary agreement was weak or non-existent, legislation provided a framework for control of production and marketing. The Coal Mines Act, 1930, introduced a marketing scheme operated by a central council and district boards, under which district and colliery quotas were allotted and prices fixed. Both centrally and at district level committees were appointed to represent consumer interests. By 1936 the districts were effectively controlling sales as well as output, and market-sharing agreements were being negotiated with European competitors. In practice the scheme was operated by the Mining Association of Great Britain. The Agricultural Marketing Acts of the early 1930s, and later the Cotton Industry Reorganisation Act, provided for some measure of autonomous control under statute in two other major industries.

The position was well summarised in the 1944 report of the F.B.I. Trade Organisation Committee:* Besides introducing tariffs,

* In an appendix to the report, *The Background of the British Trade Organisation Movement.*

> . . . the Government, although not prepared to enact a general law prescribing a "cut and dried" method of trade organisation applicable to all industries, expressed its readiness to sponsor Acts of Parliament designed to encourage schemes of self-government in particular industries and prepared to assist *ad hoc* schemes for the reduction of plant. . . . This principle was given official recognition in the Finance Act of 1935, which provided that if a scheme of reorganisation covering the majority of an industry had been certified by the Board of Trade as being of assistance in reducing excess capacity, contributions to it might be deducted from income for tax purposes.

During the early 1930s the need for a more enlightened and active policy of self-government in industry was strongly advocated by P E P, then in its early years and itself largely inspired by the failure of existing social and economic organisation to avoid or overcome the catastrophies of industrial depression and unemployment. In 1934 a P E P group engaged on problems of national reconstruction stated:

> Within the existing framework it is only under rare leadership or under intense economic pressure that appreciable moves towards better organisation for industry can be made. Yet discontent with all these obstacles and makeshifts is growing fast. More and more members of industry recognise that to halt half-way between *laissez faire* and a planned structure is to make the worst of both worlds. We have too much organisation to allow automatic readjustment to continue, and too little to secure necessary adjustments through conscious direction. Employers' associations, trades unions, industrial federations, cartels, amalgamations of firms, and so forth are all striving in their own way to bring order, and are often only succeeding in making confusion worse confounded.

This group advocated an Enabling Act "under which each industry will be free to take, under proper safeguards, those powers which it most urgently needs to set its house in order". It suggested that any industry wishing to take powers should put up a scheme to the Minister, who would refer it to an Industrial Advisory Council. The council (in some ways resembling the Import Duties Advisory Committee) would hear objections and criticisms and recommend changes before advising the Minister whether to proceed. Considerable emphasis was placed on getting the substantial approval of all interests, including consumers and trade unions, before any scheme would take effect under the proposed Act.

A campaign to secure a general Enabling Act was later sponsored by the Industrial Reorganisation League, headed by Lord Melchett. This was intended to enable a majority of producers to set up a strong central organisation notwithstanding the objections of a minority; any scheme approved by the majority of producers, the Board of Trade and a National Industrial Council would be given the force of law.

Current ideas about industrial organisation, and about the character and purposes of the bodies required, were reviewed by a committee of the Federation of British Industries in 1935. This committee considered whether the organisation of industry was adequate to meet the problems of the day, and, if more co-operation were required, whether it should be obtained voluntarily or by government compulsion, and reported its findings.*

The aims of industrial organisation were taken to be the relation of means of production to potential demand, to smooth out booms and depressions; the maintenance of fair conditions of competition; unification to enable an industry to co-operate with others, and effect common action; and negotiation with foreign industries. The committee concluded that although there had been a marked improvement towards voluntary co-operation without undue encroachment on individual enterprise, nevertheless it was necessary for there to be stronger organisation and more submission of individual interests to achieve efficient and economic production. Excess capacity had to be removed, and expansion of capacity more definitely related to demand; unity was necessary for negotiation with foreign competitors, and also to enable co-operation with financial institutions both for the finance of reorganisation and to prevent the flotation of new companies in industries where there was danger of excessive development.

The committee went on to consider how internal organisation should be stimulated, and came down definitely on the side of voluntary association. Compulsion was rejected on principle; but where voluntary associations had failed, Parliament should be asked to sanction enforcing measures. It recommended that the President of the Board of Trade should consider any scheme put

* *Report of a Committee on the Organisation of Industry* (F.B.I.), 1935.

forward by the majority of an industry to regulate output. If satisfied on the need for it, he should appoint a tribunal to examine the scheme and report on it, and legislation would depend on the tribunal's decision. The existence of such a scheme would encourage industry to reach voluntary agreement.

These proposals do not appear to have been enthusiastically supported, and further discussion along these lines appears to have been shelved with the onset of rearmament.

WORLD WAR II

The outbreak of World War II sharply interrupted the move towards closer internal regulation in industry, but greatly stimulated association activities by bringing associations once again into close and continuous touch with the Government. They participated, with varying degrees of responsibility, in the allocation of materials (and sometimes orders) to manufacturers; also drawing up and helping to administer schemes of concentration, zoning, compensation and utility production, and collecting statistics, running economy campaigns and in general acting as the principal channel of communication between Government and industry. A number of wartime controls drew members of their staff from associations—the personnel of Iron and Steel Control largely came from the B.I.S.F., and controllers were drawn from the dominant associations in the wool, shipbuilding, timber, fertilisers, leather, and cement industries.

The three hundred export groups formed in 1940 brought new responsibilities to many existing associations, and in some instances formed the basis of new ones. Some associations were also formed at government request.

Many instances could be cited of the creation of new associations and the extension of existing associations' activities as a result of wartime controls and other reasons for contact with Government. As a rule, in the major industries the formation of a new association was more a matter of consolidating existing bodies than starting the first association ever in the industry concerned. Thus the coking industry had been organised in associations of one sort or another ever since World War I; but in 1940, at the request of Government, it was established in its present comprehensive form to cover all hard-coke producers, that is coke primarily for the iron and steel industry, as the British Hard Coke Association. It was later renamed the British Coking Industry Association.

In one instance wartime reorganisation was effected before the outbreak of war. The present Cake and Biscuit Alliance had its origin in 1938, when the Food (Defence Plans) Department of the Board of Trade invited representatives of the industry to assist in devising a scheme for the allocation of raw materials, and the distribution of finished products in the event of war. The resulting Cake and Biscuit Manufacturers Wholesale Defence Committee was representative of the existing cake and biscuit manufacturers associations, a number of large manufacturers outside both, and (as it became later) the Ministry of Food. The Soap Makers and Fat Splitters Federation was also formed at the instance of the Ministry of Food, to implement the allocation scheme for the trade. The National Council of Building Material Producers is another comprehensive body formed more or less directly at the behest of the authorities, coming into existence after a report by Mr Justice Lewis in 1945 which drew attention to the need for full consultation by the Government with building material interests, and at the same time to the impossibility of consulting all the different material interests separately. The formation of other associations was stimulated by wartime measures: the Engineering Wartime Association was formed on the basis of wartime contract problems; the present British Man-Made Fibres Federation developed from the Rayon Council, founded to discuss the allocation of rayon; a powerful stimulus to the formation of the Council of Ironfoundry Associations in 1941 was the concentration policy pursued by the Government.

An example of very close co-operation between an association and Government in wartime is provided by the work of the United Kingdom Glycerine Producers. This association was formed shortly after World War I, though there had been co-operation among the manufacturers for many years before. Members marketed crude glycerine through the association, and drew a fixed profit for the sale of refined glycerine through a profits pool scheme. As a result of this close voluntary control, during World War II the needs of government departments were met by informal meetings and agreement between them and the association. No formal control was applied.

In clothing, the Apparel and Fashion Industry's Association brought together a wartime body, the Apparel Manufacturers Association, and one formed in 1933, the Wholesale Fashion Trades Association—the Apparel Manufacturers Association having been formed to provide a more widely representative organisation. The Furnishing Fabric Federation was another wartime creation.

The development of a central body in the radio industry furnishes an interesting example of wartime consolidation and change in a rapidly expanding industry. Its origin can be traced back to 1924, when the National Association of Radio Manufacturers was formed. In 1925 distribution sections were added and in 1926 these hived off as separate associations, leaving the manufacturers in the Radio Manufacturers Association. By 1939, the Radio Valve Manufacturers Association and the Radio and Electronic Component Manufacturers Federation were also in existence. In 1943, owing to the rapid development of the industry and the extent of government requirements from it, they formed the Radio Industry Council on an informal basis. Two years later, when the council was given its present form, the Radio Manufacturers Association lapsed and two new bodies were formed—the British Radio Equipment Manufacturers Association, covering the makers of radio and television receivers, and the Radio Communication and Electronic Engineering Association, covering capital communications, navigational and electronic equipment.

The British Non-Ferrous Metals Federation, to take another example of federal growth, was formed in 1945, but some of the associations which are its constituents were established more than fifty years ago. Several of these associations were represented on a Joint Committee on Terms established before 1930, which in 1933 considered the adoption of a common form of contract. A series of regular meetings was held during 1939 and 1940 and, as a result of the need for a consultative body to consider the industry's wartime problems, the membership of the Committee was enlarged and in 1941 was renamed the Non-Ferrous Metals Trade Joint Advisory Committee. Until 1945, when its functions were taken over by the Federation, it acted as the mouthpiece of the industry in negotiations with government departments and other public bodies.

At the other end of the scale, many small single-product associations were formed during the war years. A few developed out of export groups: others arose to cope with controls imposed on these industries, negotiate for supplies, and so on. Thus the Counterpane Manufacturers and Converters, the Household Textiles Association, the Handkerchief Manufacturers and the Mop Manufacturers Association were wartime creations, the first two later becoming two of the constituents of the Domestic Textile Federation. The Joint Committee of Concentrate Manufacturers was set up in 1939 and concerned itself largely with wartime controls. The Mica Trade Association was formed in 1942, in circumstances that must have applied to many other trades. The Minister of Supply established a system of import licences and

> there was in consequence much uncertainty and apprehension in the trade that a government control of distribution might be set up without adequate consultation with the trade or with, perhaps, unfair hardship to some sections.*

A deputation waited on the Parliamentary Secretary to the Ministry of Supply, the association was formed, and the Ministry negotiated with it thereafter.

SINCE 1945

With the end of the war the functions appropriate to associations in peacetime again began to engage the attention of Government and industry. Few of the associations formed during the war appear to have dissolved and there were many reasons for their continued existence. The continuation of numerous wartime controls and the preparation of reconstruction plans occupied the attention of many, while the need to regain export markets and improve industrial efficiency stimulated interest in associations as agencies for promoting industry's products and disseminating information. In some at least there was reluctance on the part of the members to disband after the wartime discovery that they had, after all, certain interests in common. Above all there was a general recognition of the closer relations to which Government and industry were permanently committed—relationships arising

* From the first annual report of the Mica Trade Association, 1943.

out of the new or extended responsibilities assumed by the State for maintaining employment, with its corollary of greater influence on investment and national expenditure in general, for location of industry, for ownership of a considerable section of industry and for the conduct of international trade. Given these conditions, if for no other reasons, associations continued in being as the rallying points of industry.

The extension of public ownership in the years immediately following the war had considerable repercussions in the associations of the industries concerned, and in the supplying and customer trades.

Although the industries supplying equipment and machinery to the coal, gas and electricity industries were all already organised in associations, the emergence of very large buyers in the form of the new public corporations must have had a considerable effect on these associations. The relationships that have developed between publicly-owned industries and their suppliers is noted later in this report. Here it is appropriate to look briefly at the fate of associations in the industries formerly under private, or predominantly private, ownership.

In the coalmining industry, the publication of the famous Reid Report by the expert committee appointed in 1944 stimulated the Mining Association of Great Britain to put forward proposals as an alternative to nationalisation. It was opposed to compulsory amalgamation, and though its financial proposals were somewhat indefinite, before the decision to nationalise had been reached the association had appointed a Director of Education and Training, and set up a committee to arrange for a detailed technical survey of the industry with a view to implementing the technical conclusions of the Reid Report.* When, shortly after, the industry came under public ownership, the Mining Association continued in existence and concerned itself chiefly with the arrangements for compensation to former owners. The association was formally dissolved in 1954, exactly a hundred years after its formation.

The dissolution of the Mining Association was, however, accompanied by the growth of a national organisation of the

* On the distributive side, too, associations were actively concerned with future plans. Before public ownership of the industry came into effect the Coal Merchants Federation of Great Britain and the Co-operative Union put forward their plan for post-war distribution of house coal. The Act, however, did not cover distribution.

small mine-owners. These smaller mine-owners had been variously organised in district associations since the introduction of selling schemes in the 1930s. In 1946, when the nationalisation Bill was introduced, the districts had to consider their future, and early in 1947 they formed the Federation of Small Mines of Great Britain. The federation, which represents some hundreds of small mines operating under licence (with an annual output of about 2 million tons of coal), continues to be the central body for negotiation with the board. The federation is closely in touch with the board on such matters as marketing, grading and pricing of coal, and conditions of employment. Draft rules under the Coal Mines Act, 1911, and the Mines and Quarries Act, 1954, are submitted to it for comment, and the federation is increasingly involved in formulating national schemes for accident and third-party insurance.

In the gas supply industry there was a variety of associations: the British Commercial Gas Association was formed in 1911 and concerned itself with commercial policy and publicity; the National Gas Council of Great Britain and Ireland was formed in 1916 and dealt with policy matters other than commercial and with labour relations through a sub-committee which later became the Federation of Gas Employers. In 1934 the British Gas Federation was set up as a co-ordinating body. During the war, in 1943, the Post-war Committee of the Federation recommended that the B.C.G.A. and the N.G.C. should combine, and this was done in 1945 when the British Gas Council was formed to represent the industry. In its report the federation opposed nationalisation and recommended that existing methods of integration should be encouraged. This view was supported by the council on its formation. Proposals for the reorganisation of the industry were also submitted by the Association of Smaller Municipal Gas Undertakings, formed in 1943 to protect the interests of this category of producers. There were also the National Federation of Gas Coke Associations and the Association of Gas Corporations—the former concerned with marketing and distributive arrangements and the latter representing the interests of holding companies. By the time the Gas Act, 1948, was passed the Association of Smaller Municipal Gas Undertakings seems to have disappeared. The Act vested in the new Gas Council the "rights, liabilities and obligations" of the British Gas Council, the

Federation of Gas Employers, the National Federation of Gas Coke Associations and its constituents, and the Association of Gas Corporations. There was no legal continuity between the former British Gas Council, which was dissolved, and the statutory Gas Council. The new council did, however, take over the premises and many members of the staff of the former council.

Similarly, in the manufacture of hard coke, the British Hard Coke Association, formed in 1941, has continued under the name of the British Coking Industry Association, while considerable changes in ownership have taken place. The National Coal Board inherited about forty per cent of the industry's total capacity, which it shares with the steel industry and a few independents.

In electricity supply there appears to have been less agreement about the changes that should be made after the war. In 1943 the Minister of Fuel and Power asked the industry to submit proposals for reorganisation. There were four associations concerned: the Incorporated Association of Electric Power Companies, which was formed in 1908 and represented the companies granted perpetual tenure of supply; the Incorporated Municipal Electrical Association, formally constituted after World War I and comprising the electrical departments of municipalities; and the London Electric Supply Association and the Provincial Electric Supply Association, representing companies granted a limited franchise. In 1944 the Joint Committee of Electricity Supply Undertakings, representing both companies and municipalities, put forward a compromise plan—there was dissension on the question of ownership—based on a policy of organised co-operation. The two principal bodies comprising the Joint Committee, the I.M.E.A. and the I.A.E.P.C., did not, however, fully support these proposals. Both put forward alternatives, that of the I.A.E.P.C. being supported also by the Provincial Electric Supply Association and the London Electric Supply Association. All these associations were dissolved on nationalisation.

In the iron and steel industry the British Iron and Steel Federation declined in importance during the war when the Iron and Steel Control was in operation. It resumed its normal activities when the control ended, and in 1945 drew up a development plan which was generally approved by the Government in the following year. From then (1946) to 1949 the federation and the industry worked under the supervision of the Iron and Steel Board, a tripartite body appointed by the Ministry of Supply in an advisory capacity.* The federation supported the view that adequate public control could be achieved by strengthening the board. In 1951, under the Iron and Steel Act, 1949, the greater part of the industry came into public ownership under the Iron and Steel Corporation.

The federation continued its work during the brief period of public ownership. Indeed, it remained essential for the running of the industry, since the corporation did not take over all the suppliers of steel: the Act covered firms, not products. Accordingly the proportion of output of steel products accounted for by firms liable to public ownership varied considerably, ranging from ninety-five per cent of some products to about twenty-five per cent of others, a fact which made effective planning very difficult. The federation, on the other hand, being organised on a product basis, could collect comprehensive statistics and accurately plan the production of steel for different users. The corporation agreed that the federation should continue to carry out all its existing functions until a long-term reorganisation had been worked out. The problem was, however, cut short by denationalisation. Under the 1953 Act, a new Iron and Steel Board was charged with responsibilities which gave it more effective planning powers, though fewer directive powers, than those of the former corporation. The board is responsible for fixing maximum prices for steel (when it thinks it desirable), approving development plans and for ensuring adequate supplies of raw material. Under this general supervision the federation performs a wide range of services for its industry.

Development Councils

Another development closely concerning the scope and activities of associations arose out of the Government's policy towards the private sector of industry, and industry's view of its internal organisation.

In 1944, the Organisation of Industry Committee of the F.B.I. reported on post-war industrial organisation, and to this end considered the structure, scope and power of associations. In

* The board represented manufacturers, unions and "independent" members. It had no statutory powers but advised the Minister, who could issue instructions to the industry under wartime regulations.

compiling its report the committee received written evidence from 130 associations. It considered the central problem to be the maintenance of individual freedom alongside wider measures of collaboration. Broadly, co-operation between Government and industry was necessary for two main problems—the balance of payments and the maintenance of full employment. But there were many other problems also calling for liaison between Government and industry. It pointed out that where no organisation had existed, the Government had pressed for wartime associations "in some cases with government nominees and backed by legal sanctions", and might be compelled to devise its own channels of administration in peacetime also if industry did not provide them. The ideal, it concluded, was for the Government to produce a framework of national economic policy leaving industrial organisations to carry it out; direct government action was not feasible when there was such a multitude of small firms in industry. Where there were associations, government departments should make them their main channel of communication. This would be done only if associations were capable of handling the problems involved.

In return for government recognition of associations as the representatives of industry the interests of consumers at large could be safeguarded by setting up a national tribunal, reporting to the Board of Trade, to which interested parties could put their case.

At the same time it was essential that associations should broaden their activities to promote not only the immediate interests of their members, but also service to customers and the community. These associations should be able not only to represent their industries adequately, but also to take the lead in improving technical and commercial efficiency.

The committee listed the following functions as appropriate to associations: communication with Government; common action, with or without other interests, on commercial and economic matters; the relation of production to consumption; fair conditions of trading and the regulation of trade practices; international negotiation; the collection and dissemination of statistics and information; uniform methods of costing; development of exports, sales propaganda and publicity; the promotion of co-operative research, technical education, improvement of service and quality.

The committee considered that there should be more co-operation between associations through the formation of federal bodies and joint councils, though on practical grounds associations controlling prices or output were necessarily formed on a narrow sectional basis and might be considered as a separate problem.

So far as membership of associations was concerned the committee was in principle opposed to compulsion and felt that associations would become more comprehensive when it was accepted that they were the recognised channels of communication with Government.

This conception of internal organisation had its parallel in the Government's policy, which, however, was formulated in terms of a need for a greater measure of central control over industrial policy and the promotion of efficiency in its widest sense. This view implied the creation at the top level of industrial organisation of bodies more broadly based than the existing associations, and capable of promoting such efficiency.

The reports of the seventeen working parties appointed in 1945 and 1946* largely favoured the latter interpretation of what associations should be and how they should be constituted. The working parties were appointed to

> Examine and inquire into the various schemes and suggestions put forward for improvements in organisation, production and distribution methods and processes in industry and to report as to the steps which should be taken in the national interest to strengthen the industry and to render it more stable and more capable of meeting competition in the home and foreign markets.

The working parties comprised manufacturers, trade unionists and independent persons in equal numbers. Eleven† of them recommended the establishment of a permanent central body to formulate policy for its industry and perform a variety of common services; two (Wool and Jewellery and Silverware) recommended new advisory bodies, and two (Glassware and Carpets) advised the strengthening of existing organisations. The Lace and Linoleum working parties suggested special bodies only for research, statistics and design.

* Cotton, Wool, Light Clothing, Heavy Clothing, Rubber-proofed Clothing, Lace, Carpets, Hosiery, Jute, Furniture, Boots and Shoes, Jewellery and Silverware, Hand-blown Domestic Glassware, Pottery, Cutlery, Linoleum, China Clay.

† Cotton, Hosiery, Light Clothing, Heavy Clothing, Rubber-proofed Clothing, Boots and Shoes, Furniture, Jute, Cutlery, Pottery, China Clay.

In 1946, shortly after the first working party reports appeared, the Trade Organisation Committee of the F.B.I. suggested the formation of advisory or consultative councils representing industry and the appropriate trade unions, with an independent chairman appointed by the Minister. These councils, it proposed, should be advisory only, the "promoting" function being that of the Minister whom they advised: trade associations could be left to implement policies arrived at in this way. The committee was strongly in favour of voluntary councils of this kind. Statutory boards, it argued, should be set up cautiously and only in exceptional cases.

The ideas behind the working parties' proposals for central bodies representing industry at a new level—that is between the trade association proper and the Government—were embodied in the Industrial Organisation and Development Act, 1947. The Act enabled the President of the Board of Trade (and certain other ministers) to set up development councils in particular industries by Order, provided that this met the wishes of "a substantial number of the persons engaged in the industry".

Under the Act certain powers were delegated to the councils: the right to raise levies, keep a register of firms and collect statistics. Beyond this they have no compulsive powers, but can undertake a wide range of activities to foster the general efficiency of their industries and advise the Minister on any matter concerning them. The councils consisted of equal numbers of employers and workpeople, and a small number of independent members.

In practice the Act had limited application. Four development councils were set up—for cotton (where the Cotton Board continued under the wider powers of the new Act), clothing, furniture, and jewellery and silverware.

The Act also provided (s.9.) that compulsory levies could be made (in the absence of a development council) for the promotion of research, exports and design. In the wool and lace industries the voluntary organisations in these industries asked that levies should be introduced. The levy in the lace industry was abandoned in 1956. In wool, the services financed by this levy continued to operate with considerable effectiveness and with the support of the industry.

This attempt to provide industry with powers of self-government under statute, and at the same time to inject a broader control over policy making, lost the support of industry almost before it had been properly started. Opposition mounted rapidly. The Government could reach no agreement on the formation of councils with the wool, boot and shoe, cutlery, pottery and china clay industries, and only in two of these, wool and china clay, were voluntary advisory bodies accepted as an alternative. Of the four councils set up, that for clothing—established only after a struggle in the Courts—was dissolved in 1952 and replaced by a voluntary body which later lapsed, and the Jewellery and Silverware Council was wound up in 1953. Opinion in the furniture industry is by no means united in favour of the Furniture Development Council. In 1954 an attempt by the Government to effect a modest extension to the Act—to enable industries themselves (as in lace and wool) to make levies for productive efficiency as well as research and exports—met determined opposition from within industry. The Bill was introduced in the House of Commons in January 1954 and withdrawn on 2 April 1954.*

Various reasons suggest themselves for this marked change in climate of opinion. The obvious one is that industry had long regarded government assistance in reorganising itself as a last resort, to be applied only in exceptional circumstances. When the fears of a post-war slump began to dissipate, so did the desire for special powers to enable better control or the reorganisation necessary to meet depression. Apart from this, the form and purpose of the councils in practice undoubtedly aroused misgivings. They were not merely advisory, they were not representative solely of the industries concerned, and although they were not intended to supersede existing associations, the fear that they would in fact do so was by no means absent. For example, one of the reasons adduced by the British Furniture Manufacturers Federated Associations in 1954 for the liquidation of the Furniture Development council was that the work of the Council was diminishing the influence and prestige of the B.F.M., whose "authority must recede" if the council continued to exist.

At least for the time being the development council idea is in

* The Bill was withdrawn because of opposition on the Government side. The Opposition, according to Mr Harold Wilson (*Hansard*, 1 April 1954, col. 2213) would "just have supported" it.

abeyance. Yet it is not one that should be written off too easily. Apart from any future variant of it that may appear, the events that led up to the Industrial Organisation and Development Act have exerted more than a temporary influence. In addition to the work being done by existing councils in cotton and furniture and in the iron and steel industry by a board which works on something of the same principles, the working party reports appear to have stimulated a number of associations into widening the scope of their activities, particularly in connection with promoting research and exports and, in general, turning attention from the defensive to the promotional type of activity. In one instance, at least, two major associations co-operated to perform one of the functions of a development council by producing a development plan for their industry, when in 1948 the President of the Board of Trade requested the Association of British Chemical Manufacturers to undertake a survey showing long-term plans and probable development. This was done in co-operation with the British Plastics Federation; some years later a follow-up survey related the industry's progress over the period covered by the first survey.

More or less simultaneous with its attempt to broaden representation and provide greater powers for the promotion of efficiency at the top levels of industrial organisation was the return of a critical government attitude towards monopolistic and restrictive practices.

The 1944 White Paper on Employment Policy forecast investigations into "the extent and effect of restrictive agreements and the activities of combines". There followed a series of reports on individual industries: films,* radio valves,† textile machinery,‡ cement,§ and building materials and components‖—the last citing more than ninety producers' associations—and the Lloyd Jacob Committee on Resale Price Maintenance, which reported in 1949. By then the Monopolies and Restrictive Practices (Inquiry and Control) Act, 1948, had come into force.

* Report of a Committee appointed by the Cinematograph Films Council, 1944.

† Report of the Central Price Regulating Committee, 1945.

‡ Report of the Committee of Investigation appointed by the Ministry of Supply, 1947.

§ Report of the Committee appointed by the Minister of Works, 1947.

‖ Report of the Committee of Enquiry appointed by the Minister of Works, 1949.

The critical attitude towards restrictive practices caused a number of associations voluntarily to review and revise some of their agreements both before and after the passing of the Monopolies Act. But since 1948 the prevalence of such agreements and industry's conviction of the need for them has kept both Government and industry preoccupied less with how to strengthen industry's internal organisations than with how to determine where the public interest lies in relation to the control of competition.

CHAPTER 2

THE PRESENT STRUCTURE OF ASSOCIATIONS IN INDUSTRY

THE aim of this chapter is to provide a brief conspectus of the range and scope of trade associations in British industries. By naming the major associations and indicating the field they cover, and also by describing where the smaller associations are found, it is hoped to give a map of the association world. This may serve as some guide to the location and area of associations mentioned in the rest of the report.

There are two broad national bodies, the Federation of British Industries and the National Union of Manufacturers, each covering the whole range of industry. Then there are between thirty and forty federal or very large associations, such as the Association of British Chemical Manufacturers, the British Iron and Steel Federation, the Wool Textile Delegation and so on. Each of these covers a complete industry. The great majority of associations are smaller bodies, serving narrower sectors of industry and, in the main, covering the production of a single type of product, or a single process in the horizontally organised industries.

This picture, however, is likely to be more misleading than illuminating if there is any idea of treating it as a precise hierarchy. An attempt to set out in detail the structure of any section of industry would show that there are a great number of independent associations, neither affiliated to a wider body, nor having attached associations themselves; that the association with the widest scope is not necessarily the most important one; that different associations cover the same trade for different purposes; that some product associations are affiliated to more than one industry-association; and that there are various other cases of overlapping and anomaly. Such a picture would also be no guide to the strength, functions and effectiveness of the various associations. In this chapter the method will be to describe the general layout and indicate roughly the relative importance of associations, rather than to establish a detailed classification by size and type.

The relationship between associations that are described as

"federated" or "affiliated" may vary a good deal. In some cases it is largely a formal matter, with some occasional consultation and co-operation, as between the Association of British Pharmaceutical Industry and the Association of British Chemical Manufacturers. In others there may be much closer integration, and the federation may provide the secretarial services of its constituents. It is always imprudent to make assumptions about the degree of influence of a federation over its affiliated or member-associations.

The general national associations

The Federation of British Industries consists both of individual firms and of trade associations. There are over seven thousand firms in membership, and nearly three hundred associations, found in all sectors of industry. The great majority are in the manufacturing trades with which this report is concerned, but some distributive firms and associations, and even the National Farmers' Union, are included. There is some overlapping, in that many individual member-firms are also members of associations; and again in that both federal associations and their constituent organisations may be members. Few major associations and very few of the largest industrial firms are outside the F.B.I.; even so about forty per cent of its industrial membership comprises firms with less than a hundred employees.

The National Union of Manufacturers, though it extends to all branches of industry, cannot claim to be so fully representative of its major units. It has between five and six thousand member-firms and is especially representative of small and medium-sized firms, employing up to about five hundred workpeople. The N.U.M. has over sixty affiliated associations, within the definition used in the report. Though many of these are small product organisations, several major associations such as the Glass Manufacturers Federation and the Council of Ironfoundry Associations are included.

The Association of British Chambers of Commerce is a third important general organisation at national level, but like other chambers of commerce it is excluded from the survey by the definition of trade association used in this report. The British Employers Confederation, the national organisation for labour matters, is similarly excluded by definition.

The standard industrial classification

A standard industrial classification,* first published in 1948, is now used for most official purposes, including the censuses of production, distribution and population. It has therefore proved convenient to relate associations to this framework, both in this chapter and in the report in general. The classification is strictly by industries, not by occupation or by ownership.

There are twenty-four major industrial groups, referred to as Orders, of which fifteen (numbers II to XVI) fall within the scope of the report. These are divided under Minimum List headings, of which over a hundred are relevant. The classification further suggests sub-divisions of these headings for use when required.

The register of trade associations printed at the end of the report follows this classification, and provides information supplementary to this preliminary survey.

NUMBER OF NATIONAL MANUFACTURERS' ASSOCIATIONS

Note: Each association is counted only once, in the first Order in which it appears.

II.	Mining and quarrying	19
III.	Non-metalliferous mining products	92
IV.	Chemicals and allied trades	87
V.	Metal manufacturing	127
VI.	Mechanical and electrical engineering	182
VII.	Vehicles	22
VIII.	Other metal goods	139
IX.	Precision instruments, jewellery	37
X.	Textiles	172
XI.	Leather and fur	17
XII.	Clothing	63
XIII.	Food, drink and tobacco	120
XIV.	Wood and cork	70
XV.	Paper and printing	75
XVI.	Miscellaneous manufactures	78
	TOTAL	1,300

* *Standard Industrial Classification* (H.M.S.O.), 1948, reprinted 1956.

The Orders and lesser headings of the standard industrial classification are suitable only for purposes of description; they cannot be used for quantitative comparison. The fact that there are more associations in one Order than another does not prove a more fragmentary style of organisation—it may only mean that one Order covers a wider product range than the other. Nevertheless it may be helpful to give some information about the number of associations in various parts of industry, if it is borne in mind that it depends as much on variety of products as on multiplicity of organisations.

It might be suggested that while comparison of numbers between Orders is of little value, some correlation might be attempted between the number of associations in an Order and other characteristics of that industry.

Business concentration—the extent to which the capacity of an industry is controlled by a small number of firms—could be held to have a bearing on the structure of that industry's associations. Unfortunately, little can be inferred from mere statistical inspection. Highly concentrated industries, in which over eighty per cent of the workers are employed by three or four firms, include wallpaper, cement, salt, asbestos cement, and dyes and dyestuffs. In each of these there are only one or two major associations; but in refractory goods and in sanitary ware, for instance, in which less than thirty per cent of the employment is concentrated in the largest firms, there is similarly only one association in each industry.* In any event it cannot be determined by these methods whether a small number of associations in an industry shows a disinclination to their formation, or, on the contrary, a highly successful and unified organisation.

Nor do other industrial characteristics, such as the rate of expansion or the proportion of output exported, obviously determine the number or strength of associations in an industry. The forces holding associations together are analysed in the section on centripetal forces in Chapter 6, "The Logic of Organisation"; by now these seem to be of sufficient strength to make trade associations practically universal in all industries, although they differ greatly in function.

* For details of concentration in industry we are indebted to the National Institute of Economic and Social Research, whose study of Business Concentration is to appear shortly.

MAP OF ASSOCIATIONS

Order I of the standard industrial classification comprises agriculture, forestry and fishing, with which this report is not concerned. The second Order includes various forms of mining and quarrying. This sector of industry is not large if coal mining is not considered; it has little direct interest in exports, and the size of firm is usually small. The disappearance of the Mining Association leaves the Federated Quarry Owners of Great Britain as perhaps the major association in the field; it includes also the National Council of Associated Iron Ore Producers and the North Wales Slate Quarries Association.

In the Order concerned with non-metalliferous mining products there are a number of major associations—the National Federation of Clay Industries, the British Pottery Manufacturers Federation, the Glass Manufacturers Federation and the Cement Makers Federation. The clay industry also includes a large number of associations concerned with special types of bricks, pipes and so on, as well as numerous local brick associations. In pottery also there are many product associations, some of which are affiliated to the federation. The Sheet and Plate Glass Manufacturers Association is separate from the Glass Manufacturers Federation, that part of the industry being dominated by Pilkington Brothers, Ltd. There are also one or two associations concerned with scientific and other specialised glass products. The Cement Makers Federation, an employers' certificated trade union, is concerned with commercial matters; there is a parallel body, the Cement and Concrete Association, largely concerned with technical services.

Many of the associations in these industries—and in metal and timber—are members of the National Council of Building Material Producers. This body represents these manufacturers only as suppliers to the building industry, and is not concerned with the other interests of its constituent associations or their member-firms.

The Order devoted to chemical and allied trades covers a wider field than is normally implied by "the chemical industry". The two largest companies in British industry and many other large concerns are centred in it. In the coke oven section the leading associations are perhaps the British Coking Industry Association and the British Tar Confederation. The Association of British Chemical Manufacturers and its affiliated associations dominate the chemical industry proper, with the Association of British Pharmaceutical Industry and the Proprietary Association of Great Britain in the pharmaceutical industry. Much of the industry organised in the British Plastics Federation is classified in this Order. In the paint industry there are two large associations, the National Paint Federation and the Society of British Paint Manufacturers, and a few small ones, including two or three dealing with the raw materials of paint. The Society of British Soap Makers is now the main soap association.

There is apparently no trade association in the petroleum industry, though there is close direct co-operation between the firms. There are in this sector associations concerned with vegetable oils, with adhesives and with other products.

Metal industries

The British Iron and Steel Federation, to judge by the range of its activities perhaps the most important of all manufacturers' associations, has interests in most parts of the iron and steel industry; but it is not entirely comprehensive and some sections of the industry and their associations are quite separate from it. The foundry-iron and iron-foundry industry, for instance, has organised the Joint Iron Council as a central body to look after its affairs. This comprises two federations of associations, the Council of Iron Producers and the Council of Ironfoundry Associations. One of these (the Council of Iron Producers) is affiliated to—though not a member of—the British Iron and Steel Federation. The Joint Iron Council regards the foundry pig iron producing and ironfounding activities represented by its two councils as a quite separate and distinct industry from the iron and steel industry represented by the B.I.S.F.

The British Iron and Steel Federation itself is organised into ten conferences, which themselves consist of product associations. These cover most forms of steel as it is supplied to the metal-using industries—ingots, billets, rails, sheets, tinplate, wire rods, heavy forgings, stainless steel and so on. The steel wire and the bolt and rivet industries are no longer associated with the B.I.S.F. Supervisory functions with regard to the main range of iron and steel products are carried out by the Iron and Steel Board, an independent statutory body. Its powers relate particularly to raw materials, prices, and industrial development.

The main association concerned with non-ferrous metals is the British Non-ferrous Metals Federation. There are several market development associations in this field, composed largely of overseas producers, which aim to promote the use of their metal—copper, lead, aluminium or zinc—in this country.

Engineering, shipbuilding and electrical goods

The next Order in the standard industrial classification covers a very wide sector of industry, employing about two million persons, nearly one-tenth of the total employed population. It includes the manufacture of a great variety of products, from heavy capital equipment to ball bearings and spring balances, of firms from the smallest to concerns like Vickers Ltd. and Babcock and Wilcox Ltd.

The Shipbuilding Conference includes virtually all the builders of ships over 500 tons. Builders of smaller vessels are organised in the Ship and Boat Builders National Federation, and marine engineers in the National Association of Marine Engine Builders. There is also the Dry-dock Owners and Repairers Central Council.

A very large part of this Order consists of the various types of mechanical engineering. The British Engineers Association includes firms and affiliated associations from many of these industries, including the Agricultural Engineers Association, the Council of British Manufacturers of Petroleum Equipment, the Machine Tool Trades Association and the Food Machinery Association. The Engineering Industries Association is an association especially strong among smaller firms in this field, and includes some electrical firms. There are a number of important associations in this sector, however, not connected with these wide organisations. They include the National Federation of Engineers' Tools Manufacturers at Sheffield, the Textile Machinery and Accessory Manufacturers Association, and the British Constructional Steelwork Association. The manufacture of office machinery is covered by the Office Appliance and Business Equipment Trades Association and the Typewriter (and Allied) Trades Federation, a body which includes distributors as well as manufacturers. Various mining equipment associations are united in the Federation of Associations of Colliery Equipment Manufacturers. The numerous other product associations in this part of industry include the British Refrigeration Association, the British Chemical Plant Manufacturers Association, and the Society of British Gas Industries.

The electrical industry's chief association is the British Electrical and Allied Manufacturers Association, whose thirty-three sections cover most types of product in this field. The cable industry is separately organised in the Cable Makers Association, and the wireless, television and allied manufacturers have four associations grouped into the Radio Industry Council. The Electric Lamp Manufacturers Association is the most important of several associations covering various types of lighting equipment. There are also a number of associations dealing with electrically-powered goods, such as the Electric Water Heater Manufacturers Association.

Vehicles

Order VII of the classification is devoted to the various types of vehicles used on roads, rail, or in the air. Two of these industries are relatively new, having been built up largely in the last forty years, and are subject to rapid technical change. Generally speaking, manufacturing firms in this section of industry tend to be large, for capital requirements are high.

The Society of Motor Manufacturers and Traders, a leading association in all respects, covers the whole motor vehicle industry (except motor cycles), including distributors and importers, though it is British manufacturers who provide the main weight behind it. The S.M.M.T. is responsible for policy matters and the provision of services, including exhibitions, to the industry. Another association covering the same field, the British Motor Trade Association, was charged with a purely executive function, that of the enforcement of the resale prices determined by the manufacturers. The cycle and motor-cycle industries have organised the British Cycle and Motor Cycle Industries Association, formerly known as the "Coventry Union", to look after their interests.

The Society of British Aircraft Constructors Ltd. is the only association in the aircraft industry. Like the S.M.M.T. and the B.E.A.M.A. it is almost as old as its industry, and has not had to be organised in an already existing industry. The part of the locomotive industry outside the nationalised railway workshops is represented by the Locomotive Manufacturers Association.

Metal goods etc.

At Light Trades House, Sheffield, there are a number of associations which are mostly federated either to the National Federation of Engineers' Tools Manufacturers (already mentioned) or the Federation of British Hand Tool Manufacturers. They are frequently concerned with price regulation in their industries. The National Hardware Alliance is a federal organisation uniting both manufacturers' and distributors' associations concerned with ironmongery, brassware, hollow-ware and similar goods.

The main association concerned with photographic goods is the British Photographic Manufacturers Association Ltd.; with clocks, the British Clock and Watch Manufacturers Association; and with jewellery, the British Jewellers Association. There is an Association of Musical Instrument Industries Ltd. and also a Pianoforte Manufacturers Association Ltd.

Textiles

Textiles, Order X, covers about a million employees, and includes all stages of production except the making of clothing. There is a horizontal structure of enterprise in the textile industries, and accordingly associations tend to be based on processes rather than products. Firms are usually small, though in man-made fibres there are Courtaulds Ltd., British Celanese Ltd. and other large companies, and in cotton some large vertical combines have developed.

In the cotton industry a statutory development council, the Cotton Board, is the only general unifying body. The Federation of Master Cotton Spinners Associations Ltd. comprises all the local associations of spinning firms. The Cotton Spinners and Manufacturers Association is a federal association most of whose member-firms are weavers, but it includes several vertical combinations. The Wool Textile Delegation federates the woollen and worsted industries of all parts of the country, and the British Man-made Fibres Federation is concerned with new fibres such as rayon and nylon: both consist, in the main, of process associations, though one or two geographical or product associations are affiliated. Other fibres also have their associations—the Silk and Rayon Users Association, the Flaxspinners and Manufacturers Association, and the Association of Jute Spinners and Manufacturers.

The Order continues with a series of headings for products manufactured from these and other fibres; each has several associations. Leading organisations in this field include the Hard Fibre Cordage Federation, the Federation of British Carpet Manufacturers, the Textile Narrow Fabrics Council, the Domestic Textiles Federation, the National Federation of Bedding and Allied Trades and the Surgical Dressings Manufacturers Association. In hosiery, the National Hosiery Manufacturers Federation is the main association; there is also the British Hosiery Manufacturers Association. Textile finishing of all types for all fibres is covered by the Textile Finishing Trades Association.

Leather

A small Order of the classification is devoted to leather and fur. Major associations in the field are the United Tanners Federation, for heavier leathers, and British Leather Federation, for light leather.

Clothing

With the exception of one or two firms in wholesale tailoring, the clothing industries still consist of relatively small firms, sometimes very small firms. Capital requirements are low and entry to the industry is very easy. Recently, however, a number of larger firms have begun to emerge in the light clothing section. The two leading associations are the Wholesale Clothing Manufacturers Federation and the Apparel and Fashion Industry's Association. The first is concerned largely with heavy clothing, suits and so on, and the second chiefly with light clothing, women's dresses, etc., but the division is by no means precise. There is also a considerable number of associations concerned with other types of garment—shirts, overalls, rainwear, children's wear, underclothing, hats, uniforms, corsets and so on; but the industry is essentially still a small-firm one, and organisation is difficult to achieve.

Footwear manufacturers' local associations, with the exception of the Lancashire one, are united by the Incorporated Federated

Associations of Boot and Shoe Manufacturers of Great Britain and Ireland.

Food, drink and tobacco

There is a large number of trades concerned with the preparation and manufacture of food, mostly producing consumer goods. The Food Manufacturers Federation has sections in many of the sub-divisions of this Order and is one of the major organisations concerned. Flourmilling interests are represented by the Incorporated National Association of British and Irish Millers and a few specialist associations. There are several associations concerned with biscuits and flour confectionery, the Cake and Biscuit Alliance being perhaps the most important. Among fish, meat, fruit and milk products there are a number of associations, some of which are affiliated to the Food Manufacturers Federation. Other important food industries are represented by the British Sugar Refiners Association and the Cocoa, Chocolate and Confectionery Alliance.

Major associations in the drink industries include the Brewers Society, a federation of numerous local associations, the Scotch Whisky Association and the National Association of Soft Drinks Manufacturers. In tobacco, the Tobacco Trade Association* was fully comprehensive but was concerned mainly with distributive matters; the Federation of Home and Export Tobacco Manufacturers Ltd. does not include the Imperial Tobacco Company.

Wood, paper and printing

Firms in the Order concerned with manufacture of wood and cork are rarely large. There is a large number of associations concerned with particular trades and products; among those with more general interests the Timber Trade Federation, the Timber Development Association and the English Joinery Manufacturers Association are the most important. The furniture sub-heading includes soft furnishings, and there is a Furnishing Fabrics Federation, a textile association in Manchester. In furniture proper the main association is the British Furniture Manufacturers Federated Associations; there is also the Furniture Development Council, a statutory body serving the industry. There are a large number of product associations in the paper and board industries,

* Wound up in 1956.

a considerable number of which are affiliated to the British Paper and Board Makers Association Incorporated. The National Wallpaper Council and the Stationers Association are independent organisations of importance.

The major printers' association is the British Federation of Master Printers. Book publishing is covered by the Publishers Association, sponsors of the net book agreement. The London newspapers are organised in the Newspaper Proprietors Association, the provincial press in the Newspaper Society, and periodicals in the Periodical Proprietors Association Ltd.

Other industries

Rubber is perhaps the most important industry not covered so far. About half the output of the industry takes the form of tyres, and this part of the industry is represented by the Tyre Manufacturers Conference Ltd. Together with the associations representing other rubber products, this association is affiliated to the Federation of British Rubber and Allied Manufacturers Associations.

Other notable associations include the Linoleum Manufacturers Association, the British Toy Manufacturers Association Ltd. and the Federation of British Manufacturers of Sports and Games Ltd. The plastics moulding industry, classified in this miscellaneous Order XVI, is covered by the British Plastics Federation, already mentioned.

To sum up, the above catalogue of leading associations is intended to show the spread of an institution rather than the distribution of particular practices. Practically all associations undertake representative functions on behalf of their members, pressing their point of view with the ministries, other public bodies, suppliers or customers. Most of them provide services for their member-firms, to assist the production or commercial side of their enterprises. Some of them have attempted to regulate the economic fortunes of the industry. Little guide to these matters could be provided in the foregoing survey; they are dealt with at length in the next part of the report, which deals with association activities. This chapter has shown what associations exist. The next part of the report is devoted to the purposes of their existence.

PART II

The Activities of Associations

INTRODUCTORY NOTE

PERHAPS the most noticeable characteristic of trade associations is their flexibility in terms both of their membership and of the functions they perform. It has already been made clear that an association may comprise a small number of manufacturers making a highly specialised product, or a very large number of firms concerned with many related products. The majority with which this report is concerned consists predominantly of manufacturers but many include distributors, suppliers of raw materials, or both.

However dissimilar associations may be in coverage, their activities are determined by two features shared by all. All members have a common interest in a particular product or process. Second, membership is voluntary in that the identity of member-firms is fully preserved and, in general, firms are free to join or not as they wish. Some interests of firms are better cared for by general associations like the F.B.I. or the N.U.M., or by geographically-based ones, usually chambers of commerce. Some activities, notably collective trading, are virtually denied to trade associations by the inherent character of the grouping.

Little can be deduced about the intensity of an association's activities simply by looking at its size and the product it represents. But there are certain broad limitations on the type of work done by associations at different levels. Thus the nature of the product itself may prevent certain types of activity—in the field of publicity, for instance—and for some purposes the single product association may, and often does, co-operate with other related associations.

It has not been possible within the scope of this inquiry to make a full analysis of the distribution of activities among associations. It can only be suggested that, broadly, industrial associations usually deal with high-level government contacts and general publicity; and product associations, or sections within associations, tend to deal more with specific problems and particular difficulties of firms, and possibly attempt the economic regulation of the trade. But there is certainly no hard and fast rule about this division of functions.

The flexible character of associations gives them considerable scope for changing the nature of their work over a period. It was seen in Chapter 1 that associations develop for various reasons; but they may continue in existence for quite different reasons, and a description of their activities cannot therefore be "timeless". The description of associations' work given in the following chapters refers to the early 1950s.

The majority of associations were formed for what can be described as "defensive" purposes, a term which includes negotiation with labour and representation to Government as well as attempts to mitigate competition in one way or another. A more recent development has been the extension of promotional and "common service" activities, some of which can be performed only by a large number of firms acting together. The description of association work given in the following chapters shows that many associations are organising such external economies in much the same way as the single large firm acquires advantages by virtue of its size. Indeed as this aspect of their work develops, associations can be increasingly regarded as substitutes for outright amalgamation in industry.

In order to examine what associations do, activities have been grouped under three main headings in this part of the report. The first concerns representational functions in which they act as a channel of communication with Government and other organised groups; the second deals with the common services which associations provide to improve the efficiency and market knowledge of their members; the third considers the most controversial aspect of trade associations, namely their employment for purposes of restricting competition. These are not, of course, watertight compartments: many associations are engaged, to a greater or lesser extent, in all three types of activity. In particular it is important to put into perspective the third aspect of association activities—restriction of competition—by indicating the extent to which associations have been, in fact, concerned with any kind of economic control.

ACTIVITIES OF GENERAL ASSOCIATIONS

The existence of the two general national associations covering productive industry—the F.B.I. and the N.U.M.—has been referred to in the previous chapter. It will be convenient at this stage to describe their activities in some detail. They are manufacturers' trade associations, and thus it would be wrong to omit them from this report, but in many ways they are different in kind from the association covering a single industry, with which the report is mainly concerned, and much of the work of the individual associations is completed through the mechanism of the national bodies. Much is also done at this level by the Association of British Chambers of Commerce and, on labour matters, by the British Employers' Confederation. But, as already explained, the definition of trade association used here precludes consideration of them.

The F.B.I. and the N.U.M. are alike in including as members both trade associations and individual firms. Many of the latter are, of course, also members of their trade associations; and both bodies, by granting a rebate on subscription rates, offer an incentive to firms to join associations in their membership. The scope of this mixed membership of the F.B.I. and N.U.M. is described at the beginning of Chapter 2. The mixed-membership principle, which is seldom found among the federations covering individual industries, is sometimes thought illogical. So far as the central organisations of the F.B.I. and the N.U.M. are concerned, however, it has real advantages. Their contacts with individual firms bring them into direct touch with their practical problems, and enable them to draw directly on the services of their experts for the work of some committees. At the same time it provides the focus for action on problems which are outside the range of any association covering a particular trade.

The chief purpose of the F.B.I. is to provide a means of formulating and promoting industrial policy, and a channel through which an authoritative view can be expressed on behalf of its members collectively. In the course of time it has developed other activities. These include the provision of services at home and overseas which promote the interests of industry in general, and also direct help in solving problems to individual member-firms, and to associations to some degree. In London these activities now occupy a staff of 160, headed by the director-general. He is helped by the general secretary and three directors (overseas, technical and home services and information) and by the economic adviser. There is also a regional staff of about fifty. Overseas the F.B.I. has full-time staff in the bigger markets and part-time representatives in the smaller.

Representation

A major part of the federation's policy work involves relations with the Government. While the individual trade associations have their own occasions for contact on matters peculiar to themselves, the F.B.I. is concerned when a problem is common to several or all industries. Such problems range from major issues of government policy—such as the British attitude to European integration—to matters of administration, such as the terms and conditions of government contracts. Recommendations on policy are generally drawn up by committees in consultation with the senior staff; but the final determination of any issue is a matter for the Grand Council, which is representative of both F.B.I. member-associations and member-firms.

Formal channels of contact with the Government are provided by membership of a wide range of bodies, ranging from the very general such as the National Production Advisory Council, whose chairman is the Chancellor of the Exchequer, to the very specialised such as the Water Softening Sub-Committee of the Ministry of Health's Central Advisory Water Committee. With some bodies, such as the Regional Boards for Industry, it is a case of making nominations rather than having direct representation. Then there are royal commissions and official committees of inquiry, to which the F.B.I. frequently gives evidence. F.B.I. office-bearers often meet the Prime Minister or his colleagues to discuss particular issues on the initiative of either side. Members of the staff are constantly meeting civil servants at any level from permanent secretary downwards.

This consultation is a two-way traffic. The F.B.I. may want to put its views on the forthcoming budget before the Chancellor of the Exchequer and officials of the Board of Inland Revenue, or to find out the Ministry of Fuel and Power's expectations about the level of coal stocks. On the other hand, the Government may wish to obtain industry's views and help on a major issue of economic policy, or its suggestions for the membership of a mission to an overseas market, or its help in entertaining foreign officials and industrialists.

The federation is also in touch with the nationalised industries partly through their consultative committees, to which it makes nominations, but equally by direct contacts.

The F.B.I. relies more upon its contact with the Government through Ministers and civil servants than upon direct action through Members of Parliament. If it has views to advance on legislative proposals it presents them to the Minister concerned and his advisers, trusting to the strength of its case and its reputation. Where its views are not accepted it has been able to get help from M.P.s or peers to put the F.B.I. point of view before Parliament.

Some of the federation's activities look inward rather than outward. The Grand Council from time to time decides to commend certain lines of action or policy to F.B.I. members and to industry at large. It is in this way that it tries to exercise its important function of industrial leadership, though it can only proceed by consent and cannot enforce industrial action. A recent example has been its appeal to firms to exercise restraint in their price policy as a contribution to restraining inflation. Another example is in fuel economy, where the F.B.I. has emphasised the need and, through booklets and articles and its own small advisory service, has suggested the means. In two special cases, the promotion of sales to dollar markets and productivity, it works with other bodies, through the Dollar Exports Council and the British Productivity Council.

It is also the means whereby members can exchange experience and ideas. Interested associations have met to discuss how they can best help their members with, for example, their export difficulties; or firms with their own research departments are brought together, sometimes with representatives of D.S.I.R. and the universities, to discuss common problems; and conferences have been held with the universities, technical colleges and schools, for each to get to know the other's needs.

As the mouthpiece of its members, the F.B.I. makes its views known and seeks public support for its case. Several times since the war it has issued general statements about the country's economic problems. Its office-bearers make speeches dealing with current preoccupations. Its monthly journal, the *F.B.I. Review*, though primarily for members, is increasingly read outside.

The F.B.I.'s work inevitably brings it into touch with other organisations. It often works closely with the Association of British Chambers of Commerce and the National Union of Manufacturers, and with the British Employers Confederation, which represents industry as employers of labour, but whose policies from time to time affect and are affected by those of the F.B.I. It also collaborates with specialist bodies such as the British Standards Institution.

Overseas activities

A feature of the F.B.I. is its extensive activity overseas. It is a member of the Council of European Industrial Federations, through which it discusses commercial and economic problems affecting Western Europe and this provides a link with the O.E.E.C. This council was, for example, the means of securing wide international industrial condemnation of export subsidies. There are also occasional meetings between the F.B.I. and individual European federations for discussions. It is represented on the British National Committee of the International Chamber of Commerce.

Overseas, the F.B.I. is represented in some ninety countries. In some of the main overseas markets it maintains a permanent staff which is involved in policy work with the government there; and on occasion head office staff may go abroad for this purpose. The F.B.I. is often instrumental in organising industrial missions abroad, and sometimes provides the secretariat for them.

For individual members interested in overseas trade it provides a wide range of services, either direct from the Overseas Department, which employs a quarter of the F.B.I.'s total staff, or from its many representatives abroad. General market reports are supplied, and detailed information about tariffs, quota restrictions and the like; firms are helped to secure suitable agents, are provided with introductions when they go abroad, and are given chances of meeting foreign buyers in this country.

Services

Sometimes through its committees, but mainly through its staff, the F.B.I. gives an immense amount of help to its individual members. Requests for information about the interpretation of legislation and government regulations, the availability of particular statistics, suitable advertising media, the basis of electricity charges, sources of supply of particular products, a large number of questions on overseas trade—some 30,000 queries of this sort are dealt with annually.* An individual firm's problems will not usually be taken up with Government but it is advised how and where to present them itself. Sometimes such problems raise points of general principle; these may then be handled through the normal policy making machinery.

A recent development of the F.B.I.'s services is the establishment of a subsidiary company, British Overseas Fairs Ltd., which helps industries and firms by organising participation in international exhibitions or all-British exhibitions overseas.

The F.B.I.'s work in providing services through which the individual firm can carry on its own business better is as important in its way as its work on matters of policy. It offers help of a kind which it would be uneconomic for any but the biggest associations to try to give, and which is quite beyond the resources of many individual firms.

The National Union of Manufacturers

The main purpose of the National Union of Manufacturers is to present to the Government the needs and views of manufacing industry as a whole. To this collective purpose, which had its origins during and immediately after World War I, has been added the secondary purpose of assisting its members in all possible ways. The National Union also provides offices and administrative staff for a number of affiliated trade associations.

The national activities of the National Union of Manufacturers are in themselves extremely varied. Formal contact with the Government is maintained by representation on various industrial committees which have been set up by the Government for consultation with industry. Chief among these is the National Production Advisory Council. This Council is served and

* An F.B.I. handbook lists twenty-eight subjects under the following headings: Company Law, Contracts, Consultants, Education, Finance, Fuel Efficiency, Imports, Industrial Research, Insurance, Market Information, Patents and Trade Marks, Publicity, Rating and Valuation, Statistics and General Intelligence, Taxation, Technical Legislation, Town and Country Planning, Trade Effluent Disposal, Trade Fairs and Exhibitions, Transport, Travel, Appointment of Agents, Certificates of Origin, Exchange and Banking Regulations, General Export Intelligence, Introductions, Overseas Tariffs and Import Regulations, Status Reports.

supported by the regional boards for industry, for membership of which the N.U.M. may make nominations. Among other government standing committees on which the National Union of Manufacturers (like the F.B.I.) is represented are the Consultative Committee for Industry, the Bilateral Trade Negotiations Committee and the Revolving Loan Fund Committee.

From time to time the National Union of Manufacturers is invited to present the views of industry to royal commissions and other government committees appointed to examine specific questions. In recent years, for example, evidence has been submitted to the Royal Commission on Taxation, the Ridley Committee on National Fuel Policy and the Verdon Smith Committee on the Census of Production. Like other national bodies, the National Union of Manufacturers is frequently asked to nominate a member to an *ad hoc* government committee.

The National Union is also represented on industrial committees which have been set up by industry itself; amongst the most important are the British Productivity Council and the Dollar Exports Council. It is one of the nominating bodies for membership of the various consumers' councils for the nationalised industries, which include the National Coal Consumers' Council, the gas and electricity consultative councils, the Central Transport Consultative Committee and many regional transport users' consultative committees.

Legislative proposals and Parliamentary proceedings which affect industry are closely watched by the National Union, and it makes direct representations to the Government, when necessary, on industrial matters. While many of the contacts already mentioned are mainly formal in character, the National Union has an informal relationship with the officials of government departments, particularly those concerned with industrial and economic affairs, to whom the views of members can always be put. It has become part of normal procedure for government departments to consult the National Union, among other industrial bodies, when advice is required on industrial or economic questions.

The National Union's journal, *The British Manufacturer*, which is published monthly, provides a link between members as well as a useful organ for the collective expression of opinion on the more important topics of the day.

Out of its original purpose to serve members collectively, the

N.U.M. has developed an organisation which serves its members individually. It has two specialised services. The first, the Export Assistance Department, provides an expert service of advice on export problems and gives members up-to-date information on world markets as well as opportunities for meeting foreign buying missions. The second, the Industrial Advisory Service, gives advice on management and production problems and, if necessary, provides practical help in putting this advice into effect. Production methods, plant layout, the improved use of labour, incentive schemes, costing and estimating procedures, management policy and organisation, and selection of executive staff are among the matters on which advice and assistance is available.

In addition to its general work, the National Union of Manufacturers continually helps individual member-firms with many non-specialised problems. Such services, which are available at all the branch offices, are becoming more extensively used by members.

CHAPTER 3

REPRESENTATION

One of the main functions of nearly all trade associations is to put the views of their members before other bodies. This type of activity is considered here under four main heads—first, relations in general with government departments; secondly, relations with the contracting side of government departments; thirdly, relations with public corporations and similar bodies; and finally, relations with other suppliers and customers.

GOVERNMENT AND TRADE ASSOCIATIONS

The subject of this section is a vital part of public administration. The purpose is to give an account of the whole range of contacts, formal and informal, which trade associations have with various government departments. This is not the place to argue the rights and wrongs of government intervention into the affairs of industry nor to explain the reasons for the assumption by the State of ever-increasing responsibilities for economic and social welfare. Here it is sufficient to observe that governmental intervention into the detailed affairs of industry has not only encouraged the formation of new organisations representing manufacturers' interests and further strengthened the existing associations of firms, but has given rise to new forms of relationship between these non-governmental organisations and government offices.

In much the same way that trade unions, once they have achieved a high degree of organisation and power, stimulate employers to combine and form associations of their own, the great concentration of administrative power in the hands of the State has frequently led to the formation of new, and often tightly organised, trade associations.

The need for voluntary organisations, fully representative of the industrial interests covered by them, is generally recognised by Government and industry alike.

From the point of view of the Government it is always a matter of great convenience to have a single consultative body for an industry. Sometimes the need for decision is urgent and time does not permit consultations with a great number of bodies or individual firms—a general view is required at short notice. Again, it is a great advantage for ministers and civil servants if differences of opinion in an industry can be reconciled inside an association before the question is brought before a department—the smaller the number of views the official has to deal with the simpler his task. The Government, therefore, is likely to welcome not only associations of manufacturers turning out similar products, but the federation of associations. But this in no way precludes the interchange of views between government departments and individual firms when this is desired by either side.

Trade associations are also an invaluable source of expert knowledge and advice on industrial matters. Ministries cannot contain specialists in all branches and problems of industry. Associations, however, can and do provide up-to-date information on the needs of particular trades. Specifically, when trade negotiations with other countries, or a conference of countries working together under the General Agreement on Tariffs and Trade (G.A.T.T.) are about to take place, the Board of Trade consults the relevant associations on the proposals likely to be discussed. Similarly, all production departments consult the appropriate trade associations on proposed regulations and legislation. This two-way traffic of information and periodic exchange of views is of considerable value to public administrators, trade association officials and business men alike. Moreover, government departments can use some associations as a ready channel of communication with firms in particular lines of business; news about trade problems, new regulations, and business opportunities can conveniently be passed on by associations through bulletins or other types of trade publications.

While it is obviously easier for government departments to deal with a single representative body or with a small number of large units rather than with a large number of small ones, the Government must ensure access on an equal footing to all bona fide organisations representing any section of an industry. Naturally, no department is anxious to deal with more trade associations than it can help, but in a number of industries there are a great many associations, most of which have to be consulted individually or must be given a hearing if a representative picture of the industry's view is to be obtained. The very existence and activity of government departments, therefore, exercises an indirect, but nevertheless strong pressure on manufacturers of similar products to organise themselves into a representative trade association which can speak with full knowledge and authority for the whole, or at least an important section, of the industry.

It is no exaggeration to say that the whole range of trade association activities is of interest to one or more branches of the Government. Two aspects of association work in particular—collective representation of the industry and economic regulation—are of direct concern to individual government departments. The departments which are most immediately affected are those which have a duty to keep track of major developments in, and give assistance to, particular industries, and, also, those which are responsible for buying supplies and placing works contracts for the public service. In the language of Whitehall they are known as "production" and "contracting" departments, but it must be remembered that this differentiation is one of function and internal organisation within ministries rather than between them.* In this chapter these two functions of the government departments concerned will be treated separately.

Production departments

Recognition of the need for collective representation on the part of industry was itself a principal motive for the formation of many associations, and one of the chief objects of trade associations is to make the views of their industries and trades known to the Government of the day. Indeed, most trade associations specifically refer, in their memoranda or other constitutions, to the need of the industry in question to "speak with one voice" in negotiations with government departments; to promote helpful, and resist unfavourable, legislative and administrative developments; to co-operate with government departments; and to act as a channel of communication between government departments and the trade. The appeal of trade associations to individual firms, especially the medium sized and smaller ones, has been as strong on this ground as on any other.

* The division in fact means that many trade associations have contact with two quite distinct branches of the same ministry. The Shipbuilding Conference, for example, is in close touch with both the policy-making departments and the office of the Director of Contracts in the Admiralty.

As the points of contact between the State and industry have become more numerous and as the range of issues on which trade associations are called upon to give advice and information, or on which they desire to make representations, has greatly increased, there has grown up a fairly clearly defined network of administrative relations, both formal and informal, between industries and government departments.

The basic principle on which rests the whole system of these relationships between firms and trade associations on the one hand and government departments on the other, is that of "sponsorship" or "responsibility" for individual industries by a number of ministries known as "production" departments.* There are eight of these, each having "responsibility" for one or more industries, so that between them they cover all the manufacturing trades in the country. The two most important are the Board of Trade and the Ministry of Supply. The Board of Trade deals with all industries which are not covered by the other production departments: this means the great majority of industry, including textiles, chemicals, iron and steel, vehicles, non-ferrous metals, rubber, paper, and that section of the engineering industry which is not directly concerned with the defence programme. The Ministry of Supply is "responsible" for the armaments, explosives, aircraft, radio, electronics and light metal industries. The Admiralty looks after shipbuilding and repairing, small boat construction, and the manufacture of nautical equipment. The General Post Office has responsibility for the telecommunication industry. The Ministry of Works deals with the building, civil engineering, and building materials industries. The food manufacturing and processing industry is the responsibility of the Ministry of Agriculture, Fisheries and Food. Government contact with the coal, gas, and electricity industries, and the oil companies,† is channelled through the Ministry of Fuel and Power. In addition the Ministry of Health is the production department for the medical supplies and pharmaceutical industries.

The present allocation of major industry responsibilities

* The terms "production department" and "sponsoring department" are interchangeable. The former, however, is the term in official use.

† There is no trade association in the petroleum industry in this country. The five major oil companies operating here are represented on the Petroleum Industry Advisory Council, which was set up on the invitation of the Minister of Fuel and Power as the successor organisation to the wartime Petroleum Board.

between these eight government departments, covering the whole field of British industry, is the result of historical factors and administrative needs. There is no general rule which demands that a particular industry comes under one department rather than another. For several centuries the Admiralty has built its own ships and supplied many of its other requirements, and this has given it a special place in relation to shipbuilding and its ancillary industries. It, therefore, accepts responsibility as a production department for merchant ships as well as for warships and also interests itself in the affairs of certain industries producing a wide range of goods mainly intended for civilian use, simply because they are required for Admiralty stores. The other Service departments have no production responsibilities, since their needs are met by the Ministry of Supply.

As far as industry is concerned, every branch of it, no matter how small, has a production or sponsoring department somewhere in the government machine, or a section of a department to which it can turn for advice and help. There are also divisions in the Board of Trade which have a general responsibility for tariff matters and export policy. Trade associations are frequently in contact with them either directly or through the appropriate sections of their production departments.

What the job of a production department is in dealing with its industries is much more difficult to define. It is certainly not a static thing and a great deal depends on the willingness of the industries to co-operate without serious reservations. The production department is the chief link between an industry and the Government. It is a repository and clearing-house for information obtained from many sources. It is in touch at one and the same time with other government departments, with a number of trade associations and trade unions, and a host of individual firms. A production department must have information readily available on the existing capacity of an industry, on the possibilities of its future development, and on present markets at home and abroad. It will often be asked for advice by prospective entrants or by firms wishing to expand and it must be able to give an answer which takes into account all the relevant factors bearing on demand, prospects, supplies of services and labour, the Government's current policy on the location of industry and many other matters involving controls of one sort or another. It must be able to take up complaints and queries, answering them itself or seeing that they get to the right place.

One of the claims often made on behalf of associations is that they help member-firms in their dealings with government departments. It is true that many firms are unfamiliar with the complexities of Whitehall, and welcome advice about the proper place to air their grievances or submit some application or other. In discussing the role of trade associations, the report of the Committee on Intermediaries* said that

> In the performance of intermediary functions the assistance rendered to their members by these organisations is mainly of three kinds. In the first place, assistance and advice is given as to the department to which any particular application should be made, the form in which it should be made and the supporting information which should be furnished. This helps to direct the application into the correct stream and to ease its course through the administrative machine without encountering unnecessary obstacles. The second branch of activity is to assist members whose applications seem to have become held up within the administrative machine. Here the knowledge of the headquarters staffs, both of the difficulties of members and of the workings of the government departments, enables the organisations to assist members in tracing the point at which difficulty has occurred in getting access (where necessary) to the official actually dealing with the matter and in disposing at an early stage of whatever difficulty may have arisen. The third branch of activity consists in taking up at the appropriate level with the government department cases where members feel that they have a grievance arising out of some decision that has gone against them. In all these activities the organisations rely upon the prestige they have acquired, both with members and with departments, and on the confidence which the departments have in the organisations. Their usefulness would be impaired were they to interfere unnecessarily or to take up cases in which there did not appear to be some genuine difficulty or in which they did not thoroughly believe. All the organisations make a practice of sifting the cases they are asked by members to take up and of putting forward only those which they believe to merit consideration.

Some associations, for example the Engineering Industries Association and the clothing associations, make a practice of giving support in this way. But though preliminary advice may

* *Report of the Committee on Intermediaries*, Cmd. 7904 (H.M.S.O.), 1950, p. 44.

be given, in the main, firms deal directly with the ministries, without the intervention of associations. Though this work is a useful service, especially to smaller firms, it is not a major aspect of the relations between Government and associations, and is not so regarded either by the majority of associations or by civil servants.

The production department has a special role in relation to controls where these still exist, such as the prohibition on exports of strategic goods and materials to certain countries. Some controls are operated by the production departments themselves, others are administered by the Treasury or the Foreign Office. In the latter case the production department acts as a channel of communication between the controlling department and the firm. It may, when passing on a firm's formal application, give general support to the permission which is being sought. What is more, it may first have been consulted informally by the firm for advice in preparing the application and for a preliminary opinion as to whether it will succeed. In fact, the production departments encourage firms to make these informal approaches, and although it cannot be bound by advice given informally, both the department and the firms involved often find it useful to be able to discuss problems freely in this way.

It is the job of the production department to be aware of the broad lines of production policy and general market conditions in the industries it covers. It must obtain as much information on what is happening in its industries as it can without losing industry's confidence. It must do everything possible to make the partnership of Government and industry a real one. This is most likely to be achieved if the civil servants and trade association officials concerned feel free to talk to each other about common problems whenever need arises. This is, in fact, the way in which much of the work of trade associations and production departments is accomplished. In many cases there is regular contact of an informal nature—a telephone call, a luncheon engagement, or a personal visit without an agenda—between the full-time officials, usually the director or secretary, of important industry-wide associations and the civil servants, usually of assistant secretary rank, in charge of the relations with particular industries. Personal contact with civil servants who have specialised knowledge of the industry is valued so highly by associations that they dislike frequent transfers of civil servants between posts within the departments.

In addition a production department is in touch with its industries at several different levels, much more formal in character. They range from routine letters sent in by individual firms and trade associations to high-level talks between a delegation from an association, or federation of associations, and the Minister and his advisers.

In the experience of the production departments, most of the major national associations know their way around Whitehall. They understand the internal organisation of the departments and the division of administrative responsibility between different levels of civil servants. They have learnt what kind of problems are dealt with at each level and they will take them directly to the person concerned. In short, they will not take a routine administrative matter to an assistant secretary and they will not ask to see the Minister about a matter which is handled by a principal. Some of the smaller associations, including those run by firms of accountants, however, have less experience of the administrative structure of the Government and are sometimes less successful in finding the right level of approach.

A number of assistant secretaries in charge of industry sections in the production departments, after consulting their diaries for the last year or two, have estimated that they spend about half their time on matters involving liaison with trade associations. The initiative comes from both sides about equally. The production department may get in touch with an association in order to expound and interpret Government policy, to seek information, or to ask the association to help in the details of administration. The trade association will contact its production department in order to communicate the view of its members to the Government and to seek its help on a variety of matters, of which export problems are nowadays the most frequent.

A representative list of topics which are discussed between trade associations and various government departments at the present time would certainly include the following:

i. Promotion of exports, and export control of goods on the restricted list.
ii. Import licensing.

iii. Tariff negotiations (including the General Agreement on Tariffs and Trade).
iv. Consultations prior to trade negotiations with foreign countries.
v. Purchase tax.
vi. Rating of industrial premises.
vii. Location of industry and land-use planning regulations.
viii. Weights and measures.
ix. Merchandise Marks Acts and Patent Acts.
x. Matters arising from restrictive practices.
xi. Proposed legislation and draft orders.
xii. Long-term and short-term supply position of raw materials.
xiii. Planning in case of a national emergency.
xiv. Health and safety regulations.
xv. Recruitment and training of staff.
xvi. Technical and research problems.
xvii. Statistics.
xviii. Exchange of economic information.

This list covers most of the subjects discussed between trade associations and government departments, but in order to get an idea of the extent to which different associations are in touch with the departments and also the purpose of these contacts, it is necessary to look at the experience of a number of them representing various industries.

Associations' experience

Generally speaking it is only the industry associations, or those representing more than a single product, that are in continuous touch with their production departments. This does not mean either that small, single-product associations are never in close touch with government departments, or that many of them do not approach the authorities on specific issues. But the experience of the departments themselves, and of associations, suggests that most of the smaller associations have few occasions to approach Whitehall. There is also the possibility that where a problem arises it will concern other related products also, and representations may be channelled through a more broadly based association to which it may be affiliated.

Some of the leading national associations (or the nominating bodies) are represented on standing committees which report to one or other of the Ministers. The National Advisory Council for the Motor Manufacturing Industry, the Shipbuilding Advisory Committee and the Engineering Advisory Council are cases in point: the Society of Motor Manufacturers and Traders, the Shipbuilding Conference and the British Engineers Association are the associations concerned. In a few associations there are standing arrangements for meetings with a department, but with the removal of wartime controls this practice has declined.

The majority of contacts with production departments take the form either of deputations consisting of the director or secretary together with the chairman or other senior elected officers of the association, who may meet the Minister or his deputies; or less formal meetings or conversations between the senior executive of the association and the principal or assistant secretary of the department concerned. The importance of arriving at a friendly understanding with government departments is well understood in the associations which have frequent contact with them. The scope of an association's work and the diplomacy needed on both sides was neatly summarised in an address by the director of a national association:

> They have been formed to promote co-operation and technical efficiency and in particular to form a medium for placing the views of their industry before government departments and for dealing collectively with the many modern problems involving negotiations with governmental and local authorities. They undoubtedly serve a very useful purpose and when free from any suspicion of monopolistic activities, are recognised by governments as the mouthpiece of their industries and as such more and more are consulted freely on the varied industrial problems with which government departments now have to deal. In fact, they do a great deal of the work of government departments and do it in a way no government official could do because of his lack of knowledge of the peculiarities of industry. During the war, many of them undertook executive work arising out of Government plans, for example in connection with the rationing of raw materials.

The recognition which government departments give to any particular association depends primarily on the statesmanlike way with which the association handles its problems and on the confidence inspired by the staff in their dealings with government officials.

> Under such conditions mutual co-operation and understanding can be established on a basis which is not only satisfactory to both parties, but can be very beneficial to the industry; the government officials will trust the staff sufficiently to inform and consult them on matters which are still highly confidential, without prejudice to the ultimate action of either party, but if there is the slightest suspicion that the association staff has failed to maintain the confidential nature of the information imparted to it, the government officials will shut up like clams and it will be a very long time before that association staff is entrusted with inside information.... Therefore, my serious advice to you is never to press your secretary to divulge what government officials have told him in strict confidence. You will do it only once, as there will be nothing to conceal in future. Government officials are very human and government departments have long memories.

The instances of contact with government departments which follow are drawn from large industry associations, and medium-sized and small associations, some of which are affiliated to broader groups and others which are not. These cases are designed to illustrate the lines on which associations have developed their contacts with production and other departments in the absence of widespread controls, and in general how they act as channels of communication between Government and industry.

Large associations and the departments

To begin with a number of the leading industry associations, the Society of British Aircraft Constructors is in contact with several departments, of which the most important to it is the Ministry of Supply, its "sponsor". It has less frequent contacts with the Air Ministry, the Ministry of Transport and Civil Aviation, and occasionally with the Board of Trade, the Ministries of Education, Labour and others. Relations with the Ministry of Supply are very close on a wide range of subjects including the procurement, design, development and manufacture of aircraft and guided weapons, and their associated equipment. On the technical side the Society co-operates with the Ministry of Supply in a number of special committees and panels concerned with design, development and production. Initiative for meetings comes from both sides. From time to time the society is brought into the activities of other official committees, and has given evidence before the Select Committee on Estimates of the House of Commons.

The British Man-Made Fibres Federation is continuously in touch with the Board of Trade, either providing information on request or making representations on the industry's behalf. The operation of the General Agreement on Tariffs and Trade, the relaxation of restrictions on Japanese imports into certain Colonial territories, the difficulties of exporters dealing with various overseas markets, the submission of cases to oversea governments against higher import duties—these are typical instances of submissions recently made by the federation. It has also been actively pressing for the inclusion of man-made fibres in specifications for fabrics used in the public service, the forces, hospitals, etc., with considerable success. The Board of Trade, for its part, frequently consults the federation on such matters as market conditions and problems in various overseas countries, and generally takes its view as the industry's representative body.

Contact with Government on many fronts is maintained by the Association of British Chemical Manufacturers. Within a few years of its formation the association was actively sponsoring the Key Industry Duty under the Safeguarding of Industries Act, 1921. Later, as a result of representations to the Import Duties Advisory Committee, it secured additional duties on a large number of products made in this country, and the addition of several important raw materials to the free list. During the passing of the Patents and Designs Bill, 1932, the A.B.C.M. secured important amendments to the Bill. Following World War II the Association took part in submitting proposals—which took three years to draw up—to the Patents Committee, and many of these were subsequently incorporated in the Patents Act, 1949. Since 1930 the association has maintained close relations with the Poisons Board, putting forward its views on modifications to the Poisons List and Rules. The association, which consists of both makers and substantial users of chemicals, is usually in a position to put forward a comprehensive view to the various departments with which it deals.

In 1948 the President of the Board of Trade requested the association to undertake a survey of the chemical industry, and this was done in collaboration with the British Plastics Federation. The association is frequently in touch with the Board of Trade, especially with the Tariffs Division, and is consulted by the Import and Export Licensing departments on general matters concerning applications for licences. For this purpose it keeps itself informed about supplies and home demand for a wide range of chemical products. It has also been consulted by the Board of Trade and the Home Office in connection with regulations governing the transport of dangerous chemicals. On matters affecting safety and health the Association of British Chemical Manufacturers is also closely in touch with the Factory Department of the Ministry of Labour, and the Medical Research Council. Some years ago, in conjunction with the Home Office and the Department of Scientific and Industrial Research, the association financed an investigation into methods of detecting various toxic gases met with under industrial conditions, and helped to draw up specifications for a protective respirator. This work is now being revised and extended in conjunction with the D.S.I.R. In co-operation with the Factory Department, the Association of Tar Distillers, the British Chemical Plant Manufacturers Association and the Institute of Petroleum, it has drawn up a set of precautions for use in the distillation of inflammable liquids. Other government departments with which it is in contact are the Ministry of Agriculture on problems of pest control and the Home Office on civil defence.

The officers of the Federation of Master Cotton Spinners Associations maintain close personal touch with the permanent officials of many government departments on questions affecting the industry. From time to time, the federation finds it necessary to make official representations on behalf of the spinning industry to either Ministers or their departments. Within recent months such questions as the reopening of the Liverpool Market, unfair foreign competition, G.A.T.T., and duty on imported machinery have been the subject of discussions with the Board of Trade. Negotiations frequently take place with the Chief Inspector of Taxes in the North-West on taxation questions. The Federation Rating and Valuation Department is in constant touch with the Inland Revenue on the question of mill valuations for rating assessments, and the Federation Accident Department is in almost daily contact with the Factory Department of the Ministry of Labour on questions arising under the Factories Acts. The federation, in collaboration with the spinning trade unions, originated discussions with the Ministry of Labour which eventually led to the recent introduction of the Mule Spinning (Health) Special Regulations, 1953, for the industry. Federation representatives act on the Textiles Committee of the International Labour Organisation and have representatives on various committees set up by the government departments.

Members of the Council of the British Engineers Association, representing mechanical engineering, serve on the Engineering Advisory Council. The association is frequently approached by government departments with requests to nominate industrial representatives to serve on official committees; it is also consulted on questions arising out of bilateral trade negotiations and exports. Subjects on which it has tendered advice and information to government departments include the suspension of import duty on steel, industrial derating, and legislation on inventions and designs.

The British Iron and Steel Federation is in contact with several government departments; for example, the Board of Trade and the Ministry of Labour. It has been associated with periodic government working parties set up to consider such questions as the long-term demand for steel and requirements of steel plates. The federation also submits evidence from time to time to various government committees, either direct or via the Federation of British Industries (for example, the Verdon Smith Committee on the Census of Production). The B.I.S.F. also has direct contact with various statutory bodies such as the National Coal Board and the British Transport Commission. The most important recent development in this sphere arises from the appointment of the Iron and Steel Board under the Iron and Steel Act, 1953, to supervise the industry; regular contact and co-operation have been established between the B.I.S.F. and the Iron and Steel Board at all levels. The general purposes of the B.I.S.F.'s contacts with government departments and statutory bodies is to put forward, on behalf of the industry as a whole, the co-ordinated views of its various sections, and to assist the Government in the implementation of its economic policy.

As already mentioned, the Society of Motor Manufacturers and Traders is the nominating body for the National Advisory Council for the Motor Manufacturing Industry, which was set up by the Minister of Supply in April 1946, in order to provide a means of regular consultation between the Government and the motor manufacturers of the country. It sits under the chairmanship of the Permanent Secretary to the Board of Trade and it consists of eight manufacturing members nominated by the President of the Board of Trade on recommendations put forward by the society; representatives of the ministries most closely involved, namely Supply, Transport and Board of Trade; together with two representatives of the trade unions and one independent member. The council has devoted its attention to many matters affecting the motor industry, principally to the vital question of promoting a greater volume of exports, to the allocation of steel when steel was in short supply, and so on. To date the council has held about forty meetings and its first public report was largely responsible for the alteration made in taxation, from the horsepower to the flat-rate tax, which has assisted the manufacture of larger engines to meet overseas demand. The S.M.M.T. is also able to maintain close liaison with the Board of Trade in that the Director of the society is joint secretary of the National Advisory Council with a representative of the Board.

In 1943 the society instituted a Parliamentary and Legal Council, formed of representatives of the Society and of the British Cycle and Motor Cycle Industries Association Ltd., the Institution of British Carriage and Automobile Manufacturers, the Motor Agents Association and the Scottish Motor Trade Association. This council from the industry's side replaced the Motor Legislation Committee, formed in 1918. The council reviews and advises on all legislative measures affecting the motor industry, makes representations to the Government on its behalf, and co-operates with user organisations where joint interests are involved.

The society may, of course (and often does), put a case to the Government on its own or jointly with other associations. In 1950 and again in 1953, for instance, a number of purchase tax concessions were secured after approaches to the Treasury in one or other of these ways. Representations were made *inter alia* to the Chancellor of the Exchequer and Members of Parliament on vehicle taxation, to the Ministry of Transport on the permitted speed of heavy vehicles, and to the Treasury on capital issues control and hire-purchase regulations. In general, the policy of the society aims to influence, so far as possible, impending legislation in the interests of the motor industry and motor users, and when legislation has come into force, to press for amendments and adjustments in the light of experience.

The principal function of the British Non-Ferrous Metals Federation is to provide a central secretariat and to put forward the agreed views of the industry in discussion with government departments and other trade organisations. The Board of Trade is now the federation's parent ministry. Until the recent concentration in the Board of Trade the Federation had to concern itself with the Ministry of Supply and the Ministry of Materials. While controls lasted there were monthly meetings at the Ministry of Supply concerned with all the subjects of government control—metal supplies and prices, end-use controls, import and export licensing, and inter-governmental problems handled through the International Materials Conference in Washington and O.E.E.C.—and with exchange of information and statistics of interest jointly to the government departments and the industry. The agendas for these monthly meetings were jointly composed and each side took the initiative in bringing forward subjects for discussion. With the departure of controls the meetings have become quarterly, and latterly have taken place even less frequently than that.

Apart from formal meetings, there is a great deal of informal consultation between the civil servants and the officers of the federation. During the period of control and since, the meetings have been between officials. The director of the federation has headed a team composed of the directors of the main federated associations, and this group has reported to the federation and to the associations. The federation always seeks to send to the departments those best able to advise, and while the officials have covered broad questions of control and have advised the departments on commercial questions applying to the industry as a whole, in technical or specialist matters the federation draws upon the directors and staffs of member concerns for the particular knowledge required. In recent months the Board of Trade has been given advice or information on the trend of home trade and export business, on tariffs, on statistics, including Census of Production requirements, and on the supply of raw materials. Although the Government has ceased to act as importer of raw materials, the Board of Trade still holds metal stocks and it has frequently been advised on questions arising in connection with the disposal of copper stocks.

The experience of the Cake and Biscuit Alliance furnishes another good example of contact with Government which, although neither so close nor so essential to the alliance's membership as it was during the war, is still a very large part of its work. The departments chiefly dealt with are the Ministry of Agriculture, Fisheries and Food, the Board of Trade and the Inland Revenue. An important subject of contact with the first is the interpretation and administration of the hygiene regulations of the new Food and Drugs Act. During the initial drafting stages of the Hygiene Regulations a sub-committee of the alliance maintained contact with the (then) Ministry of Food and secured various amendments to the original proposals. Another topic discussed with the Ministry was the Sugar Bill, upon which joint representations were made with the Cocoa, Chocolate and Confectionery Alliance, the Food Manufacturers Federation, other bakery associations and the Co-operative Wholesale Society. The alliance supplies the Ministry with four-weekly returns of biscuit production. There have also been contacts concerning the codification of names of products; a Code of Practice for the Biscuit Industry was published in 1949. Some approaches are on entirely *ad hoc* problems; for instance, during a rail strike arrangements were made for the movement of essential ingredients.

The export of biscuits and cake is the concern of the Board of Trade as well as the Ministry. The alliance is from time to time in contact with the Board of Trade and with the External Relations Division of the Ministry through its own Export Committee, to which government representatives are sometimes invited. The aim of the alliance is to widen its export markets by securing the alleviation of foreign import restrictions. There is contact with the Board about export and import licences. The Board of Trade and other ministries are responsible for packaging, marking, labelling and weights and measures orders and are frequently in touch with the alliance about these things. A recent piece of legislation which has involved the alliance in negotiations with the two departments and with Inland Revenue is the new Rating and Valuation Act.

Although there is now no continuous co-operation with departments engaged in the same task, as there was during controls, relations with the Government are still fairly frequent and close. The initiative may come from either side, and the government connection may include attendance at a committee of the alliance, for instance the Export Committee.

A Cake and Biscuit Manufacturers Export Group was formed during the war, and is still in existence. Its members are drawn from the alliance, and it receives the services of the alliance staff free. In addition there are separate export committees for cake and biscuits. The committees work with the Ministry of Agriculture, Fisheries and Food and the Board of Trade in their efforts to procure the lifting of foreign restrictions against their products, and upon such matters as export licences, foreign regulations and special prices for sugar used in goods for export. The Biscuit Export Committee undertakes the scientific testing of all biscuit and cake before shipment to the States: this is to prevent rejection of the goods under the strict food and drug regulations of the U.S.A. During the period of controls the alliance would not allow replacement of ingredients for these export orders until it received back the certificate of approval issued by its laboratory. This sanction is no longer possible, but these certificates of analysis are still voluntarily remitted to the alliance by members.

The British Plastics Federation is in regular contact with the Board of Trade, the industry's sponsoring department, over export matters and statistics, with the Ministry of Works on matters concerning plastic fitments for housing, and with the Engineering Industries Division of the Board of Trade on plastics working machinery. Its numerous technical activities also bring the federation closely in touch with all the service departments, the Forest Products Research Laboratory, the Factory Inspectorate, and the Fire Research Testing Station. The work of the former Export Group is now done by the federation, which keeps closely in touch with the Export Services Branch of the Board of Trade, passes on export information and gives member firms introductions to overseas markets. From time to time the federation has made representations on specific issues: it was instrumental in securing a reduction in purchase tax on certain plastic articles, in reducing freight rates for a number of plastic materials after negotiations with the railway and shipping authorities, and, after approaches to the Inland Revenue, in obtaining more favourable wear-and-tear allowances for moulding and laminating presses and other processing machinery.

Smaller associations and the departments

So far these examples have been drawn from the work of large industry associations, many of them of a federal character. Those which follow give an idea of the experience of less general and, in some instances, quite small associations representing the manufacturers of a specific product.

The British Coking Industry Association, although by no means small in terms of staff, activities and income, satisfies the condition of being concerned with a fairly specific product with a clearly defined market. Its relations with Government are close, but almost entirely informal since the ending of official control over wholesale coke prices and supplies. In place of the former statutory control there is now a gentleman's agreement between the Ministry of Fuel and the B.C.I.A. to control profit margins. Half-yearly figures of costs and proceeds, based on a standard costing system, are collected by the association and forwarded to the Ministry of Fuel. Profit margins on coke sales are then negotiated with the Ministry. In this way an entirely voluntary control is exercised over prices of coke produced by B.C.I.A. plants (the retail price of domestic coke, with which the B.C.I.A. is less concerned, is still subject to official control). Official control over coke supplies waned rapidly as supplies increased. The Ministry's Coke Supplies Officer (Hard Coke), who is chiefly concerned with ensuring supplies for the iron and steel industry, is also an official of the National Coal Board, and sits on B.C.I.A. committees dealing with supply questions.

The British Chemical Plant Manufacturers Association, although less frequently in touch with government departments than it was during and shortly after World War II, continues to have frequent dealings with the Board of Trade on such matters as import and export licensing, import duty remission, bilateral trade quotas. For example, if a United Kingdom chemical manufacturer applies for a licence to import a piece of chemical plant from the U.S.A., the import licensing department of the Board of Trade, in order to conserve dollars, will seek the opinion of the Engineering Industries Division of the Board on whether comparable British plant is available, and they will in turn consult the association. There is similar consultation in respect of applications for remission of duty on imported machinery. There is frequent day-to-day contact with the Board of Trade, both with the sections dealing with the various export markets and with those handling inquiries for chemical plant. When bilateral trade agreements are being negotiated, the association provides a brief for the negotiators in so far as the industry's interests are concerned; such briefs are submitted to the Board of Trade through the sponsoring ministry. The association is also in touch with the Export Credits Guarantee Department about members' credit insurance problems.

The Apparel and Fashion Industry's Association, formed in 1947 by the amalgamation of two existing associations chiefly owing to the need for contact with government departments, finds that such contacts continue to be an important part of its work in spite of the ending of controls and rationing. It has dealings with the Board of Trade over exports and imports, trade activities, importation of machinery, statistics, distribution of industry and other matters, and with the Treasury and Customs and Excise on purchase tax. The Factory Department of the Ministry of Labour administers the Factories Act and so A.F.I.A. has some contact with it. It has negotiated with the Ministry of National Insurance on the question of 'broken-time' payments by employers. The association acts on government committees and is a nominating body for certain other committees.

The Typewriter and Allied Trades Federation, which represents importers, wholesalers and retailers as well as manufacturers, co-operates with the Ministry of Labour in the Government Training Scheme. One of the federation's most important connections is with Her Majesty's Stationery Office, which controls all the typewriters and office equipment used in the forces and civil service. After the war, H.M.S.O. arranged for the orderly disposal of their surplus machines through the federation, who organised it so that there was as little disruption of the market as possible. H.M.S.O. partly finances the Lost and Stolen Typewriter List, on which about one-eighth of the machines that appear are government owned. Contacts are made about six times a year. The federation is not at the moment represented on any government committee but it may be asked to sit on specialist committees as occasion demands.

Since the removal of control over barley supplies and the replacement of the official export quota by a voluntary one, the Scotch Whisky Association's contacts with Government have diminished considerably. It still remains frequently in touch with Customs and Excise, which is responsible for ensuring that whisky is not taken out of bond until exported, or the duty paid on it, for certain labelling* requirements and for issuing the certificates of age and origin required by many overseas countries. Various matters arising from the Customs and Excise Act are also taken up with this department. The association is also in close touch with the Board of Trade on matters affecting trading conditions in other countries, such as trade treaties, labelling and packaging requirements, tariffs, methods of computing duties, and foreign countries' import requirements and quotas. The association also briefs the Board of Trade for trade discussions, and on occasion the Board has made representations on its behalf against the raising of overseas tariff barriers to the detriment of whisky exports.

Examples of associations whose contacts with Government are primarily or exclusively through wider bodies are provided by the Federation of Calico Printers, the Rayon Weaving Association and the Association of Jute Spinners and Manufacturers. The Federation of Calico Printers normally has few occasions to be in touch with Government, and then it can put its viewpoint through the Cotton Board, the Textile Finishing Trades Association or the British Man-Made Fibres Federation, on all of which it is represented. Similarly, the Rayon Weaving Association finds that many of the questions it could raise with government departments apply also to other sections of the industry and can be channelled through the Man-Made Fibres Federation, although occasionally it gets in touch with the Board of Trade on its own account. The Jute Spinners and Manufacturers used to negotiate directly with departments from time to time, but since 1947 all relations with Whitehall are handled through the Jute Trade Federal Council.

Many of the smaller associations have very few contacts with government departments, and months may pass without any such contacts. The experience of the Aluminium Holloware Manufacturers Association must be typical of many. Immediately after World War II there was close collaboration with the Board of Trade in a scheme for promoting new output, and in connection

* The association has pressed successfully for more informative labelling on whisky.

with exports. More recently contacts with departments have become few and far between. The association is kept informed by the Board of Trade of trade talks pending with other countries so that they can add their representations if need be, and there are routine contacts on statistics; but apart from this, there are long periods during which the association has no need to get in touch with any government department.

Parliamentary lobbies

It is possible for trade associations, like other special interest groups, to press their case to the Government not only through the administration but also through Parliament. For British industry this must always be a subsidiary or reserve approach. No pressure group is so strong as a party whip, and a determined Minister can in most circumstances carry his policy. Still, there may be some profit from parliamentary activity. A Minister may be weak, or he may be conciliatory; or, at the least, the views of the trade association may achieve some welcome publicity.

A number of Members of Parliament, mostly on the Conservative side,* are themselves connected with firms in industry, and it is probable that these firms are members of trade associations. Again, some industries are geographically concentrated, and therefore dominant in certain constituencies. It is hence not difficult for an association in such an industry to find Members interested in its cause.

Most major associations, therefore, have occasional contacts with Members who are prepared to express the views of the industry in the House, because they or their constituents are concerned in it. Normally these contacts are *ad hoc* and infrequent. When there is no legislation afoot or no crisis in the industry they scarcely exist. At other times an association may work more closely with a group of M.P.s; but in any case its best hope lies in persuading the Minister or his civil servants that its case is right, rather than in creating Parliamentary hostility to the Minister's intentions.

Some trade associations, it is true, maintain closer liaison than this. The Federation of Master Cotton Spinners Associations, for example, keeps a watch on all Bills introduced into Parliament,

* A Labour M.P., Mr Victor Collins, has for long been President of the Employers' Federation of Cane and Willow Workers Associations.

and finds it necessary on occasion to suggest amendments; sometimes by direct approach to the department concerned, and also by having them moved in the House by a Member. There is also considerable circulation of information to Lancashire M.P.s. The Engineering Industries Association also maintains very close relations with a number of private Members, who co-operate in many ways and will ask questions in the Commons if necessary on engineering and financial topics. One or two association officials are themselves Members.

A few associations have more elaborate arrangements. The Glass Manufacturers Federation has formed a Parliamentary Group, which consists of Members from both sides of the House interested in the industry, and which works in conjunction with the Executive Committee. The activity of this group secured a reduction of purchase tax on cut glassware. But this degree of formality is rare. It would be surprising to find an association that could not have its views pressed in the House; but it would be equally surprising if any of them used this as more than a secondary strategy. Moreover, incessant Parliamentary activity only serves to annoy the departmental civil servants who have to provide ministerial briefs, and who are the officials responsible for direct dealings with the industry. More common is the attempt to keep Parliament informed by supplying bulletins and other literature, either to selected groups or to all Members. It is perhaps this service that has the greatest general value; "lobbying" proper has, in Britain, only occasional significance.

CONTRACTING DEPARTMENTS AND TRADE ASSOCIATIONS

So far as the contracting departments* of the central Government are concerned, trade associations fall into two prime categories: those which, in the experience of the departments, do not appear to concern themselves with the prices charged by their members; and those which do. Most of the associations which

* The principal contracting departments of the Government are the appropriate divisions of the Ministry of Supply, Ministry of Health, Ministry of Works, the Admiralty, the General Post Office, War Office, Air Ministry and H.M. Stationery Office. There are also the Crown Agents for Oversea Governments and Administrations, but they are not a department of the central Government.

come into the first category have approached the contracting departments from time to time on a variety of matters which affect their members either individually or as a whole.

In contrast, the associations falling into the second category have, on the whole, much less to do with the contracting departments; principally because these associations make far fewer approaches to them. Such contact as there is, is usually brought about on the initiative of the departments which are affected by their activities, and usually concerns conditions of contracts and specifications, or price-fixing.

The subjects discussed can be broadly grouped under five main headings:

i. Conditions and terms of contracts.
ii. Prices, including profit margins, rebates, quantity discounts, and cost investigations.
iii. Tendering procedure and allocation of orders among suppliers in special circumstances.
iv. Guarantees of workmanship and materials.
v. Technical and research problems.

Probably the most common of all the matters discussed by the contracting departments with trade associations is the phrasing, interpretation and application of conditions of contracts. Standing committees have been set up by the government contracting departments and by several of the major trade associations to deal with it.

On the Government side there is the Contracts Co-ordinating Committee, which has been in existence since 1920. Its main functions are to promote uniformity among government departments on contracts policy and practice; to prevent overlapping and competition between departments; and to secure co-ordination of action for the maximum of economy. The main committee has delegated much of its work to two sub-committees, the General Purposes Sub-Committee and the Works Sub-Committee. There is also an Accountants Sub-Committee.

The General Purposes Sub-Committee is concerned with the details and problems of government contracts procedure and conditions. Its chairman is a director of the Contracts Division of the Ministry of Supply, which also provides the secretary. The sub-committee consists of representatives of the Admiralty, Air

Ministry, Ministry of Health, Post Office, Stationery Office, Ministry of Supply, War Office, Ministry of Works, Treasury and Treasury Solicitor. This sub-committee drew up the document published as *Standard Conditions of Government Contracts and Stores Purchases* and is responsible for its periodic review. These standard conditions are accepted by practically every firm which has dealings with government departments. The Ministry of Works provides the chairman for the Works Sub-Committee in the person of its Director of Contracts, and a civil servant of the same ministry acts as its secretary. This sub-committee deals mainly with building and civil engineering works contracts and the materials and manufactured goods required for them. Departments represented are the Treasury and the main departments concerned with works contracts. A representative of the Treasury Solicitor attends all meetings. The sub-committee is responsible for the publication of the *General Conditions of Government Contracts for Building and Civil Engineering Works* (CCC/Wks/1)—a twenty-two page document now in its eighth amended edition, which serves as the standard form of contract for government building and civil engineering work.

The co-ordinating committees established by the contracting departments have their counterparts, in a number of cases, in standing committees of trade associations specifically set up to deal with conditions of contracts and cognate matters. Thus the Society of British Aircraft Constructors has a Contracts Advisory Committee which advises the members as to whether draft instructions and conditions introduced by the Ministry of Supply are acceptable or not. The British Electrical and Allied Manufacturers Association, through its Contract Conditions Committee, is constantly engaged in revising the *B.E.A.M.A. Conditions of Sale and Contract*, which in its several editions covers practically every type of contract in the industry outside those with the Government. The British Engineers Association maintains a Terms of Contract Committee, which, in conjunction with the Institution of Mechanical Engineers and the Institution of Electrical Engineers, is working out standard conditions of contract for the mechanical and electrical engineering industries. The British Non-Ferrous Metals Federation issues *Standard Conditions of Sale and Supplementary Provisions*, and many other trade associations do the same.

The Locomotive Manufacturers Association draws up standard contract conditions from which members will not depart without the Association's permission. The Crown Agents have discussed with the Association the interpretation of the L.M.A.'s safeguarding clauses applying to orders taken, compared with the Crown Agents' Conditions of Contract. The B.E.A.M.A. has standard forms of variation clauses to cover changes in costs of goods manufactured during the currency of contracts, but these are not accepted by the Ministry of Supply without investigation in each case.

Some associations prove useful to the contracting departments if it is proposed to introduce a new condition or instruction which the issuing department thinks is likely to be controversial. The Society of British Aircraft Constructors, for example, is invited to make comments at the drafting stage and this obviates the necessity of writing to individual firms, for conditions and terms accepted by the Society will usually be accepted by the industry as a whole, though the Society cannot bind its individual members. Other associations such as the British Electrical and Allied Manufacturers Association and the British Engineers Association are also occasionally consulted by the contracts divisions of the Ministry of Supply when matters affecting their particular industry are under consideration.

In many cases trade associations themselves take the initiative in approaching individual contracting departments to discuss new terms and conditions of contract and suggest amendments to existing ones. In the recent past, the British Federation of Master Printers has approached H.M. Stationery Office to discuss general problems affecting government printing work executed under contract by outside contractors.

Some of the major associations have more regular contact with the appropriate government contracting departments. Thus, officials of the Shipbuilding Conference correspond with, and often meet, the Director of Navy Contracts and his senior officers. Discussions between them deal with incentive schemes, guarantee clauses and other matters.

The form in which tenders are to be submitted to government departments is another subject that is discussed by trade associations and the contracting departments.

The Ministry of Works Directorate of Contracts, to take one

major example, negotiates with some individual trade associations and federations in the building industry on such matters as the limit of firm price tendering and the extent of cost variation to be allowed above the limit; the limit of lump sum tendering above which bills of quantities would be used; tendering procedure, including such items as the time to be allowed for tendering and the exhibition of drawings; methods of advising results of tenders and the amount of information that should be given with such advice; nomination of sub-contractors for specialist work and the degree of relationship between main contractor, sub-contractor and the Ministry.

Tendering procedure and buying practices are also discussed between trade associations at all levels, including the F.B.I., and the contracts divisions of the Ministry of Supply, Ministry of Health, H.M. Stationery Office, Admiralty, the General Post Office and the Crown Agents for the Oversea Governments and Administrations.

For a variety of reasons, a few trade associations allocate the orders obtained by their members from major purchasers. The practice is not one which the contracts divisions will support in ordinary circumstances, but when materials and productive capacity are scarce a trade association can be extremely useful in helping a department to find additional sources of supply. During the war, for instance, a number of the associations in the clothing industry were used by the Ministry of Supply for this purpose. Also the British Salt Federation, the British Metal Windows Manufacturers Association Ltd., and the Hard Fibre Cordage Federation have, during periods of scarcity in the past, co-operated with one or other of the ministries and allocated contracts to firms nominated by the associations.

A slightly different example is provided by the Surgical Dressings Manufacturers Association, which has been asked by the Crown Agents to allocate a proportion of member-firms' output to fulfil orders placed by the Crown Agents' principals when there is a marked increase in total demand. The Crown Agents are also in touch with the British Iron and Steel Federation and the British Iron and Steel Corporation over export allocations of semi-manufactured steel products.

Some associations, of course, allocate orders among their members as a means of direct economic regulation. The contracting departments may, therefore, be faced with a tight price ring and it may be necessary for them to enter discussions with the organisations concerned. The Telephone Cable Makers Association is one association which allocates the orders placed by government contracting departments among member-firms. They also decide a common price schedule for the main products manufactured by their members.

In cases where there is agreement by a trade association to quote similar prices or otherwise arrange the prices to be tendered, or where competitive tendering is not possible, the contracting departments may seek the co-operation of the trade and its association so that they can carry out cost investigations of the products of "representative" firms to satisfy themselves that these tendered prices are fair and reasonable. Such co-operation has been generally forthcoming and the examination of pricing data by accountants of government departments is increasing.*

Only a few trade associations negotiate about actual list prices, rebates and discounts with the contracting departments in time of peace. Some trade associations allow their members to charge lower prices or give annual rebates to government departments.

Co-operation between trade associations and government contracting departments is of considerable value in establishing common standards and specifications. For instance, the three service departments and the Ministry of Works purchase building paint answering to their specifications from an approved list of manufacturers: the specification required is the British Standard wherever one exists, but if there is none then the product may correspond to either a D.E.F. (Defence) or C.S. (Civil Supply) Standard.

The Boot and Shoe Manufacturers Federation, United Tanners Federation, British Leather Federation, and the National Association of Cut Sole Manufacturers assist the Ministry of Supply

* The Ministry of Health, Ministry of Works, Ministry of Agriculture, Fisheries and Food, the General Post Office and one or two other departments do a great deal of it. Among the associations which have allowed the contracting departments facilities for sample checking of costs and prices are the Shipbuilding Conference, Dry Dock Owners and Repairers Central Council, British Electrical and Allied Manufacturers Association, High Speed Steel Association, Black Bolt and Nut Association of Great Britain, Woodscrew Manufacturers Association, White Lead and Lead Oxide Convention, Plaster Makers Conference, Surgical Dressings Manufacturers Association, the Telephone Cable Makers Association and several associations in the clothing industry.

in selecting offers of sole and semi-chrome upper leather to be reserved as supplies to boot manufacturers holding contracts with the department. The Admiralty has had discussions with the Inter-Port Naval Traders Association to ensure that only a standardised quality of uniform clothing is sold to naval ratings.

Some trade associations assist the contracting departments in finding solutions to technical and research problems. The Coil Spring Federation is one of these and it has formed the Coil Spring Federation Research Organisation to undertake this sort of work. In 1956, three association firms were co-operating on a research project for the Ministry of Supply, each tackling the same problem along different lines and sharing the results of their investigations. The Admiralty have supported and given contracts to the research institute of the marine engineering industry known as Pametrada, which is financed mainly by the industry and partly by the Government through the D.S.I.R. The British Disinfectant Manufacturers Association recently held discussions with the Crown Agents on efficacy tests for certain disinfectants.

The two-way traffic between trade associations and the contracting departments extends into many other fields of common concern. Some associations occasionally make representations to the departments concerned about delays in acceptance of tenders or in payment of bills, but as a general rule contact on these matters is made through the F.B.I.

Special problems are sometimes dealt with by setting up *ad hoc* administrative machinery. At the end of the war there were discussions between the Admiralty and the three associations representing chain cable manufacturers to determine the best means of disposing of chain cable and gear so that it would not flood the market to the detriment of future production. The trade associations concerned, as well as the trade unions in the industry, were represented on a consultative panel which met at regular intervals until the market returned to normal. The Ministry of Supply, the department chiefly concerned with the disposal of wartime surpluses, had scores of such schemes. Nearly all of them were abortive, because the enormous demand for goods far exceeded the manufacturing capacity of the firms.

From time to time the contracting departments may seek the assistance of trade associations to tackle a particular problem. Thus the Crown Agents have made arrangements with the Tyre

Manufacturers Conference regarding special marking of tyres to prevent pilferage.

A final example of close contact is that provided by a committee set up in 1953 by the Ministry of Supply to improve liaison with the cotton industry. The Contracts Division of the Ministry is also represented on this and it includes all the various associations connected with the industry. It meets whenever any matter of general importance is under discussion.

The Ministry of Health: a case study

The following account illustrates the relationship that has developed between trade associations and one of the contracting departments. The Ministry of Health was chosen not because it is typical of all, but because it has a very wide range of contacts with associations. Through its Supplies Division and Cost Investigation Branch* the Ministry has contact with trade associations in four main ways:

i. It maintains liaison with the appropriate trade associations in certain matters concerning the production of drugs and medical supplies generally, for example, the production of spectacle frames and lenses used by the National Health Service and the arrangements for supply of X-ray equipment.
ii. It confers with trade associations (about general conditions of contracts, for example) in its capacity as central purchasing agent for drugs and medical supplies, including surgical appliances for the National Health Service in England, Scotland and Wales and for the Armed Forces.
iii. It acts as a clearing house for information and co-ordinates the exchange of views between government departments, principally the Board of Trade, and the medical supplies industry through its trade associations on many matters of common concern, chief of which is the question of export and import policy.

* The Cost Investigation Branch is not part of the Supplies Division, but is responsible to the Accountant-General, of whose Division it forms part. Broadly, the Supplies Division exercises the "production" functions and is responsible for all Ministry purchasing, both for the Service departments and the National Health Service, as well as for general supply questions arising within the N.H.S. The Cost Investigation Branch is responsible for investigating costs and profit margins of manufacturers and wholesalers supplying important products for the National Health Service.

iv. Where convenient it discusses with trade associations the reasonableness of prices charged for supplies used in the National Health Service. For this purpose, the Cost Investigation Branch may seek the co-operation of the associations in carrying out investigation of the costs and profit margins of manufacturers and wholesalers. The Department of Health for Scotland is associated in all such discussions and investigations.

The Supplies Division of the Ministry is the central purchasing agent for drugs and other medical supplies required by the armed services. It also places contracts for the supply of certain drugs and other medical supplies to all National Health Service hospitals in the United Kingdom; there are additional contracts applying only to hospitals in Scotland and Wales. Moreover the Ministry is responsible for the nation-wide distribution of new drugs as yet in short supply, such as new antibiotics. All major items of X-ray equipment are purchased centrally by the Ministry and X-ray films are available to hospitals under the Ministry's contracts.

Pharmaceuticals. In its capacity as buyer of drugs for the armed services, and the hospital service in Scotland and Wales, the Ministry of Health (Supplies Division) has occasional contact with the Association of British Pharmaceutical Industry. It may receive representations from the association about general contract conditions and packaging charges, but does not discuss actual prices with it. The Ministry, which is the production department for drugs and other medical supplies, acts as a clearing house for the exchange of views and information between the industry and many government departments, chiefly over export policy in general and also over particular trade agreements before they are finally negotiated.

The Ministry receives regular trade returns from the Association of British Chemical Manufacturers and also from the loosely organised British Insulin Manufacturers. In particular, statistics relating to production, imports and exports are given by the trade. The Ministry would like to persuade member-firms of the Association of British Pharmaceutical Industry to send in returns of trade figures, but so far they have not been successful.

The Ministry is occasionally in touch with the Botanical Section of the London Chamber of Commerce in connection with problems affecting the import of drugs and raw materials for the manufacture of drugs.

The Ministry was consulted by the Association of the British Pharmaceutical Industry about a proposed change from Imperial to metric measures in wholesale trading, since such a change (ultimately agreed) would affect supplies to hospitals and the service departments. The A.B.P.I. has a "price-recommending" system for a range of standard drugs and preparations. With the co-operation of the Association, the Cost Investigation Branch of the Ministry has carried out an inquiry into the costs and profit margins of manufacturers in this field.

Surgical dressings. The Supplies Division has dealings from time to time with the associations covering surgical dressings and plaster. Both these associations agree prices for certain standard products such as B.P.C. Standard dressings, and a substantial part of the Ministry's contract purchases are subject to these prices. With the co-operation of the trade association concerned the Ministry's Cost Investigation Branch has carried out inquiries into the production costs and profit margins of a number of manufacturers.

Surgical instruments and equipment. The Ministry has now very little contact with the main trade associations in the surgical instruments and equipment industry, but it worked very closely with them during the war. Prices are competitive and the associations concerned are not price-fixing organisations. At the request of the Board of Trade in 1951, the industry was asked by the Ministry to look into its productivity.

Laboratory apparatus. For many years the Ministry of Health has found that manufacturers of certain types of scientific glassware, particularly beakers and flasks, decline to quote for contracts to supply in bulk and that quotations received from laboratory furnishers, the wholesalers, are to a large extent identical. Nevertheless, there is some price competition for contracts between members of the association.

X-ray apparatus. The major items of X-ray equipment used by the National Health Service are brought under central contract by the Ministry, and the X-ray Section of the British Electrical and Allied Manufacturers Association occasionally makes representations on design and production and other matters. The contracts placed by the Ministry are subject to cost investigation. The association has put a number of grievances before the Minister during a recent interview with him.

Ophthalmic optical supplies. To meet the demand for spectacles provided by the National Health Service the Ministry set up a number of working committees with the appropriate trade associations, before the National Health Service Act came into force, to consider production questions and to decide on the standard spectacle frames to be supplied to patients. As supply has now for some time matched demand, these committees no longer meet.

The Ministry is, however, in frequent contact with the Association of Wholesale and Manufacturing Opticians and its affiliated bodies the British Metal Spectacle Manufacturers Association and the Ophthalmic Prescription Manufacturers Association. A committee of experts (not representing trade associations) set up by the Ministry to advise on the suitability of spectacle frames for the National Health Service continues to meet as required.

There is no independent price fixing by any of the associations in the ophthalmic optical trade. The Ministry of Health, after discussion with the trade associations concerned, fixes the rates at which opticians are reimbursed for supplies of optical appliances used in the National Health Service. For this purpose, the Cost Investigation Branch, with the co-operation of the associations, inquires as necessary into the production costs of lens manufacturers, frame manufacturers and prescription houses.

Dental equipment and supplies. The Ministry of Health buys dental goods only for the armed services and is, therefore, a marginal buyer. It has now very little contact with the former Association of Dental Manufacturers and Traders, which has changed its name to the Association of British Dental Traders. The activities of this association and its members were referred in 1949 to the Monopolies Commission for investigation. As a result of the Commission's report, the Dental Goods Order came into force in 1951 and the Association made substantial alterations in its rules to eliminate the practices criticised by the commission.

Hearing aids. The provision of hearing aids under the National Health Service has led to an interesting development. Although there are a number of small manufacturers of hearing aids joined together in the Hearing Aid Manufacturers Association, the Ministry of Health has arranged for the production of about

100,000 government aids a year with the General Post Office. Many of the parts for the aids are manufactured by specialist firms in the electrical and radio industry under Post Office contracts and the aids are then assembled by other firms under other G.P.O. contracts. This had to be done because the member firms of the Hearing Aid Manufacturers Association are small producers whose higher working costs make them uncompetitive in the mass production field. The association has made representations to the Ministry about the existing arrangement, but as the government aids are very satisfactory, the Department has not felt able to purchase commercial aids or to make them available to National Health Service patients.

Surgical appliances, artificial limbs and invalid vehicles. The Ministry places contracts for surgical appliances supplied through the Hospital Service to individual patients. The appliance industry is not highly organised but the Ministry maintains useful contacts with the Surgical Instrument Manufacturers Association and its Scottish counterpart. Infrequent meetings are held at which the Ministry announces and discusses fresh developments and association representatives are able to express their views. Less regular liaison is maintained with the Incorporated National Federation of Boot Trades Associations, which represents the interests of some surgical footwear makers and with the St Crispin's Society of Shoemen.

The Incorporated Guild of Hairdressers, Wig-Makers and Perfumers represent the interests of a number of the larger wig makers under contract to the Ministry, and specialist members of the guild occasionally discuss with the Ministry problems arising from the operation of the wig contracts and offer advice on various aspects of hair work production.

Contracts are also placed for the supply of artificial limbs and invalid vehicles of all kinds to disabled persons. There is no association of invalid vehicle manufacturers but design, production and cognate matters are discussed with the individual manufacturers. The interests of artificial limb makers are covered by the Artificial Limb Section of the Surgical Instrument Manufacturers Association.

In addition to these more or less regular contacts, occasional contact is made with the United Tanners Federation and the Oak Bark Tanners Association on the availability and quality standards of leather and with the Surgical Appliance Manufacturers Association, which represents the interests of a major group of subcontractors producing a limited range of surgical appliances. The Hairdressing Manufacturers and Wholesalers Association on occasion speak for some of the wig producers, and the British Council of Retail Distributors has in the past presented general objections to the contract timetable and procedure for procuring wig supplies.

PUBLIC CORPORATIONS AND OTHER PUBLIC BODIES

Relations with the ministries are not the only possible representative functions of trade associations. Contacts may develop between them and other public bodies, especially when these are large purchasers of the products of association members. Among such bodies, the position of public corporations, local authorities and hospital groups has been examined in the course of the inquiry. In a few instances public corporations themselves belong to associations of manufacturers, but here it is intended to study only the contacts that have developed between public bodies and associations of their suppliers.

None of the local authorities and hospital groups interviewed in the course of the inquiry were in touch with manufacturers' associations, although all were aware of the existence of many associations concerned with the fixing of prices and terms of sale. The major public corporations, however, have extensive dealings with associations, ranging from regular meetings at which many subjects, including prices, are discussed, to occasional meetings on specific problems.

The extent and frequency of the direct contact between buyers and associations seems to depend chiefly on the size of the buyers' purchases. Where these are small in relation to the output of association members, as in any one local authority, there is little incentive for either side to meet the other. The association does not want to give the authority preferential terms, and the authority prefers open tenders to any form of commitment to association members.

Where the buyer is of the size of a nationalised industry there is more likelihood of closer contact, for these may well be virtually the sole domestic purchasers. The development plans and purchasing policies of the public corporations concerned are of major importance to association members, and the inherent bargaining strength of the corporations probably induces a greater inclination towards unity among manufacturers. The fact that a substantial buyer, such as a corporation, can do much to break up an association which it believes to be acting unreasonably must also encourage both sides to arrive at an understanding. Where prices are not in question, equally important negotiations take place on technical requirements such as standardisation, expansion plans, equality of contractual terms offered, and so on.

The relations between associations and public corporations are described in this section from the point of view of three leading corporations, rather than from the experience of the very many associations concerned. Notes on the position of the National Coal Board, the British Transport Commission, and the Central Electricity Authority are given here, but the contacts of other corporations may be no less extensive. However, British European Airways, the Gas Council and the various area gas boards, though well aware of associations among their suppliers, have little, if any, direct contact with them. The Port of London Authority deals with many associations, but with the exception of the Society of Motor Manufacturers and Traders, these consist of merchants and importers rather than manufacturers.

The National Coal Board

The National Coal Board deals with a large number of trade associations. Broadly speaking, these fall into two groups: those concerned with specialist colliery equipment and those concerned with products used by other industries as well. The board's contacts with the specialist associations are fairly frequent; their contacts with the non-specialist associations are less frequent, but vary with the nature of the purchases concerned.

The Federation of Associations of Colliery Equipment Manufacturers, formed soon after World War II, includes most associations whose members manufacture equipment for use in collieries, whether they specialise in such equipment or include it among a wide range of products. There is a periodical meeting between F.A.C.E.M. representatives and N.C.B. officials, and a good deal of co-operation between technicians from both sides. The Federation does not exercise any degree of control over its constituent associations, but is rather the instrument whereby they co-operate from time to time.

The specialist equipment associations include the Council of Underground Machinery Manufacturers, the Pit Tub and Mine Car, the Coal Preparation Plant, and the Skip Plant and Winding-Engine Manufacturers Associations. None of these associations is concerned with price-fixing and the board's contacts with them is on technical problems, contract conditions and the like.

The Council of Underground Machinery Manufacturers was established before 1939 and was recognised by the Government as a representative body for allocation purposes during the war. It is now completely representative of the older-established firms. There are some new firms outside, though perhaps there is a tendency for all to join in the course of time. It affects the board mainly in that it has negotiated common contract conditions with the board and in that its members co-operate with Coal Board engineers on problems of design. It also co-operates with the board over priorities and raw material problems in periods of shortage.

The Pit Tub and Mine Car Association is a smaller organisation containing both large and small firms. One large firm in the industry remains outside. This association's activity has been most noticeable during periods of shortage, during the war, for example, when it pressed the interests of its members very strongly in order to get supplies of material.

The Coal Preparation Plant Association arranges contract conditions and co-operates with the board on design and technical matters. It has undertaken the allocation of materials when this was necessary. The board have worked out some limited arrangements on standardisation with the association.

The Skip Plant Association is an association of four firms set up since the war, administered in London, with which the N.C.B. collaborates on technical matters.

As its name indicates, the Winding-Engine Manufacturers Association comprises the makers of equipment for colliery shaft winding operations. Joint consultation with the National Coal Board takes place on matters of mutual concern. The Association contains some very large firms as well as smaller ones. There is some overlapping membership between the Coal Preparation Plant Association, the Skip Plant Association, and the Winding-Engine Manufacturers Association.

Other associations in F.A.C.E.M. include the British Electrical and Allied Manufacturers Association, the Locomotive and Allied Manufacturers Association, the British Pump Manufacturers Association, the Aerial Ropeways Association, the Federation of Wire Rope Manufacturers, the Locked Coil Ropemakers Association, and the Miners Electric Lamp Manufacturers Association. (This last, which consists of one large firm and a number of smaller ones, has no connection with the Electric Lamp Manufacturers Association.)

Among these associations, the N.C.B. has most contact with the British Electrical and Allied Manufacturers Association and the Locomotive and Allied Manufacturers Association. The B.E.A.M.A. discusses and recommends contract conditions for member-firms. Though the B.E.A.M.A. itself is not a price-fixing organisation, some trade groups serviced by it collaborate on price levels; for example, flame-proof electric motors are all offered at a standard price; and so are non-flame-proof motors, transformers, and the products of a "winder group". The L.A.M.A. is greatly concerned with the exchange of ideas on the technical side – specifications for steam locomotives, for instance, were set out in collaboration with Coal Board engineers. Standard conditions for contracts are also fixed.

The board is aware of the existence of very large numbers of associations concerned with items of non-specialist equipment and stores. Where the board is a big buyer, contract conditions and terms may be negotiated with associations. Again, where the board is a big buyer and the associations fix prices, these prices are discussed. The board's negotiating technique varies according to the proportion of sellers represented by such associations. Thus the board is more or less closely in touch with associations covering steel products, conveyer belting, electrical goods and engineering tools. Where prices are fixed by associations the board claims to make extensive use of non-association firms.

The British Transport Commission

The Supplies and Production Department of the British Transport Commission, which is responsible for co-ordinating the purchasing policies of the regions, is in touch with a very large number of manufacturers' associations. The nature and frequency of the contact depends on the size of the purchase involved and the extent to which the commission is the principal buyer. When the commission is virtually the sole purchaser of a particular item, meetings are frequent.

There is no permanent machinery for joint discussions with any association. Those most frequently met are the Locomotive Manufacturers Association, the Railway Carriage and Wagon Building Association, the Wagon Repairing Association, the Cast Iron Chair Association, the British Electrical and Allied Manufacturers Association, and the Cable Makers Association. The principal matters discussed are conditions of contract and production problems, and, with some but not all, price levels. Meetings with other associations are less frequent but cover much the same ground, most of these others being concerned with prices.

The department finds many associations of considerable value on production questions, for instance, on helping to distribute orders so as to achieve the maximum possible output, and in some cases on technical matters. But although relations with some associations, principally those mentioned above, are in general close and useful, it is felt that the majority of others could be more co-operative, particularly about their pricing arrangements.

Many products extensively used by the commission are manufactured in its own workshops, and at least one association (the Cast Iron Chair Association) has claimed that its members can make the goods more efficiently, and urged that the commission should cease production.

The department is not aware of any tendency towards greater cohesion among associations as a result of the commission's existence; indeed, it would regard such a development as an indication that its buying policy had become sufficiently keen to encourage a more united front on the part of manufacturers. In principle the department favours the existence of associations among its suppliers, but at the present time, when many of them appear to the department to be somewhat inflexible in their attitude, its experience of associations is not always satisfactory.

The Central Electricity Authority

The Central Electricity Authority and the area electricity boards are closely in touch with a number of manufacturers' associations through standing joint committees. The C.E.A. have also been approached at various times by a number of associations on specific matters.

There are joint standing committees with the British Electrical and Allied Manufacturers Association, the Cable Makers Association and the Water-Tube Boilermakers Association. Until comparatively recently there was also a joint committee with the Electric Lamp Manufacturers Association, and *ad hoc* meetings of the electricity boards' side of this committee with the Electric Light Fittings Association, the National Association of Manufacturers of Electric Lighting Equipment and the Electric Discharge Lamp Auxiliaries Council were also held on occasion.

The joint standing committee with the Water-Tube Boilermakers has not met for some time, although close collaboration on technical matters is maintained through the Boiler Availability Committee and also by *ad hoc* meetings between the authority's engineers and representatives of the manufacturers on specific problems.

The joint standing committee with the B.E.A.M.A. meets quarterly, the chairmanship alternating yearly between the electricity boards and the B.E.A.M.A. The representatives of the B.E.A.M.A. are, in general, drawn from the members of the Council of the B.E.A.M.A. for the year, and on the electricity boards' side, membership includes the two deputy chairmen of the authority and some four or five chairmen or deputy chairmen of the area boards elected by the area board chairmen to represent them, together with the interested chief officers of the authority and two of their divisional controllers. This joint committee has appointed several sub-committees to deal with such matters as general conditions of contract, contract price adjustment clause, standardisation of switchgear, transformers, turbo-alternators, etc., and meters. There is also a technical sub-committee on electric cookers on which the British Electrical Development Association is also represented.

The main joint committee, at its meetings, reviews the work of the sub-committees and endorses their recommendations. Any such endorsements or other decisions taken by the joint committee are, however, subject to ratification by the C.E.A. area boards and the B.E.A.M.A. separately by report to their organisations. In addition, the joint committee discusses any matters of common interest which are put on the agenda at the request of either side.

One of the more important standing items is a review of plant breakdowns in power stations and methods of overcoming them, including discussion of the necessary division of manufacturers' resources between new production and repair work. A typical agenda might also include such items as sales development publicity and the examination of any criticisms by electricity boards or the B.E.A.M.A. members of a particular matter of joint interest.

With the Cable Makers Association there is a similar structure of a main joint committee and technical sub-committees on standardisation and also on conditions of contract and contract price adjustment. Representation of the electricity boards' side is drawn from selected chief officers representing the authority and area boards under the chairmanship of an area board deputy chairman. Representation on the C.M.A. side is, as in the case of the B.E.A.M.A., made through members of their council, and in general the same procedure is followed as in the joint committee with the B.E.A.M.A.

The C.E.A. and area boards attach considerable value to these joint committees, not only for their obvious advantages in bringing user and manufacturer together, but also because they afford a venue for clearing up minor misunderstandings without unnecessary waste of time.

Originally both these joint committees had sub-committees on prices, but these have been discontinued as it was found that, in general, questions regarding prices demanded consultation at higher level. Now, when prices, or the connected subjects of discounts and rebates, are discussed, small *ad hoc* meetings are arranged for the purpose. Although the authority is reticent on this point, it seems probable that, like the National Coal Board, it negotiates prices with associations in fields where it is a substantial buyer, and varies its technique of negotiation according to the comprehensiveness and attitude of the associations concerned.

There are also contacts between the C.E.A. and area boards with the various specialised groups connected with the B.E.A.M.A., such as the Associated Manufacturers of Domestic Electric Cookers, the Meter Manufacturers Association and so on. Generally speaking, such meetings are held to study the possibility of further standardisation or simplification with the object of price reduction.

The authority and area boards, not undertaking manufacture themselves, are not members of any manufacturers' associations, nor are they members of the Electrical Fair Trading Council, although they have indicated to that council that they are prepared to recognise them as the appropriate body through which to deal on matters within their purview.

RELATIONS WITH OTHER SUPPLIERS AND CUSTOMERS

Just as the existence of a powerful single buyer, in the form of a government department or a public corporation, encourages its suppliers to work closely together, so the existence of one strong association tends to promote collective action on the part of firms which supply its members, and firms which buy from its members. In many instances, of course, problems of supply were principal motives in the formation of associations in the absence of any counterpart association of suppliers and customers. The growth of the Cocoa, Chocolate and Confectionery Alliance, for instance, and of the British Wood Wool Manufacturers Association, is closely associated with problems of supply, and, in the case of the Wood Wool Association, of sales outlets also. The Wood Wool Association succeeded in improving a supply situation which is in the hands of one big seller, the National Coal Board, and in developing a major market in which the Ministry of Supply predominates. The same "countervailing power" motive, where one association is formed in order to balance the power of another which represents suppliers, is clearly brought out in the case history in Appendix A (p. 313). But, whether it was originally a principal reason for their growth or not, many manufacturers' associations have some degree of contact with others which represent suppliers and customers. Subjects of discussion range from questions of availability of supplies, patterns of demand and technical requirements to contract conditions, price levels and discounts.

In most of the larger associations representing whole industries rather than single products there is some element of supplier/customer relationship within the association. This is true, for example, of the Society of Motor Manufacturers and Traders, the Society of British Aircraft Constructors, the British Plastics Federation, the Radio Industry Council and the Association of

British Chemical Manufacturers, all of which include either individual manufacturers or product associations concerned in various ways with the same product.* In other instances, distributors as well as manufacturers belong to the same association.

The Society of Motor Manufacturers and Traders also belongs to this category; other examples are the National Hardware Alliance and the Typewriter and Allied Trades Federation. In a few cases, as in the Glass Manufacturers Federation, suppliers of raw material and machinery are admitted to membership (in the case of the G.M.F. to associate membership). But there are always suppliers and customers outside the ambit of even the most comprehensive association.

Before looking at some examples of associations' representational activities as buyers and sellers, some general observations must be made about these aspects of their work.

The first is that in their capacity as buyers, representations on price levels made by associations to their suppliers' associations appear to be only of a general character, if indeed the subject is discussed at all. Clearly representations about prices must be general in the case of large associations acting on behalf of the whole industry; but even where more specific product associations are concerned, prices do not seem to be the subject of formal representation or discussion. With some exceptions, member-firms seem to prefer to negotiate as buyers on their own, leaving the association to act as a background body which will raise general questions of supply. Yet the very existence of an association must have some effect on the attitude of sellers.

Secondly, many associations explicitly exclude, in their rules, any discussion of selling price, and in practice extend this rule to buying prices also. In many cases, too, there may be large numbers of associations concerned with selling to any one association's members. On the other hand, associations which themselves fix prices may feel some reluctance to interfere with similar arrangements on the part of their suppliers.

In discussions on this question, a few associations have observed that whereas small firms tend to suggest that the association should use its bargaining strength to reduce buying prices, larger firms

* In such instances the parent body does not usually concern itself with the supplier/customer relationship of its constituents, since its principal aim is to represent them externally as manufacturers.

prefer to leave the association out of it, because they can get better terms independently.

As representatives of their member-firms as sellers, many associations are in touch with distributors, either for the purpose of maintaining a list of approved wholesalers, agreeing discount rates or, in the case of associations representing manufacturers of consumer goods, for maintaining resale prices. Others fix prices and discounts without prior discussion with distributors or other associations of manufacturers; these appear, as a rule, to have few contacts with associations of customers. Again, others fix neither prices nor discounts but collaborate with their customer associations on other points of common interest. Price-fixing and other forms of economic regulation, however, are surveyed in a later section of this report. Here the emphasis is on representations made between associations on more general problems, and the examples which follow serve to illustrate the methods and purposes of such contacts.

Permanent liaison committees or formalised regular meetings between associations in their supplier/customer roles seems to be exceptional, though they are found in a number of important industries. The British Iron and Steel Federation and the British Coking Industry Association have a joint committee to consider coke supplies to blast furnaces; the Shipbuilding Conference has a liaison committee with the General Council of British Shipping; the Society of Motor Manufacturers and Traders meets the Motor Agents Association and the Scottish Motor Trade Association in the Joint Committee of Vehicle Manufacturers and Retailers; the National Paint Federation meets its customers (merchants and contractors) in two joint committees; and there are a few other instances among the industry associations. In the great majority of cases, however, discussions appear to be organised on a less formal basis as occasion demands. A number of the larger associations are represented on a wide variety of bodies by an appropriate member of the staff: the British Electrical and Allied Manufacturers Association is represented on over thirty other organisations, some of them users of electrical equipment, and the Society of Motor Manufacturers and Traders is similarly represented on over a dozen other bodies. This form of representation is directed to representing the interests of their members as buyers or sellers only in a very broad sense.

The Glass Manufacturers Federation provides examples of the chief methods by which contact with suppliers and customers is maintained. Besides admitting suppliers of raw material and machinery into associate membership it keeps in touch with suppliers' associations such as the Silica and Moulding Sands Association, while on the customer side it has joint technical committees with the Closure Manufacturers Association, the Food Manufacturers Federation and the food machinery makers; it also has less formal meetings with user representatives such as the Brewers Society and the Toilet Preparations Federation.

A group of customers of members of the British Iron and Steel Federation, the National Association of Iron and Steel Stockholders, is affiliated to the federation and has periodic meetings with it. The federation is also frequently in touch with a group of suppliers—the National Council of Associated Iron Ore Producers—and with non-affiliated suppliers—the National Coal Board, the British Transport Commission, the National Federation of Scrap Iron, Steel and Metal Merchants and the British Coking Industry Association—and customers, among which are the Society of Motor Manufacturers and Traders, the Shipbuilding Conference and the British Constructional Steelwork Association.

The British Man-Made Fibres Federation, whose thirteen member-associations between them cover every phase of man-made fibre production and use, from the initial processing of raw material to selling the finished cloth, works closely with a number of user organisations, in particular with the Incorporated Society of London Fashion Designers in arranging exhibitions, and with the Retail Trading Standards Association on the question of nomenclature.

The Society of Motor Manufacturers and Traders maintains a department concerned with transport problems, which is in touch with the railway authorities and shipping conferences.

The Federation of Master Cotton Spinners Associations has regular negotiations with the Liverpool and Manchester Cotton Associations on terms and conditions of sale for raw cotton, and is also in touch with appropriate bodies in the cotton-growing countries on questions of quality. Conditions of supply, including prices, are taken up with the machinery manufacturers.

Many of the external contacts of the British Plastics Federation arise out of its widespread technical work, for instance with the

Society of British Aircraft Constructors in connection with the Society's drawing-office handbook on plastics materials.

Turning to associations concerned with a smaller group of products, or a single product, an indication of how such an association can keep in touch with suppliers and customers through a wider body is given by the Federation of Calico Printers which, along with customer- and supplier-associations, is a constituent of the British Man-Made Fibres Federation. The Calico Printers have informal meetings with the Cotton and Rayon Merchants Association (also a member of the B.M.M.F.F.). Other customer contacts are made through the Manchester Chamber of Commerce, while the Association of British Chemical Manufacturers and the Colour Users Association are contacted as suppliers of raw materials. Similarly the Jute Spinners and Manufacturers meet some users in the Jute Trade Federal Council. The Scotch Whisky Association is in touch with the Wine and Spirits Association representing the retailers, and with the National Farmers Union on questions of barley supply. It is also in occasional contact with overseas associations of importers. The British Aluminium Hollow-ware Manufacturers Association holds meetings with wholesalers, the hardware factors, and retailers, the National Federation of Ironmongers, and is in touch with suppliers, the aluminium rolling mills. A recent report on the work of the British Refrigeration Association provides examples of representations to suppliers of raw materials of importance to the refrigeration industry. In two instances attention was drawn to the comparative prices of American materials; in a third case, the needs of its members, both as regards quantity and standard size were made known to the manufacturer concerned.

CHAPTER 4

ORGANISATION OF COMMON SERVICES

THE preceding chapter has been concerned with the representational side of associations' activities: aspects of their work which by definition depend on the existence of other groups, whether these consist of government departments, other public bodies or other associations. In this section it is intended to describe the main types of common services they have developed, which can be broadly described as promotional. These do not primarily involve representation to other groups, but arise out of the recognition that some things can only be done, and others done more effectively, by collective action, and are equally part of the external economies which associations organise for their industries.

The provision of these services has brought industrial associations into many spheres of activity: the organisation of exhibitions, press and public relations, publications, international conferences, research and productivity studies, the collection of industry statistics, and much else besides. It was seen in Chapter 1 that some associations were started in order to organise their industry's exhibitions, for example, while many others, formed primarily to represent their industries to Government or in negotiations with labour, later extended their services to include such matters as publicity and market information. This extension of promotional work was considerably stimulated immediately after World War II. The reasons for this have already been touched upon. Co-operation, virtually enforced on most industries during the war, continued for purposes of reconstruction planning and undoubtedly many firms were impressed by the extent to which they could work together with advantage and without relinquishing their autonomy to any significant extent. The general recognition of Government's new responsibilities in the field of economic and social policy tended to keep associations in being, with similar effects. The influence of the working parties and development councils was a further stimulus to associations to widen their horizons, while the assimilation of numerous export groups (or the growth of new associations from them) opened up further possibilities for collective action. The importance of rapid technical change and, with the emergence of new industries, the recognition of inter-industry competition also contributed to the development of promotional, as distinct from the primarily defensive, aspects of associations' services.

Before attempting to describe the chief types of common services at present organised by industrial associations, a word must be said about the activities performed at different levels, and by different types of association. It is evident that activities affecting industry as a whole, such as organising discussions with universities on advanced education, or formulating policies for participation in exhibitions overseas, can only be undertaken effectively by top-level organisations such as the Federation of British Industries. Many product associations participate indirectly in activities or services organised by more broadly based associations which represent the industry groups of which the product associations form a part, just as they do where representations have to be made to Government on issues that affect not only their own but also other related interests and products. Thus even where certain types of promotional work could be done by the individual product association, it may be more worth while to leave them to be done by a broader industry association.

The character of the product itself may impose certain limits on the scope of an association's promotional work. The association may consist of makers of products which are used primarily, or solely, by other manufacturers, or of processors whose work is some stages removed from the final product. Then it is unlikely that it would be worth while for the association to arrange publicity or exhibitions on its own. Much less dependent on the type of product or the level of association is the limitation imposed by the number and size of member-firms. An association representing only a handful of small or medium firms is necessarily limited in scope by the fact that it depends on subscriptions. The advantages that might be gained by extending the range of services provided by the association might, from the members' standpoint, be outweighed by the cost of the staff and establishment this may involve. The economies of large size apply also to associations in this respect, and probably for this reason many of the more specific product associations are ticking over in readiness for an occasion demanding collective action, usually in the form of making a representation to Government, rather than continuously engaged in providing a number of different services.

Thus, associations would differ very considerably in the scope of the services they provide, even if these services depended solely on their own character and size. But there are, of course, other influences which arise from the extent to which manufacturers wish to co-operate and from what they regard as the most important aims of their association. The chief purpose of many associations is the control of competition in one form or another; beyond this they do little apart from making occasional contacts with government departments. Others which are not concerned with prices in any way exist primarily because their members wish to present a united front to Government, and negotiate with suppliers and customers from time to time, but the members have not the desire, nor the association the resources, to do much else.

In practice, therefore, the range of services provided by associations varies a great deal. But it is possible to distinguish the main lines along which their activities have developed, and here it is intended to describe the main types of services organised by the largest industrial associations, and by a number of the more active smaller ones representing single products or processes. For this purpose these services are grouped under two broad heads, the first covering activities which promote the commercial and trading interests of member-firms, the second dealing with activities whose chief effect is to improve the industry's productive efficiency.

TRADING AND COMMERCIAL SERVICES

The promotion of members' commercial and trading interests by an association can take many forms and it would be possible to classify them in many different ways ranging from detailed lists to two or three broad headings. Here the activities are examined in two main categories, the first covering the promotional and publicity work of associations, and the second covering information and advisory services to members. The first deals with associations' activities as the channel of information from their industries to their markets, and the second deals with their collection of information and its dissemination back to their members, together with the provision of services which facilitate members' trading activities.

Promotion and publicity

Exhibitions. Many associations are responsible for organising exhibitions for their industries, and some of these displays have acquired an international reputation. Among those which organise annual exhibitions, the Society of Motor Manufacturers and Traders have over fifty years' experience. The holding of exhibitions was one of the society's first activities, and indeed one of the chief reasons for its formation. From about 1903 onwards the industry's exhibitions have been entirely organised and run by the S.M.M.T. The International Motor Exhibition at Earls Court is held annually. In 1953 paid attendances were 613,000 (more than double the pre-war figure), including 6,000 accredited overseas buyers. The International Commercial Motor Transport Exhibition, which started in 1907, is normally held every two years.

In 1949 the society added the Smithfield Show and the Agricultural Machinery Exhibition to its programme in the interests of its tractor and agricultural machinery manufacturing members. For this event the society has entered into an agreement with the Smithfield Club and the Agricultural Engineers Association, and undertakes much of the organising and administrative work. All three events, which are international in character, are widely publicised overseas, and free admission is offered to overseas visitors. Within the past few years exhibitions of British motor vehicles and automative products have also been held in New York and Toronto.

The society exercises effective control over the industry's exhibitions by means of the Exhibition Bond, a voluntary agreement which binds members who sign it not to support any event not approved by the society; in return they obtain certain benefits such as reduced charges, and priority in the allotment of stands in the society's exhibitions. The bond is signed by practically all members who enter the society's shows and by many others who support this principle.

The Society of British Aircraft Constructors is the exhibition authority of the aircraft industry, and is wholly responsible for the displays and exhibitions which over the past eight years have become synonymous with the name "Farnborough". In this instance, also, members undertake by voluntary agreement to seek the society's permission for the showing of aeronautical goods of all kinds at public exhibitions within the United Kingdom. Like the S.M.M.T., the Machine Tool Trades Association had its origin in exhibition affairs, and since 1912 it has been responsible for staging the International Machine Tool Exhibition, which is held every four years.

The National Radio Show is the chief medium of publicity of the Radio Industry Council. It is intended chiefly to display the domestic products of the industry, but a secondary object is to attract recruits, and for that purpose a technical training display and a servicing exhibit are included. The Office Appliance and Business Equipment Trade Association promotes the annual Business Efficiency Exhibition, held alternately in London, and Birmingham or Manchester. The British Engineers Association sponsors the Engineering and Marine Exhibition and, as many other associations do also, keeps members informed about other exhibitions of interest to them at home and overseas. The Engineering Industries Association organises an annual London Region Display, a cheaply run exhibition for the small firm, primarily intended to attract overseas buyers. The British Food Fair is organised by the Food Manufacturers Federation and is held every two years.

A variation on the annual exhibition is the permanent display centre such as those of the British Man-Made Fibres Federation and the Glass Manufacturers Federation. The London office of the Man-Made Fibres Federation includes a display centre in which fashion shows are frequently held, often in collaboration with fashion groups. Other exhibitions are put on in conjunction with bodies concerned with education and design. The Glass Manufacturers Federation has a permanent exhibition, The Story of Glass, at its headquarters in London, which are themselves more of a display centre for the industry than simply administrative premises for the association. Its purpose is mainly educational and a large number of school visits are arranged. The exhibition shows the history, raw materials, processes and products of the whole glassmaking industry and there is space for exhibitions concerned with particular aspects of the industry. In addition there are facilities for showing films, and a library of the glass industry.

Many associations which do not themselves organise regular exhibitions on their own account collaborate with other bodies, or organise occasional displays at strategic points. Thus the British Iron and Steel Federation is represented from time to time at exhibitions such as the British Industries Fair and Fuel Efficiency Exhibitions. A model steel works was constructed a few years ago and exhibited at the Ideal Homes Exhibition and various other exhibitions around the country. Arrangements were made for this model to be shown during the greater part of 1955 in the Imperial Science Museum.

An example of the considerations entering into a decision to hold industry exhibitions is provided by the British Chemical Plant Manufacturers Association, which organised small exhibitions in 1926, 1931 and 1936. After the war opinion among the membership was divided on the subject of the most suitable time for resuming chemical plant exhibitions. For several years during the post-war reconstruction period, while order books were overfull and deliveries protracted through difficulties in raw material supplies, there was little need for an exhibition. Eventually the association sponsored a chemical plant exhibition which was held in 1953 jointly with the regular Engineering, Marine and Welding Exhibition. At the instigation of the association a chemical engineering conference was held concurrently with the exhibition, organised by the Institution of Chemical Engineers and the Chemical Engineering Group of the Society of Chemical Industry. It is planned in the summer of 1958 to hold a chemical and petroleum engineering exhibition sponsored jointly by the association and the Council of British Manufacturers of Petroleum Equipment.

The Cake and Biscuit Alliance is another association which holds exhibitions from time to time. A few years ago it held an exhibition, one section of which was an industrial display by manufacturers, the other consisting of a display of many varieties of biscuit shown with appropriate food and drink.

The number of associations which collaborate with other bodies, sometimes other associations, sometimes trade journals, together with those which take stands at the British Industries Fair, probably runs into many dozens. To take some examples, the Incorporated Federated Associations of Boot and Shoe Manufacturers run exhibitions in association with the Shoe and Leather

Fair Society, the export committee of the association running its own stand to help overseas visitors; the Employers Federation of Cane and Willow Workers have held exhibitions at the Guildhall, London, in co-operation with the Worshipful Company of Basketmakers; the Association of Jute Spinners and Manufacturers have taken part in displays featuring the jute industry as a whole, and also in the National Packaging Exhibition. The brick and tile sections of the National Federation of Clay Industries collaborate in staging biannual exhibitions. The Wholesale Clothing Manufacturers Federation and the Shirt, Collar and Tie Manufacturers Federation hold displays in collaboration with the Outfitters Annual Conference, in which makers of garments outside the scope of the federation are invited to participate. The Apparel and Fashion Industry's Association co-operates in the London Fashion Fortnight along with the Man-Made Fibres Federation; it has also put on a television show with the B.B.C. and helped to put on special shows at the London Coliseum with the International Wool Secretariat and *Woman's Own*. Another joint venture developed within the past few years is the exhibition of British Industrial Instruments sponsored jointly by associations of manufacturers of British Industrial Measuring and Control Apparatus, Scientific Instruments, Lampblown Scientific Glassware and the British Electrical and Allied Manufacturers.

Some associations themselves take stands at the British Industries Fair. In the early 1950s the B.I.F. catalogues of exhibitors included the British Iron and Steel Federation, the British Non-Ferrous Metals Federation, the British Plastics Federation, the Cable Makers Association, the Gauge and Tool Makers Association, the Fancy Goods Association and about a dozen others.

Press and other publicity. Publicity of one sort or another is one of the growing points of associations' activities. Although only a small number of associations have a full-time Press officer, many others have shown greater awareness of the advantages of a favourable climate of public opinion during recent years and some have developed extensive publicity services.

Naturally, those industry associations whose products are frequently in the news are those with the strongest Press or information departments. The Society of British Aircraft Constructors has an information department to which a Press officer is attached, and a considerable volume of material about the aircraft industry is circulated to newspapers and technical publications throughout the world. Similarly, the Press and information department of the Society of Motor Manufacturers and Traders publicises the activities of its industry at home and overseas through Press conferences, news releases, and editorial material. It also operates an information service to deal with inquiries from firms, organisations and the public. The Radio Industry Council has a public relations committee and a staff Press officer. Both the Federation of British Rubber Manufacturers and the Council of Ironfoundry Associations have appointed Press officers, within the past few years, to facilitate the spread of news about their industries.

The Association of British Chemical Manufacturers has also taken more interest in publicity during recent years. As a first move it produced and distributed widely a *Press Guide to British Chemicals*, a book which lists names of chemical manufacturers; a wide range of chemical products or fields of work, together with the names of the manufacturers concerned; and trade names of products and their makers. A publicity committee of the association exchanges experience and discusses methods and media of publicity. The Shipbuilding Conference keeps Government and the Press supplied with information about shipbuilding, by acting as a source of material for articles contributed to trade and technical journals by office bearers such as the president, vice-president and others. Quarterly statistical summaries compiled by the conference are issued to the Press, to government departments, banks, trade sections of overseas embassies and so on. Reprints of Press comments on these figures are widely circulated.

The Glass Manufacturers Federation has also considerably increased its publicity services with the appointment of a public relations officer and the development of a policy with three chief aims in mind—to persuade the public that British glass is better than either foreign glass or the products of competitive industries, to keep members informed of developments in those competitive industries, and to encourage the recruitment of suitable entrants to the industry.

Joint advertising on behalf of an industry or product is another method of publicity that has increased during the past ten years or so. Only a few associations undertake it as a regular feature of their activities, but many obviously find it a convenient and effective part of a campaign extending over a relatively short period. Among the most familiar joint advertising campaigns are those of the British Iron and Steel Federation for the steel industry, the Brewers Society for beer and the International Wool Secretariat for wool. Joint advertising is also conducted for timber, leather, linoleum, carpets and salt-glazed drainage pipes.

Less prolonged joint advertising to support a particular campaign is fairly widespread. When wartime controls were in force a common advertising campaign based on the slogan "Biscuits Keep You Going" was run by the manufacturers through their associations. Towards the end of the war the Society of British Aircraft Constructors administered a special eighteen-month prestige advertising campaign overseas as the first step towards expanding exports. The Council of Ironfoundry Associations ran a Press advertising campaign in 1953. Smaller associations which have used this medium to reach the public are the Gunmakers, and the British Pressure Cooker Manufacturers. Within the past few years, the former has undertaken a limited amount of Press advertising to suggest to the shooting public that they should submit their repairs to association members, who will be known by the fact that they exhibit the association sign. The establishment of the British Standard for pressure cookers was followed by an intensive advertising campaign, lasting for a year, in the national Press and women's magazines, which served not only to popularise reliable pressure cookers but also to make known the significance of the B.S.I. Kite Mark. The English Joinery Manufacturers Association ran a national advertising campaign to counteract the intensive advertising of metal window manufacturers. A special advertising and publicity committee was set up for this purpose, and reprints of the advertisements, with small stick-on labels illustrating the slogan "You'll be glad you chose wood windows", were distributed to all members. This was not, strictly speaking, a once-for-all effort, since it is the association's intention to continue the work of making the public (to quote its 1955 report) "wood-window minded". Similar motives were doubtless behind the Corset Weeks organised by the Corsetry Manufacturers Association in collaboration with the Corset Guild; these have been discontinued in favour of an editorial publicity campaign run by the association itself. The Tie Manufacturers Association continues to organise an annual Tie Week.

Other associations do not themselves undertake advertising, but give advice, on request, to members about advertising media. The Jute Trade Federal Council, for example, has a public relations officer, and any member of the Council's constituent associations can call on his services for general publicity work, including advertising and exhibitions. The British Engineers Association publicity committee has compiled a list of overseas journals for the use of member firms' advertising departments.

A few associations are also employing films as a general publicity measure. The British Iron and Steel Federation is producing a wide range of films both for training purposes and to give general information about steel; some of its films are specially designed for television. The National Federation of Clay Industries has produced a film about bricks which is available to borrowers and is accompanied by brochures for distribution. The Mechanical Handling Engineers Association has produced two films, *Mechanical Handling* in 1948 and *Conveyers as your Servants* as a supplementary in 1952. The British Engineers Association and the B.E.A.M.A. have collaborated in producing a guide to industrial film-making.

So far as publicity and information to other branches of the trade (as distinct from the public at large) is concerned, most industries are well served by trade journals and most associations have close contacts with their trade press. Many in fact rely largely on trade journals for their communication with suppliers and customers. In some cases, independently published journals act as the official organs of associations. The Typewriter Trades Federation and two kindred bodies, the Office Appliance and Business Equipment Trades Association and the national association of distributors, have such a journal as their official spokesman, and the Gunmakers Association is similarly served.

Other associations publish their own journals—usually in addition to journals and bulletins circulated only to members. Some, such as *The British Jeweller*, the official organ of the British Jewellers Association, published by the British Joint Association of Goldsmiths, Silversmiths, Horological and Kindred Trades, are on general sale; others are distributed free.

Since 1915, the British Electrical and Allied Manufacturers Association has published for general sale *The Beama Journal*, a monthly review of electrical engineering. *The British Iron and*

Steel Monthly Statistical Bulletin, which was published until the end of 1955, usually contained articles of general or topical interest on steel; these have been reprinted and are issued free of charge. The B.I.S.F. now publishes a quarterly called *Steel Review*, which contains similar articles. The quarterly *Wool Textile Bulletin*, issued jointly by the Wool Textile Delegation, the Export Group and the Wool (and Allied) Textile Employers Council is also free and is widely distributed; it is primarily intended for interested Members of Parliament, government departments, local authorities, etc. The brick section of the National Federation of Clay Industries issues the *Brick Bulletin*, a free publication containing general and technical information for users as well as producers, which has a circulation of about 16,000 among architects, surveyors, builders, government departments, local authorities and schools. The National Council of Building Material Producers circulates *B.M.P. Weekly Information* to its constituent associations and also to local authorities, architects and others, about 1,300 copies a week going out. Some associations give wide circulation to their annual reports; that of the British Chemical Plant Manufacturers is sent to twenty-four trade journals and a number of kindred associations.

Apart from regular publications of this kind, many associations also produce occasional pamphlets for specific purposes. Thus the Glass Manufacturers Federation issues literature to publicise its permanent exhibition, or to serve as a handbook to schools for the encouragement of recruits to the industry. The Council of Ironfoundry Associations produces numerous booklets and brochures about its industry in general, or particular aspects of it, and circulates these widely to customers and others. The British Chemical Plant Manufacturers Association published a leaflet describing how the association can help buyers of chemical plant for distribution to visitors to the Chemical Plant Exhibition in 1953. The British Coking Industry Association has issued a leaflet to the trade on coke suitable for domestic appliances. The British Aluminium Hollow-ware Manufacturers Association counteracted misleading statements alleging that aluminium hollow-ware was inimical to health by publishing, and circulating through the retail trade, a brochure containing extracts from the reports of various scientific bodies and the other investigators showing that such statements are entirely without foundation.

Directories and buyers' guides. While it usually takes a fair-sized association to run exhibitions or establish extensive publicity services, the publication of directories or buyers' guides as a means of getting in touch with customers is within reach of smaller organisations, and a great variety of trade guides of all kinds is published by associations. Some of those published by the larger associations are very comprehensive and demand the continuous attention of a staff engaged in compiling them. The S.M.M.T. has a Registers Department which is occupied chiefly with the production of the *Register of the Motor Industry*, an annual directory of manufacturers, wholesalers, dealers and repairers. This, although intended primarily for the information of members, also has an extensive circulation outside, and its contents are not restricted to member-firms. The B.E.A.M.A. directory is among the most elaborately produced, being over 1,000 pages long and containing classified details of its member-firms' products in four languages.

The Association of British Chemical Manufacturers publishes *British Chemicals and their Manufacturers*, a directory listing some 10,000 different products, their makers and other information. It is published once every two years and widely distributed, free, at home and abroad. The British Chemical Plant Manufacturers Association also produces a biennial directory, *British Chemical Plant*, which includes an address list of members with the names and addresses of their overseas agents, when they wish to publish them; an illustrated section containing members' advertisements; and a classified index of products with a key in French, German and Spanish. Each edition of 5,000 copies is circulated, free, to chemical plant users at home and abroad from a list compiled by the Association. The British Engineers Association, the Brewers Society, the Federation of Master Printers and the Federation of British Rubber and Allied Manufacturers Associations are among other associations which produce very substantial directories.

Some associations do not publish an annual directory on these lines, but produce booklets from time to time setting out names and products of members. The Mechanical Handling Engineers Association, for example, exploits the photogenic character of its industry by producing a large brochure showing recent installations of mechanical handling equipment in a wide variety of uses, and giving a quick-reference guide to the products of each member-firm.

The Surface Coating Synthetic Resin Manufacturers Association, in collaboration with the British Plastics Federation, in 1955 produced an index of its producers which is available to the paint and printing ink industries.

Special promotional bodies

In some industries the need to promote the use of materials or products is regarded as sufficiently pressing to warrant the setting up of special bodies to carry out this work. The single-purpose association is used in other connections also, for instance to attend to commercial regulation, but at this point it is intended to look only at those concerned with promotional activities.

In 1953 the British Carpets Promotion Council, a body sponsored jointly by the British Carpet Manufacturers Federation and the International Wool Secretariat, was formed. Its activities provide a good example of some of the methods of collective product promotion. The council was set up to undertake a promotion scheme which opened with extensive advertising in the trade press, a series of meetings with manufacturers and wholesalers' travellers to explain the Council's aims, and the issue of 7,000 campaign books to carpet retailers. This was followed by the issue of some 9,000 packs of display material, and the start of intensive sales training courses in several centres throughout the country for the selling staffs of retailers. Contacts were also made with the Wholesale Floorcovering Distributors Association and with the National Association of Retail Furnishers. These preparatory activities culminated in the Carpet Fortnight, which was supported by Press and poster publicity. More than 2,000 printing blocks were issued to retailers for Press advertising, and two booklets were produced, one for the consumer—about 90,000 of these were distributed—and the other for salesmen. Other features of the campaign were Press competitions, a window display competition organised by a leading trade journal, and a short television programme.

This type of organisation has something in common with the development associations which have been set up in a number of industries. These exist chiefly in non-ferrous metals, but also for timber and cement and concrete. In non-ferrous metals there are development associations for aluminium, copper, lead, tin and zinc. Their growth is stimulated because there is a lack of direct contact between the producing and using branches of the industries, or because of the growth of competing products, or for both of these reasons.

Among these development associations there are certain differences in organisation, and in particular they have different degrees of contact with users. For instance, there are three associations of zinc users which share staff and offices with the Zinc Development Association, and work in collaboration with it; the copper and lead development associations are not similarly integrated with their user-organisations, while the fact that the aluminium producers are also the largest fabricators gives the Aluminium Development Association a measure of integration in a different way. There are various other differences, but the basic purpose of these development associations is the same: to promote the use of the products they represent.

The accounts of the copper, zinc, and cement and concrete associations which follow illustrates the range of activities that can be undertaken. It should not be inferred, of course, that each of the other development associations has the same range of activities, or that the same methods are used.

The Copper Development Association was founded in 1933, and is a pioneer among development associations. The association is financed mainly by the copper-producing countries of the British Commonwealth, the trade associations representing the copper and brass fabricating industry and a few of the leading British fabricating firms. Its affairs are controlled by a council which delegates most of its functions to a management committee. The association is a non-trading organisation whose aim is the extension and improvement of existing applications of copper and the development of new uses. Its services are available to all without charge or obligation.

The main function of the association is to provide technical information and advice on applications of copper and copper alloys and to provide a link between research and industry. It does not itself engage in research, for which facilities already exist, though members of the staff are in close contact with the researches carried out by such bodies as the British Non-Ferrous Metals Research Association. The C.D.A., through its staff, is represented on a large number of committees of the British Standards Institution, including all those which are considering standards for copper and copper alloys. The association maintains close contact with technical bodies in Britain, France, Germany and America, including the recently formed International Wrought Non-Ferrous Metals Council.

The technical staff of the association answer many thousands of technical inquiries every year. The staff are greatly assisted in this work by the use of the C.D.A. library, which contains a collection of information on copper and copper alloys which is unique. Published literature is regularly scanned and all useful information is recorded.

The technical officers of the association, particularly the building engineer and his assistants, are frequently asked to visit inquirers at their offices and works to discuss their problems. They also annually give hundreds of lectures and demonstrations at the request of schools and craftsmen's organisations.

The other main activity, and one which contributes to the high reputation of the association, is the issue of publications, for which no charge is made. So far fifty publications have been prepared and issued, and they include those particularly suitable for engineers, builders, plumbers, architects, metallurgists and other technologists, as well as a few of more general interest. Some of the early issues have now been abandoned or superseded, but even so there are at present twenty-eight different publications available, and the rate of distribution of these has steadily increased until now more than 100,000 are despatched annually to all parts of the world.

Twice a year a bulletin is issued privately to members. This gives an account of the work of the association, and also a technical survey of published information dealing with copper and its alloys. The technical survey is also published separately from the bulletin and is sent to anyone who expresses a need for it.

To publicise its services to the thousands of new entrants to industry every year and to renew existing contacts, the association takes part in four major exhibitions, namely, the British Industries Fair (Birmingham section), the Engineering and Marine Exhibition, the Building Exhibition, and the Electrical Exhibition. Hundreds of inquiries for information are received on the C.D.A. Stand at these exhibitions. The association maintains permanent displays at the Building Centres in London and Glasgow, and the Engineering Centre in Birmingham. Display material is often sent on loan to small exhibitions arranged by the science departments of schools and colleges. Wall charts relating to the use of copper in building and the extraction of copper from its ores, and wood panels with mounted ore specimens, are distributed to technical colleges and schools. Window displays on applications of copper are arranged throughout the year by the C.D.A. in the Northern Rhodesian Government office in London.

The association has a number of films for distribution, mostly on copper production, and in 1955 made its own first film, *Copper Flashings*, in colour; another was in preparation in 1956.

The Zinc Development Association was established in 1938. Little of the metal consumed is found in the United Kingdom, but there is a considerable fabrication industry here. The Commonwealth producers formed the Z.D.A. so that accurate information about possible uses of the metal would be readily available for British consumers, and so that no opportunity would be lost of securing the fullest use of the metal, where appropriate.

The three associations of zinc users which share staff and offices with it were formed towards the end of and immediately after World War II. These are the Zinc Alloy Die Casters Association, the Hot Dip Galvanisers Association, and the Zinc Pigment Development Association.

The Z.D.A. is supported by all the zinc smelters, and most of the mining companies in the British Commonwealth. All but three of its eighteen members are situated overseas. The Zinc Alloy Die Casters Association has forty-eight members in the United Kingdom, two in the Commonwealth and an affiliated association in Australia; the Hot Dip Galvanisers Association has eighty-five United Kingdom members and twenty-four in the Commonwealth, and also thirty-six corresponding members in Europe and America; and the Zinc Pigment Development Association has nine members, all in the United Kingdom.

The Z.D.A. itself is concerned strictly with developing the uses of zinc, and not with its production: that is to say, it is the sales activities of its members that it seeks to promote. However, the Z.D.A. takes care to encourage the efficient use of zinc; it is sufficiently independent to be able to regard sound advice as more important than maximum immediate sales. It would not hesitate to discourage the use of zinc for unsuitable purposes, for example. The essential function, therefore, of the Z.D.A. is to provide a technical advice service to customers. Though the association is looked upon as the representative body in this country for all zinc interests, relations with government departments are now a secondary matter: various ministries consult the Z.D.A. from time to time, but there are no control or supply problems to call for constant negotiation.

Publicity is a major activity. Advertisements are always of a semi-technical nature, and are placed in journals concerned with scientific and industrial subjects. The *Zinc Bulletin*, published quarterly, contains illustrated notes and articles on the uses and applications of zinc; this has a circulation, at home and overseas, of about 25,000 copies. In addition, *Z.D.A. Abstracts* is published monthly, giving brief summaries of all articles published on the technical aspects of zinc and zinc uses, with a circulation of about 4,000. There are also many internal news letters and digests on technical questions, and more than seventy books and manuals have been produced on many problems of zinc techniques. A technical representative of the association visited consumers in India, Australia and Africa. The association takes part in the Building Exhibition and the Engineering Exhibition. Its displays are always of a technical character.

There is considerable interchange of information both of a technical and market nature between member-firms, and each association has a technical committee which helps to circulate advice between firms. Any member may put a problem before these committees through the association without revealing its identity to the committee. Research is in the hands of a research committee, which co-ordinates the work being done on the uses of zinc for the industry. The Z.D.A. provides money for the British Non-Ferrous Metals Research Association, and also for particular projects carried on by other bodies. Many firms also contribute individually to the research association. Some co-operative research is also undertaken by members. Standardisation is carried out in co-operation with the British Standards Institution, the Z.D.A. preparing draft standards and nominating members to B.S.I. committees.

The association has a staff of thirty-three, of whom fifteen, including the director, hold technical qualifications. Distributing centres in Canada, Australia, India and South Africa supply Z.D.A. literature on request and forward technical inquiries to the Z.D.A. for reply.

At present the Z.D.A. is concentrating upon the extension of its interests in Europe. Industrial teams and members of the staff visit the Continent frequently, and a European General Galvanising Committee and a European Pressure Die Casting Committee have been set up. A representative of the association visits the United States every year. Conferences are being held more frequently, and there is a possibility that the association will interest itself in safety and similar questions, as a further effort to improve the efficiency of the using industries.

The Cement and Concrete Association, which was formed in 1935, is non-profitmaking and is not connected in any way with the sale or manufacture of cement. Commercial matters are the province of the Cement Makers Federation (in the same way as the Aluminium Development Association is distinct from the Aluminium Industrial Council). All manufacturers of Portland Cement in Great Britain and Northern Ireland, of which there are eighteen, are members of the Association, and membership is confined solely to manufacturers. The association provides users of cement and concrete with a free and impartial source of technical information and advice based equally on long practical experience and on the findings of a modern research station. It employs a staff of over two hundred, including qualified engineers, architects, research workers, technical assistants, public relations officers and general office staff. They are under the control of the director, who is assisted by the technical director, the director of information and the secretary.

Similar associations in Australia, New Zealand, South Africa, Eire, Jamaica, India and Egypt are affiliated to the Cement and Concrete Association on a fee basis. The association also has a reciprocal arrangement with the Portland Cement Association of America for the exchange of literature, technical and research reports, etc., and has contact with many organisations all over the world, to whom it sends selected information and literature and from whom, in turn, it receives similar service. In Britain the association has branch offices in Edinburgh and Manchester.

The Cement and Concrete Association is regularly consulted by various government departments on technical problems. Close contact is maintained with the Building Research Station, and the Road Research Laboratory, and the association contributes to the Committee for Co-operative Research with the Road Research Laboratory. Technical service is given free to inquirers. The Building Division deals with all structural matters, housing and factories, bridges and all types of concrete finishes; the Roads Division handles everything connected with road construction and soil cement stabilisation. Research is carried out at the research station at Wexham Springs, near Slough, where all aspects of the use and behaviour of cement and concrete are studied. This is aimed at greater knowledge of the behaviour, uses and potentialities of the material; testing which would normally be the work of professional experts is not undertaken. All the knowledge obtained as a result of these researches is freely available.

In education, the association co-operates with teaching institutions all over the country, mainly through the supply of literature for distribution to students. Grants have been made both to research students and to universities for the purchase of equipment. A Chair of Concrete Technology at Imperial College has been founded by the cement industry and a lectureship at Leeds University has also been financed by the association. The Cement and Concrete Association has given particular encouragement to some fifty technical colleges running the City and Guilds *Concrete Practice* course. A film strip has been prepared and issued together with teaching notes to most of the colleges running the course, and a summer school is run annually for the lecturers. Intensive training courses, usually of one week's duration, are held by the association at its training centre. These specialised courses are intended to keep industry informed of developments and modern techniques in the field of concrete technology.

The association has its own printing department, and produces many of its brochures and publications. Most of these are of a technical nature and are available free on request. Two magazines are also available on subscription: *Concrete Quarterly* is of general interest and gives information and photographs of concrete work being undertaken or projected in all parts of the world; *The Magazine of Concrete Research*, published three times a year is more specialised. Both these magazines have a wide circulation at home and abroad. Since 1935, the association has issued more than six hundred different publications. A comprehensive reference and lending library is maintained, and a photographic section of the library includes photographs and lantern slides which are also let out on loan to lecturers and others.

In 1949, the association was instrumental in forming the Prestressed Concrete Development Group, and in 1952, the Paving Development Group. In 1954, a joint committee on structural concrete was formed to take over the work formerly done by the liaison committee of the Cement and Concrete Association and the Reinforced Concrete Association.

Market information and services

The second main group of activities which have the effect of promoting members' trading and commercial interests comprises the collection of market information and its dissemination to members, together with the provision of other services which enable firms to extend their markets or reach them more effectively. This is in a sense a representational activity; but it is included in this chapter to emphasise the service which the spread of information gives to member-firms. In describing their activities a distinction is made between those relating to home, and those to export, markets. This has been done partly because the methods of collecting information differ considerably, partly because the increased attention which many associations have devoted to export matters has led them to make separate arrangements for handling overseas information.

Export markets. A number of the larger associations have overseas departments which handle export matters. A few have permanent representatives in their chief export markets, while others organise overseas visits by their members, or disseminate reports about trade conditions overseas. Among the services provided by these associations which have a considerable exporting interest are the circulation of statistics and market intelligence, sometimes in special export journals; fairly continuous contact with production departments on the preparation of briefs for trade negotiations, the lodging of objections to increases in overseas tariffs and so on; and an information service for members' individual inquiries. Smaller associations which do not have special staff dealing with exports may simply circulate overseas information in their bulletins and deal with individual inquiries as they arise;

and many have export committees which examine export matters and advise on appropriate action.

The Society of British Aircraft Constructors, the Society of Motor Manufacturers and Traders, the British Electrical and Allied Manufacturers Association and the British Engineers Association are among those which have developed extensive export services, each on rather different lines.

The Society of British Aircraft Constructors has an export officer who prepares briefs for British negotiators engaged in trade talks that cover aircraft interests, and it passes on to its members a great deal of information about overseas developments, and very many inquiries received from potential buyers. It also prepares much statistical and other information for members interested in exports.

The Society of Motor Manufacturers and Traders has an overseas department which deals primarily with the export development of British motor products. Working in the interests of the British Manufacturers' section of the society, it maintains close contact with the Board of Trade and other government departments concerned with exports; prepares briefs on behalf of the industry for United Kingdom negotiations engaged in trade talks; and handles all questions arising out of them. The society can claim to be the only trade association, apart from the F.B.I., with overseas staff representatives covering all the most important markets of the world. A part of this department's work is directing the activities of these representatives, eight in number, who between them cover Australia, New Zealand, Europe, Africa, India, the Near, Middle and Far East, South America and North America. They are the observers and "trade ambassadors" of the industry in their territories. They maintain high-level contact with their local governments, make representations on questions such as tariffs and legislation, report regularly to the society on market conditions, furnish statistics, and in many other ways smooth the path for the British exporter. In addition the overseas representatives and their parent department both handle numerous inquiries from individual manufacturers.

Attached to the overseas department is the society's shipping secretary, who acts as secretary to the shipping committee. He deals with problems connected with the transport of vehicles and accessories both at home and overseas. An important part of this section's work is negotiating with the various shipping conferences over shipping difficulties and freight rates.

The overseas department publishes a weekly export information news-sheet incorporating reports from its overseas representatives and items from the *Board of Trade Journal*, the daily and technical press, etc. This is circulated free to all manufacturers interested in export—about seven hundred in all. In addition, the statistical department produces the *Customs Tariff Service*, which gives details of duties, etc., in about sixty overseas markets, and the *Overseas Registration Service*, which gives details of the number of vehicles and/or new registrations in a hundred and twenty different territories overseas.

In the electrical industry, the British Electrical and Allied Manufacturers Association's oversea committees have been in existence since 1915; today there are nine of them in operation acting as overseas intelligence branches. The oversea committees' work under the guidance of the B.E.A.M.A. export panel and the export department of the association, which is the link between the association and the oversea committees. In addition to the usual activities in connection with the promotion of overseas trade, the association assists the Government with trade agreements with the Dominions and foreign countries. In 1940 it organised twenty-five electrical export groups at the request of the Board of Trade. (These have now been dissolved as they no longer meet a genuine need.) The B.E.A.M.A. export department offers its services to all electrical manufacturers, whether members or not. The *B.E.A.M.A. Export Bulletin* is produced monthly for the guidance of electrical exporters generally.

The British Engineers Association's technical and overseas division deals with inquiries from overseas and promotes export trade. It handles numerous inquiries; provides an interpreter and translation service; and furnishes status reports to members. Advice to members on overseas representation is backed by records of more than seven thousand overseas firms and eight hundred associations concerned with mechanical engineering. This division also maintains a library of home and overseas trade and technical publications and market reports. There is also an expert committee, drawn from member-firms, which studies and reports on broader policy issues. Its work covers the examination of overseas markets, the relation of the home to the export market; the regulation of imports; credit facilities; and Government organisation abroad. Up-to-date information is secured through members' frequent visits to overseas markets. Among its publications the B.E.A. has produced a number of monographs dealing exclusively with export markets, such as *Exports*, a descriptive and statistical account of the export trade and current export practice, and *India*, a sixty-page memorandum introducing exporters to the Indian market.

The director of the British Engineers Association attends an annual gathering of the directors of engineering associations of about seventeen or eighteen European countries. This is an informal group which discusses problems of common interest, e.g. the progress of G.A.T.T., and considers arrangements for the International Mechanical Engineering Conference, which is held every two years. The B.E.A. is also asked, from time to time, to send a representative to meetings of the O.E.E.C. mechanical engineering committee, though as a matter of course it provides a brief to the Board of Trade.

The type of service offered by other associations whose overseas contacts are less extensive can be illustrated by a few examples. Export policy in the iron and steel industry, for instance, is coordinated by the British Iron and Steel Federation's steel production and supplies committee. The export department deals with such matters as liaison with government departments, general information for sections of the industry on export regulations and queries on export matters. Advice is given, for example, on import restrictions affecting steel in overseas markets, bilateral trade agreements and export licences, where required. By a special arrangement, the British Steel Export Association is responsible for selling heavy steel products abroad on a centralised basis. Exports of other forms of steel are handled by firms themselves or through merchants.

A number of associations provide extensive information services on which individual members can draw. The British Chemical Plant Manufacturers Association collates a wide range of information about its members' main overseas markets, maintains a register of agents to assist members in choosing such agents, gives personal introductions to travelling members, deals with queries relating to export controls, export credits, conditions of contract, export licensing, tariff rates, and so on. The Export Committee of the Boot and Shoe Manufacturers provides an advisory service on marketing, conditions of sale and foreign tariffs. (About a hundred and twelve different markets are distinguished.) The committee has contacts with commercial representatives overseas and foreign embassies in the United Kingdom.

As already noted, in the wool textile industry export promotion is financed from the proceeds of a levy under s. 9 of the Industrial Organisation and Development Act, 1947. This levy was initiated by the Wool Textile Delegation, which has a majority on the Council of the National Wool Textile Export Corporation, the body through which the export group is financed. The group is particularly active in promoting and safeguarding its members' interests overseas. Within the past few years the group has taken part in numerous tariff inquiries and representations. The Export Corporation conducts major promotional campaigns in the U.S.A. and Canada, and, by radio, in the Middle East.

In the Cake and Biscuit Alliance there are separate export associations for cake and biscuits, and also the Cake and Biscuit Manufacturers Export Group, which is serviced by alliance staff. The committees work with the Ministry of Food and the Board of Trade in their efforts to procure the lifting of foreign restrictions against their products, and upon such matters as export licences, foreign regulations and special prices for sugar used in goods for export. A special aspect of the work of the Biscuit Export Committee is the scientific testing of all biscuit and cake before shipment to the United States. This is to prevent rejection of the goods under the strict food and drug regulations there. During the period of controls the alliance would not allow replacement of ingredients for these export orders until it received back the certificate of approval issued by its laboratory. This sanction is no longer possible, but these certificates of analysis are still voluntarily remitted to the alliance by members.

Most associations which have large export interests are in touch with United Kingdom Trade Commissioners overseas, and occasionally associations collaborate in making joint submissions on matters affecting exports. Thus, within the past few years, the Furnishing Fabric Federation and Export Group submitted evidence to the South African Board of Trade and Industries, opposing a proposed application of duties on furnishing fabrics. This evidence was supported by the Cotton Board, the Man-Made

Fibres Federation and other textile bodies, and was placed before the Board by the Senior Trade Commissioner at Pretoria, whose guidance in compiling the evidence was later acknowledged in the federation's annual report. The Scotch Whisky Association, much of whose work is concerned with export matters, is also closely in touch with British embassies abroad. This is supplemented (as in the case of many other associations), by occasional visits to overseas markets by the association's secretary.

The collection and circulation of statistics relating to exports is an extensive activity, in the sense that most associations which have any export interest produce some figures, though only the larger ones do so regularly or in detail: the British Iron and Steel Federation is one example. The number of associations that collect statistics from members for this purpose, however, is limited, and apart from some of the larger industry associations it is exceptional to find a comprehensive statistical service. The collection and dissemination of statistics is more fully described below, where home market services are considered, since the majority of associations do not publish export statistics separately.

Before turning to associations' activities which are concerned more with the home market, reference should be made to a special arrangement for exporters operated in the man-made fibres industry. Through the Central Rayon Office, Ltd.—a body which exists for bringing together, on an entirely voluntary basis, yarn producers, weavers, dyers, printers and merchants—firms engaged in the different sections of the industry agree to produce fabrics for certain markets at keenly competitive prices. The scheme applies to bulk-produced cloths of standard quality; long runs make cheap production possible, and by agreement among the firms concerned profit margins are reduced at every stage of manufacture. Consequently the final product can compete with the lowest prices anywhere. The operation of such a scheme is simplified by the comparatively stable price of the raw material used in fabric production. The rules of the Central Rayon Office provide for standard qualities and prices, and its only function is to negotiate with representatives of the various sections of the industry: securing business is the responsibility of the normal commercial channels.

Statistics

Apart from activities specifically aimed at improving export prospects by enabling firms to sell overseas on the basis of better knowledge, or under more favourable conditions, there is a wide range of association services which concern domestic market conditions and services.

It has already been pointed out that the statistical services provided by associations vary a great deal both in quantity and quality. This is as true in the home market as in exports. Some of the larger associations provide regular series of statistics covering many aspects of their industries' activities, drawing on member-firms for returns to supplement official figures. Not all are published, but they may be used for the guidance of policy-making or for the information of firms which themselves contribute to the composite figures.

Among associations which produce detailed and comprehensive statistics are the British Iron and Steel Federation, which publishes monthly statistical bulletins and a statistical year book (now, in both cases, jointly with the Iron and Steel Board); and the British Coking Industry Association, which compiles figures of production, disposal and raw materials supplies on behalf of the Ministry of Fuel in addition to figures of costs and proceeds, coke quality and gas analyses. Other associations which supply statistics to government departments are the National Federation of Clay Industries, the Cake and Biscuit Alliance and the Glass Manufacturers Federation. The last-mentioned collects monthly returns of the production, sales and stocks of glass containers, and prepares a monthly index of production in other sections of the industry. Other associations which produce comprehensive industry figures are the Federation of British Carpet Manufacturers and the Boot and Shoe Federation.

The collection of statistics for wartime purposes undoubtedly stimulated the collection and distribution of information in this form, and, in a few cases, industries have taken over statistical services which they wished to undertake for themselves. Since 1945 the British Non-Ferrous Metals Federation has been responsible for the compilation of the industry's statistics formerly undertaken by the Ministry of Supply. The federation has a statistics department, which, as well as its own work, carries out the work of the British Bureau of Non-Ferrous Metal Statistics.

This bureau was founded in 1947 by the federation, the British Overseas Mining Association and the British Non-Ferrous Smelters Association. It is directed by a council of members of these three bodies, which jointly subscribe to its funds what is needed beyond the revenue from the sale of publications. The bureau publishes a monthly bulletin which, until the return to free dealings in non-ferrous metals on the London Metal Exchange, published only figures relating to the production, consumption and export of copper and zinc in the Commonwealth and to the output of products in the United Kingdom, but which since 1954 has expanded to include statistics of the whole world and of other metals. Many private companies, trade organisations and government departments abroad provide regular statistics. In addition to these statistics the larger affiliated associations compile statistics showing the trends of orders, and uses and sizes in demand, in conjunction with the federation.

In much the same way the Wool Industry Bureau of Statistics was formed by the Wool Textile Delegation when the Wool Control was wound up. Collection of information for the bureau, which is provided on a completely voluntary basis, is, nevertheless, almost completely comprehensive. All firms who submit returns to the bureau receive a four-page monthly summary of statistics free; in addition there is a full monthly bulletin of statistics available to members of constituent associations on a low subscription, and also to others at a slightly higher rate.

A number of associations also collect statistics which are not published generally, but circulated only to members. Thus the Society of British Aircraft Constructors, the Cotton Spinners and Manufacturers, the National Paint Federation and the National Association of Drop Forgers and Stampers, among many others, often collect statistics which are treated confidentially and circulated to the members concerned. The Shipbuilding Conference, which has built up a very efficient and comprehensive statistical department, covering shipbuilding and shipping at home and overseas, collects much of its information in this way.

Many of the Shipbuilding Conference records are compiled from detailed and confidential information supplied by members. The latter are kept regularly supplied with composite statistics derived from this information, together with analyses of Lloyd's Register of Shipping Returns and information systematically drawn from home and overseas trade journals. The work of the statistical department is impressive both in the amount of information collected and its thorough analyses.

A considerable amount of this information is not of a character which can be made generally available (except in very general terms as in the quarterly statistical summaries which are published). Information from individual firms is treated confidentially, and the conference is naturally reluctant to put more knowledge than necessary in the hands of overseas competitors. The detailed facts at its disposal do, however, enable the conference to forecast trends in the industry and base its policies on as much information as possible. Among other associations which provide detailed statistical information are the Cocoa, Chocolate and Confectionery Alliance and the Federation of British Rubber and Allied Manufacturers Associations.

Other market services

Other services which help member firms in their trading capacities cover a very wide field; passing on inquiries from prospective customers to members, advising individual members on transport, insurance, patents, valuation and similar matters are the daily incidentals of many associations. A number run status and credit bureaux, many provide legal advice on request and some undertake support of members' cases in the Courts when they involve a point of principle deemed to be important to the industry as a whole.

PRODUCTION SERVICES

Broadly speaking, the services described so far are those which promote sales opportunities, although, of course, better knowledge of markets and trade must also improve the possibilities of production planning. It is now intended to look at association services which have a more decided bearing on production efficiency through their effect on techniques and methods of production, and on the conditions under which production is carried on. This means looking at associations not so much as channels of communication with markets, but more as channels of communication within the industries they represent and as organisers of services which in one way or another improve the productive efficiency of member-firms.

Technical information and services

In a broad sense, a great deal of associations' work consists of organising the interchange of information, in so far as they act as a means of transferring the experience and knowledge of some firms to the benefit of the rest. This is true, in particular, of all the production—as distinct from sales—services with which this section is concerned. They are also the means of exchanging information in the somewhat narrower sense of the actual passing of knowledge and experience between individual firms or groups of firms in the same industry. To begin, it is worth looking briefly at some of the arrangements that are made to facilitate this kind of communication. The Society of British Aircraft Constructors, for example, distributes a technical information bulletin which sets out the results of company research and development in production techniques, and many other bulletins which make available to designers the experience of both military and civil aircraft operations are also published within the society. In the boot and shoe industry the association brings together groups at different levels and of different techniques, factory managers, representatives of research and professional associations, to discuss problems and exchange information. These groups are reproduced at local levels, and a factory exchange system, like that of the British Productivity Council, has been arranged.

The Association of British Chemical Manufacturers operates an industrial information service for its members; this pools the (non-confidential) experience of firms in overcoming production difficulties and makes it available to others. The service is extensively used. Replies to inquiries, which appear in the association's weekly bulletin, are sent to members on request. The Engineering Industries Association produces the fortnightly *National Capacity Gazette*, which provides the latest details of capacity and materials available and required, of premises and storage facilities, and of business and export opportunities. In the Federation of Master Cotton Spinners Associations, certain members give the federation details of their experience of improved machinery and methods. This is kept under a code number and is available to other members, but no indication of sources is disclosed without permission. The National Association of Drop Forgers and Stampers has a technical committee to which difficult problems may be passed by the association's technical officer, and the committee decides which other firm in the association the inquirer should be put in touch with to get the information. This association also runs an annual technical convention. One of the functions of the technical department of the Society of Motor Manufacturers and Traders is to arrange meetings to consider proposed new regulations affecting motor vehicles, and circulate drafts to members for comment. It also acts as a clearing house for technical problems put to it by manufacturer- and user-members of the society.

A less tangible and less formal, but none the less important, form of communications exists, of course, in the committee structure of associations, which bring together what is often a significant proportion of member-firms for periodic meetings. Partly for this reason a note on committees has been added as a tailpiece to this chapter.

Standards. Virtually all the larger associations, and very many of the small ones also, are the standards authorities for their industries and as such are in touch with the British Standards Institution. Some, including a few of the smaller associations, also work out their own "industry" standards which may or may not ultimately become British Standards. A number of the larger bodies have long-established links with the B.S.I. and are among its strongest supporters, and within the past ten years the more widespread recognition of the utility of adopting standards relating to dimensions, quality, methods of test, nomenclature and so on has brought many smaller associations into this field of work.

The larger industry associations have special departments dealing with standards, and, behind these, numerous technical committees concerned with different products or processes. In the iron and steel industry, for example, the great bulk of steel production is based on British standards and a section of the British Iron and Steel Federation is concerned with co-ordinating work within the industry during the progress of a new standard. In the aircraft industry the Society of British Aircraft Constructors is the standardisation authority. Since 1938 it has introduced some six thousand standards for use in the manufacture of aircraft and their equipment, They range from complicated items such as complete control columns, rudder bars and pilots' seats to more general standards such as rivets, bolts and small engineering parts. The society's standardisation work, which involves continuous revision to keep pace with technical progress in aeronautical engineering, has earned high tributes from the authorities both at home and overseas. Through the society several hundreds of senior engineers in the aircraft industry serve on those committees of the British Standards Institution which deal with aircraft standards introduced for general use.

In 1955 the Society of Motor Manufacturers and Traders set up a reorganised and enlarged standards department to expand the work formerly done by its technical department. The new department works under a Standards Board of senior executives, and is concerned with four categories of standards: dimensional, material and qualitative, safety and performance, and technical and test procedure. Like the Society of British Aircraft Constructors, the S.M.M.T. has a number of its own standards in addition to those adopted by the B.S.I. Many of the S.M.M.T. standards are adopted, after an interval, by the B.S.I. A very wide measure of agreement has been reached on tyre and wheel standards. The S.M.M.T. publishes details of these in book form: for agricultural and industrial vehicles, and cars and commercial vehicles, in alternate years. The Tyre and Wheel Technical Committee of the society, which draws up these standards, works in very close co-operation with its counterpart, the Tire and Rim Association of America. As a result it has been possible to work out and adopt interchangeable sizes of tyres and rims for Britain and the States.

The Federation of British Rubber and Allied Manufacturers Associations has roughly sixty nominees on various B.S.I. committees at any one time; it also works with the International Standards organisation, where, owing to the experience of the British rubber industry in evolving methods of test, a very large measure of international agreement for British Standards in this field has been secured.

The British Plastics Federation, whose most extensive activities are in the field of technical information, standardisation and quality control, carries out numerous technical investigations, and on the basis of these collaborates with the B.S.I. in preparing specifications of plastics materials and methods of test. In 1954, for example, the federation helped in the preparation of eighteen British Standards published in that year, three of them resulting from specifications prepared by the technical committees of the federation.

The British Electrical and Allied Manufacturers Association, which took a leading part in setting up the former British Engineering Standards Association (now the B.S.I.) has some forty technical committees considering the standardisation of various products. One thousand three hundred expert representatives of its member-firms serve on over 200 B.S.I. electrical standards committees. The association pays particular attention to the effect of home and overseas standardisation on export trade. It has taken a leading part, through the British National Committee, in the International Electrotechnical Commission, which is concerned with specifications and technological co-ordination throughout the world.

In chemicals, the Association of British Chemical Manufacturers was largely responsible for initiating the organisation of British chemical standardisation; its work in this field led to the reconstitution of the former British Engineering Standards Association into the B.S.I. The association is well represented on B.S.I. committees and has done a great deal of work on standardised nomenclature for chemicals. In 1948 a joint technical committee was set up and after a hundred meetings produced a work which has since been issued as a British standard, *Recommended Names for Chemicals used in Industry*.

A growing number of associations in textiles, such as the Man-Made Fibres Federation and the Wool Textile Delegation, are now concerning themselves with standards, especially standard methods of test and nomenclature, and there are many examples to be cited from other industries. Thus the British Industrial Measuring and Control Apparatus Manufacturers Association is represented on about fifteen B.S.I. committees, chiefly concerned with standardising components and terminology. Through the B.S.I., the Boot and Shoe Manufacturers have agreed specifications for miners' boots and children's shoes. The Federation of British Manufacturers of Sports and Games is represented on B.S.I. committees considering standards for such items as boys' shinguards and sports goods bought in bulk by education authorities and the services. The Gunmakers Association, independently of the B.S.I., has issued charts showing standard shotgun and rifle chamber sizes, and standard choke sizes for 12-, 16- and 20-bore shotguns. The Cake and Biscuit Alliance, in collaboration with the Tin Box Manufacturers Federation, has contacts with the B.S.I. on standards for biscuit tins.

In the relatively new industry of pressure cookers, the British Pressure Cooker Manufacturers Association initiated standardisation because a number of pressure cookers on the market were considered to be unsafe, and accidents to users could have discredited pressure cookers in general. After consulting the British Standards Institution, the association set up a committee which produced a draft standard in six months; this was then revised by a technical committee of the B.S.I. and a British Standard for Domestic Pressure Cookers (No. 1746) was issued in 1951, about a year after the association and the B.S.I. had taken the problem in hand. After inspection by the B.S.I. and some slight modifications, all the five association firms were given the right to use the B.S.I. certification mark, and now all the cookers carry the B.P.C.M.A. guarantee label, incorporating the kite mark. This was the first British standard to be issued for a product in common domestic use.

The English Joinery Manufacturers Association is also extensively engaged in standards work. It is represented on some thirty B.S.I. committees, and runs a scheme under which firms can make and sell products under the E.J.M.A. Certification trade mark. The mark covers a number of specifications, including kitchen units, storage fitments, windows and doors. Some of the specifications have been issued as British Standards, others are E.J.M.A. specifications.

The extent to which standards are utilised in the engineering group of industries is emphasised by the existence of an association of users of engineering products. This is the Engineering Equipment Users Association,* which was founded in 1950 to promote the interests of users chiefly through preparing specifications which are subsequently taken up by the B.S.I. Its work covers materials handling equipment, instruments, gears, pumps, ball and roller bearings, storage tanks, heat exchangers and various items of electrical engineering.

Research. Many associations, mostly the larger bodies, are closely linked with the research agencies of their industries. In some instances they were responsible for starting research groups which have since become research associations jointly financed by industry and the Department of Scientific and Industrial Research.

* There is also a Machinery Users Association, a much older body, formed in the 1890s, which concerns itself not with standards but with rating problems.

A few examples will illustrate the type of relationship existing between trade and research associations in industries where co-operative research is extensively practised.* In the electrical industry the British Electrical and Allied Manufacturers Association, in collaboration with the Institution of Electrical Engineers and the then newly formed Department of Scientific and Industrial Research, established the British Electrical and Allied Industries Research Association (E.R.A.). The B.E.A.M.A. is represented on its council and the majority of members of the association are members of the E.R.A., contributing financially and in other ways to its work; for example, by undertaking special tests for the E.R.A. and by serving on its committees. In addition to the financial support given to the E.R.A. for collective research, it is estimated that more than fifteen million pounds are spent annually on research and development by individual B.E.A.M.A. firms.

The Cake and Biscuit Alliance works in close co-operation with the British Baking Industries Research Association at Chorleywood. Advice and help is obtained for members upon such matters as colouring and additives. The alliance is also interested in the possibility of the establishment of a joint biological testing station for the food industries.

Because of the specialised and advanced nature of the problems associated with the design and production of aircraft and aero engines, the industry can receive little assistance from the D.S.I.R. The Society of British Aircraft Constructors collaborates, however, with the D.S.I.R. wherever a joint effort can be of mutual advantage. The society was responsible for setting up the Aircraft Research Association to build and operate a transonic wind tunnel and a supersonic wind tunnel. These are intended primarily for use by aircraft designers on day-to-day problems, so helping to release the research facilities at government establishments for more fundamental work. The society has direct relationship with the Research Association of the Light Alloy Industry. It is also in close and daily touch with the government research establishments working in the field of aircraft and guided weapons, such as the Royal Aircraft Establishment and the National Physical Laboratory.

* For a detailed and comprehensive survey of co-operative research, see R. S. Edwards, *Co-operative Industrial Research* (Pitman), 1950.

During World War I, the Iron and Steel Institute (the industry's technical society, open to individual membership, founded 1869) organised research committees for the industry and, in the inter-war years, a number of research committees were organised jointly by the institute and the British Iron and Steel Federation. These committees reported to the Iron and Steel Industrial Research Council, a B.I.S.F. body on which were representatives of the Iron and Steel Institute and the D.S.I.R.

The British Iron and Steel Research Association (B.I.S.R.A.) was founded as a regular research association in 1945 by the B.I.S.F. in consultation with the Iron and Steel Institute and with the support of the D.S.I.R. There are several close links between the three organisations; for example, the B.I.S.R.A.'s governing council is largely appointed by the B.I.S.F. and partly by the institute. The director of the B.I.S.R.A. is the research director of the B.I.S.F. and he makes a general report on the work of this research association at each quarterly meeting of the B.I.S.F. Council. The B.I.S.R.A. receives industrial finance mainly from the B.I.S.F. and is also helped by a grant from the D.S.I.R.

The British Coking Industry Association is another strong supporter of research. The British Coke Research Association is supported jointly by the B.C.I.A. and the D.S.I.R., and half the association's annual income of £130,000 goes to the Research Association. The same is true of the Boot and Shoe Manufacturers Federation. The Society of Motor Manufacturers and Traders is similarly the chief supporter of the Motor Industry Research Association, formed in 1946.

To take two examples from the textile group of industries: the Wool Industries Research Association, the first of its kind to be set up by industry (it was started in 1918) receives substantial support under a levy, the basis of which was prepared by the Wool Textile Delegation. Grants are also made to Leeds University and various technical colleges. The British Cotton Industry Research Association (Shirley Institute) is guided by a council on which nominees of the trade organisations, including trade unions, play a large part. Liaison officers of the institute visit members of the Federation of Master Cotton Spinners to carry out mill trials. The facilities of the institute are available to all federation members. The federation takes a close interest in the work of the Shirley Institute, and up to a few years ago made large donations towards its maintenance; the funds are now largely obtained through a levy collected by the Cotton Board from all firms engaged in the cotton industry. An annual contribution to the Shirley Institute is also made by D.S.I.R. In 1951 a private company, Shirley Developments Ltd., was set up for the commercial development and exploitation of results of the institute's research, with the object of making developments more rapidly available to members. Representatives of the federation are on the board of management. Publications are received regularly from the D.S.I.R. and the Federation Technical Information Service forwards relevant extracts to members.

Costing. Several associations, taking note of the growing awareness of the value of standard costing and budgetary control, have prepared and published estimating and costing manuals on modern methods of costing. Among them are the Federation of Master Printers and the Federation of British Rubber and Allied Manufacturers' Associations; the latter, in 1954, distributed a booklet free to all members of its affiliated associations describing new methods and techniques in detail and setting out various processes and noting difficulties which might arise.

Education. Within the past few years more associations have shown interest in education, some in order to stimulate recruitment, others to raise standards of technical proficiency, others again to stimulate research in their particular fields; and some for all three reasons.

One of the earliest instances of an association's education activities is provided by the National Association of British and Irish Millers, which in the 1880s sponsored courses and examinations in flourmilling technology at the City and Guilds of London Institute. Nowadays all associations have education committees. That of the British Electrical and Allied Manufacturers Association collaborates with the Institution of Electrical Engineers in the preparation and constant review of a model syllabus for the training of electrical engineers. It also joins with the Institution of Electrical Engineers and the educational authorities in assessing the numbers of trained engineers periodically required by the electrical manufacturing industry. In the post-war years the association, in collaboration with the Federation of British Industries, has launched the B.E.A.M.A. Group Training Scheme for overseas students. With the help of the B.E.A.M.A. an increasing number of training places for South American, Arab, Indian and Pakistani students are found in the industry. The association is represented on many committees of the Institution of Electrical Engineers, the F.B.I., the Radio Industry Council, the Regional Advisory Council for Higher Technological Education and others concerned with national education problems. In 1951 the B.E.A.M.A. endowed the Chair of Electrical Engineering at Cambridge University with the capital sum of over £72,000 subscribed by member-firms.

The Engineering Industries Association has been concerned to find means of improving the training of apprentices in smaller firms. The object was to overcome the difficulty of limited training facilities in small and medium-sized firms and enable them to offer the same standard of training as the larger companies. The scheme evolved entails pooling the training resources of a number of firms. By this means a comprehensive training course can be established. The scheme is controlled in each area by a committee of representatives of the participating firms, the youth employment services and educational bodies.

The British Man-Made Fibres Federation furnishes literature, display boxes, wall charts, and so on, to schools and consumers, and provides lectures for the staffs of large stores, and for women's organisations. Within the industry, it provides more specialised courses for employees at various levels; in 1954 it had its first summer school at Christ Church, Oxford, for younger executives drawn from all sections of the industry. The British Non-Ferrous Metals Federation, on its formation in 1945, set up a subcommittee to consider recruitment and training in the industry. Its work has included the preparation of a scheme in conjunction with the School of Industrial Metallurgy at Birmingham, for students to be trained in members' works during vacations. The federation records particulars of courses and release schemes which exist in member-firms for further education and specialised training. In 1946, several associations in conjunction with the federation covenanted to subscribe £120,000 over ten years for the promotion of the science of metallurgy at Birmingham University. In addition a number of bursaries, scholarships and prizes for technical and other schools are provided by various constituent associations.

The British Coking Industry Association also has extensive

educational activities, granting university scholarships for those wishing to train to become coke-oven managers, and running refresher courses and training for management. In 1955 the B.C.I.A. spent some £10,000 on their educational activities. The Council of Ironfoundry Associations has a close interest in recruitment and training; it has organised conferences on training, and in addition makes, through the Joint Iron Council, a substantial annual grant to the National Foundry College, and has given £5,000 towards the cost of equipment. It also supports the National Foundry Craft Training Centre at West Bromwich, and has produced numbers of training films and film strips. The Society of British Aircraft Constructors' practical help to recruitment, which started in the 1930s, now includes post-graduate scholarships awarded annually for courses at institutions such as the College of Aeronautics.

The British Engineers Association, the British Refrigeration Association, the British Chemical Plant Manufacturers Association, the Apparel and Fashion Industry's Association, are among others which are active in this field. The British Chemical Plant Manufacturers Association, for instance, is in close contact with the Institution of Chemical Engineers, advises members on problems of education and training, and is often approached by students for advice and assistance in obtaining works training. The British Refrigeration Association is represented on the Board of Governors of the National College for Heating, Ventilating, Refrigeration and Fan Engineering, to which it has made a financial grant. It has also endowed a research scholarship, and offers its assistance to technical colleges in obtaining equipment for instructional purposes.

A growing interest in educational matters led to the reconstitution of the Screw Manufacturers Association, one of those serviced by the Birmingham Chamber of Commerce. Up to 1944, the association was named the Metal Thread Screw Manufacturers Association, and dealt with all trade matters, including labour, materials and prices, but since its reconstitution as the Screw Manufacturers Association it has concentrated on encouraging and promoting education in its industry; the other activities have been absorbed by kindred associations (including a Metal Thread Screw Association). On being established as the Screw Manufacturers Association, it negotiated with education authorities for the introduction of suitable classes for two grades of apprentices, and now runs its own apprenticeship scheme and awards certificates.

Organisation of services: association departments and committees

In looking at the chief association activities in this way, there are inevitably many omissions, since there are activities on which only one or two associations are engaged. In order to fill some of these gaps, and to give a more composite picture of various associations' services, it is worth looking briefly at the structure of departments and committees developed in different associations. This method of description is not without its own dangers of omissions and distortions. Not all committees are equally active, not all are permanent, and mere titles can cover many activities or few. On the other hand, a description of this sort helps to indicate the spread of activities of different kinds among associations.

The larger associations have specialised departments dealing with subjects which are of continuous or permanent interest, and committees dealing with problems which may be long- or short-term. Most of the smaller associations set up committees to deal with specific issues, and these committees exist so long as the problem continues. The departmental and committee structures outlined below were those current in the early 1950s; committees dealing with purely domestic matters, such as finance committees, have been omitted.

The Federation of Master Cotton Spinners, the British Engineers Association and the Society of Motor Manufacturers and Traders are examples of associations whose work is organised under specialist departments. The Federation of Master Cotton Spinners has departments dealing with industrial accident insurance, production efficiency, transport and fuel. In addition there are specialist committees on wages, rating and taxation, doubling, weaving, accidents and redeployment. The work of the B.E.A. headquarters staff is divided into eight sections: administration, economic research, exhibitions, external relations, intelligence and statistics, legal and secretarial, publications, and technical and overseas. There are also expert committees on policy, education, exports, technical matters, taxation, terms of contract and transport. The Society of Motor Manufacturers and

Traders is organised in seven departments: exhibitions, overseas, records and registers, statistics, legal, technical and standards, and press and information. Like many other large associations, the S.M.M.T. has a number of product sections which discuss problems specific to them.* In other associations there are no formal departments, but expert staff may be appointed to co-ordinate the work of a special committee, for instance, on safety problems, productivity or public relations.

The Association of British Chemical Manufacturers, in addition to the committees of the seven product groups into which its membership is divided, has standing committees on fuel efficiency, industrial information services, marking of containers, patents and trade marks, publicity, trade effluents, traffic and works safety. The Council of Ironfoundry Associations has committees on safety, transport, recruitment, training and education, market development and productivity. The Society of British Aircraft Constructors has six main committees on the technical side alone—on airworthiness, research and technological development, education and technical information, standards, production technique, materials and equipment—and there are numerous panels and sub-committees. In all, nearly four hundred of the industry's senior technicians serve on this committee structure, which is now being closely paralleled in the field of guided weapons. The Boot and Shoe Federation has main committees on labour, trade and production, exports, public relations, and liaison with the research association. In the British Plastics Federation, the most important standing committees are the main technical committee and the publicity committee; but its six product groups have about twenty technical committees between them.

The Glass Manufacturers Federation, which has six product sections, has committees covering the whole industry on publicity, factories and hours, raw materials, purchase tax and education; and others covering specific sections of the industry include committees on weights and measures, legislation and standardisation and packaging codes. The British Iron and Steel Federation has about fifteen committees dealing with subjects under frequent discussion; they include steel production and supplies, development, international trade relations, price policy, costs, statistics,

* The British Paper and Board Makers Association has no fewer than forty-two product sections.

accident prevention, training and public relations. There are standing committees of the National Paint Federation on arbitration, development, packaging, statistics, transport and raw materials; and to take a final example from the food industries, the Cake and Biscuit Alliance has eleven regular committees covering cake and biscuit export, packaging, ingredients, production, transport and distribution.

CHAPTER 5

COMMERCIAL REGULATION

THE third main aspect of association activities with which this part of the report is concerned is the control of competition, more commonly referred to under the general heading of restrictive practices. In contrast with other activities described earlier, this side of association work has occupied public and official attention in varying degrees for the past sixty years or so, not only in Britain, but also in all other industrial countries.

In Britain, legislation dealing with restrictions on competition is relatively recent. Indeed, if this report had been written some ten years earlier it would have been necessary to devote a much larger part of it to examining market control exercised by associations in industry. In the event, the operations of the Monopolies and Restrictive Practices Act, 1948, and the passing of the Restrictive Trade Practices Act, 1956, have made it unprofitable to attempt a detailed account of the methods of collective commercial regulation, or to pass judgment on whether, or to what extent, they are in the public interest. The fourteen reports of the Monopolies Commission published up to the middle of 1956 have revealed the main ways in which the forces of competition are controlled, and the 1956 Act sets up machinery to determine whether such practices are justified or not.

It would be surprising, however, if the regulation of commercial activities through associations were quickly to pass beyond controversy as a result of these developments. Under the 1956 Act associations will be required to register agreements or arrangements specified from time to time, and these may subsequently be prohibited or permitted to continue. This process itself will undoubtedly stimulate fresh discussion about the virtues and limitations of competition—especially in the event of possible trade recessions in future—and, if competition is to be controlled in certain instances, in whose hands control should be vested. Market power cannot be considered entirely as an economic problem; and though its exercise may be closely controlled, nevertheless its potential may still be an influence with other groups concerned. This, in broad terms, raises questions about the accountability of centres of power in the economy. These are not problems which arise only in connection with trade associations, since they are implicit in any discussion touching on the reconciliation of sectional interests.

So far as commercial control by associations is concerned, the policy problems to which they give rise could perhaps be briefly stated in this way: the cost of greater efficiency may be greater market control (as in the case of the single large firm), but the market power exercised by an association is not necessarily counterbalanced by improved efficiency. Secondly, there may be some forms of market control which cannot be justified on grounds of efficiency alone, if indeed at all. Thirdly, there is the problem of providing an effective means of adjudicating on types of market control and supervising the operation of those that may be deemed to be justified at any given time.

In this report it is not the intention to discuss the issues of monopoly and restrictive practices in any detail. Apart from the reports of the Monopolies Commission itself there is a considerable body of literature on the subject; and the 1956 Restrictive Trade Practices Act in any case opens a new phase in official policy towards restrictions on competition. Nor, it must be emphasised, are any judgments intended here in the treatment of the subject. The aim of this chapter is the more modest one of attempting to put the problem of commercial regulation into perspective in relation to the functions performed by associations as a whole, by looking first at the main forms of control employed and at the conditions of such control, in order to distinguish the types of association engaged in it. Then, in order to indicate more clearly the size of this problem in relation to the total number of associations, an attempt is made to indicate the industry groups where, in the experience of buyers of all kinds, commercial control by associations prevailed in 1955 and early in 1956.

At the outset it should be observed that by no means all, not even a majority, of manufacturing associations are concerned in any way with commercial control. Among those which are, agreements vary widely in scope and effectiveness, and some of the associations concerned also have extensive activities of the type described in earlier chapters.

Forms of control

Before looking at the type of associations concerned with effective restriction of competition, a word should be said about the main forms of control employed. Not all agreements which restrict competition are the subject of controversy. It is widespread practice among associations to draw up standard contracts and conditions of sale, for example, and while this may be regarded as a limitation on competition, few would suggest that the practice is undesirable from either the buyer's, the seller's, or the public's point of view.

For agreements that are the subject of criticism and controversy one can turn to the reports of the Monopolies Commission. From these reports, which deal almost exclusively with the activities of associations, many practices can be distinguished. These include price-fixing, quota systems, exclusive dealing, discriminatory rebates, collective boycott, restriction of association membership, and restriction of supplies to customers.

In its report on collective discrimination* the Monopolies Commission distinguished six types coming within its terms of reference. Two of these dealt with collective agreement on resale price maintenance and its enforcement. This is banned under the 1956 Act (though certain types of agreement on resale price maintenance may be allowed). The others, notably exclusive dealing and aggregated rebate arrangements, are, the report observed, often associated with price fixing.

Information obtained in the course of the P E P inquiry, together with a study of the products suggested to the Board of Trade for reference to the Monopolies Commission, established that (apart from products subject to collective enforcement of resale price maintenance) the majority of the products listed in the commission's report on collective discrimination were also cited as being covered by collective pricing agreements. In addition a very large number of others were named, both in the suggestions made to the Board of Trade for reference to the commission, and in the P E P inquiry, which do not appear in the report on collective discrimination. That is, common pricing arrangements are often, but by no means always, supported by discriminatory arrangements; the two can exist separately. In this report price

* Monopolies Commission, *Collective Discrimination* (H.M.S.O.), Cmd. 9504, 1955.

agreements alone have been selected in order to give an idea of the extent to which competition is controlled to a greater or lesser degree. They are the most pervasive in manufacturing industry, and other practices (again excepting collective resale price maintenance) are usually found as supports of price agreements.

First, however, how far is it possible to distinguish the type of association concerned with controlling competition?

The legal forms adopted by associations give some guide to the scope of their activities in this connection. These forms are described in more detail in Chapter 8; for present purposes it is enough to note that, of those manufacturers' associations which are registered or certificated trade unions, about fifty in number must have adopted these forms in order to enforce restrictive conditions on their trades.* Some of these are known to be concerned only with the collective enforcement of resale price maintenance: others are concerned with ensuring common prices among their members. Since, however, associations which may be trade unions in the eyes of the law are not obliged either to register or certify themselves as such, this is hardly an adequate guide.

A somewhat better indication is provided by the two hundred or so associations which are registered as companies, for these cannot legally be trade unions; that is, they cannot engage in restriction as a main activity. On the other hand, registration as a company does not guarantee that members of an association do not agree on common prices, and some in fact do, though possibly not as part of formal association business. At the other extreme a few associations specifically exclude pricing or other commercial agreements in their constitutions. But both types are rather exceptional, and it is fairly safe to assume that the majority of associations registered as companies do not engage in activities designed to control prices of competition. The remaining thousand or so associations of manufacturers have no public record of their existence, or of their legal status.

There are certain other conditions, relating to membership, which determine associations' activities in this field. An association which represents makers of products which are not closely

* In some instances, it is possible that this form was sought only for purposes of negotiation with labour; but this could only occur among a few of the certificated associations, which are not obliged to lodge a copy of their constitutions with the Registrar of Friendly Societies.

competitive can obviously have little interest in controlling competition. This is most evident in the national bodies, the Federation of British Industries, and the National Union of Manufacturers, whose members have many interests in common as manufacturers but, taken together, are not in competition one with another. The same is true of the other multi-product associations. Thus, for example, the Association of British Chemical Manufacturers represents manufacturers of many different and non-competing products and therefore has no interest in matters concerning prices or the control of competition. In other words, a fair degree of similarity of product is an essential condition of the regulation of competition, and it is among the single-product associations that such agreements are found. It is true, of course, that within a number of the larger multi-product (or "industry") associations there are groups of manufacturers or member-associations who collaborate to restrict competition. But they do not do so through the parent body, which does not, and in most cases could not, exercise such control. The majority of associations which are mentioned by name throughout this report are of this general character and hence have nothing to do with regulating competition.

As might be expected, too, it appears that geographical concentration tends to facilitate collaboration among manufacturers, especially among the smaller firms.

These conditions do not, however, provide more than a rough indication of the type of association which is in a position to control competition. Many which could, do not; and many attempt to control prices but cannot do so effectively owing to the presence either of non-member firms, or of waverers in the ranks.

A SURVEY OF PRICE FIXING

In order to get a general picture of the extent to which restraints on competition exist in industry, inquiries were made among government departments, public corporations, local authorities and hospital groups, and large and small firms in their capacity both as members of associations (in the case of public corporations and firms) and as buyers (in all cases).

Of the firms that were aware of price-fixing associations among their suppliers, none were in touch with these associations. Public bodies vary in the extent to which they are in touch with price-fixing associations among their suppliers. In most cases, if not all, the number with which they are in touch regularly, or even occasionally, forms only a small proportion of the total number of associations known to them. In one instance a public purchasing department cited no fewer than a hundred price-fixing associations whose activities affected it as a buyer. About half the associations exercised close and effective control over their prices, while the other half were not so successful, at least so far as this particular buyer, a substantial one, was concerned. In this instance there was practically no contact between the buyer and any of the associations. In two other similar cases, some fifty and seventy price-fixing associations were named.

From the evidence of these sources the information relating to price fixing has been selected. The grounds for this selection have already been mentioned, but it remains to define price fixing more closely. In the majority of instances the evidence related to common prices for the same product, the prices being reached from an average of costs submitted by member-firms. In many cases the fixing of discounts was also noted, apart from agreement on discounts (but not selling prices) as a method of control employed for consumer goods. A number of associations were also mentioned as agreeing on price increases only. Most of the arrangements on pricing were voluntary, in the sense that defaulting member-firms were not subject to any penalty, other than the extreme sanction of expulsion, which was seldom applied, but in some cases there was provision for fines for non-observance of the agreed prices.

There is, of course, considerable variation in the rigidity of price agreements. They range from the rigid price ring which brooks no outsiders and guards its prices jealously, to the gentleman's agreement, or simple price leadership. For this reason, some distinction has been made, in considering price agreement, between the industries where such agreements—in the experience of the majority of buyers—were most effective, and those where some of the buyers could purchase outside the agreed price. In a number of instances some of the more substantial buyers observed that although non-association firms existed, they could not supply the product in the quantity, and often of the quality, that was required.

A point arising from the condition that products must be fairly standard in order to be eligible for price fixing is that in industries where some equipment is custom-built it is generally free from the common price or price limits agreed for standard work. Similarly in some industries, but not in all, the prices of goods for export are not subject to agreement.

There are also what may be termed the exceptional cases. A few associations, among them those concerned with glycerine and hard coke, voluntarily keep their production departments informed of price changes and the reasons for them, thus in effect receiving an independent check on the fairness of the prices.* Iron and steel products under the aegis of the Iron and Steel Board are subject to maximum prices; and two products were mentioned by buyers in the P E P inquiry as having maximum, not minimum prices fixed by the associations concerned—the products are Scotch whisky and certain jute goods. In a few instances buyers observed that non-association prices tended to be higher.

Finally, it should be noted that in addition to the omission of discriminatory practices, common tendering has been excluded from the account given below, except where the tenderers are also manufacturers. The same applies to "reporting" associations, which tend to exist in industries where the costs of tendering for a job may be quite substantial. Some of these merely act as clearing-houses of information about inquiries for tenders which have been received. Members are given the names of others who have received the same inquiries, and thereafter they are left to discuss informally which is in the best position to do the work. Others use "reporting" more directly for allocating work. Price arrangements existing outside manufacturing industry are omitted.

The extent of price agreement

In the course of this inquiry into the extent of price agreement operated by associations, some 250 different associations were named by the various sources that were approached. Although this part of the inquiry was made as comprehensive as possible, complete coverage cannot be claimed. Partly for this reason, but also because, at the time of writing, the impending operation of the Restrictive Trade Practices Act may well have caused some

* As noted in the section in Chapter 3 on government and trade associations, cost investigations are carried out on various products at government request.

associations to revise their agreements, the names of associations are not used in this section of the report. (It is possible that this and other material collected during the present inquiry may be used by P E P for a follow-up study after the 1956 Act has been in operation for some time.) The method of presenting the material on the basis of the Standard Industrial Classification is set out in detail below.

The evidence of the various sources used in the P E P inquiry shows about 240 products or closely related groups of products to be covered by price agreements of varying rigidity. There is a roughly corresponding number of associations, though in some instances the association as such may not actually include price agreement among its activities; and as already mentioned, the descriptions given below refer to conditions as they were in 1955 and early in 1956. They may have changed considerably before the Restrictive Trade Practices Act came into force.

Of these 240 products, about half were cited as being covered by fairly rigid agreements. For the rest some of the buyers were able to get better terms from association members, or deal outside the association.

When the 240 products are grouped according to the Standard Industrial Classification they are found to be quite widely distributed among different industries. But there are noticeable concentrations of price-fixing associations in some industries, especially metal products and electrical engineering, and noticeably few in the clothing and food groups.

In presenting the information in more detail, the Standard Industrial Classification has been used as a framework. As is explained elsewhere in the report, the S.I.C. consists of twenty-four Orders, or main industrial groups. Order I covers agriculture, forestry and fishing, Orders XVII to XXIV cover building and contracting, public utilities, transport, distribution, commerce, administration, professions, and miscellaneous services. Orders II to XVI cover manufacturing industry, and it is only with these Orders that this report is concerned. Arrangements restricting competition which exist outside the industries found in Orders II to XVI are accordingly excluded.

Each Order is in turn subdivided into Minimum List Headings, each covering a specific industry or group of products. To take an example, Order II covers mining and quarrying; there are six

Minimum List Headings in Order II, each covering a particular group of products: coal; iron ore; stone; slate; clay, sand, gravel and chalk; and "other". The Minimum List Headings are numbered in sequence from 1 to 299, though numerous gaps are left to enable additions to be made in the future. Orders II to XVI, covering manufacturing industry, account for the Minimum List numbers 10 to 199.

These Orders with their Minimum List Headings are shown in detail in the Register of Associations at the end of this report, where 1,300 or so manufacturers' associations are classified according to the S.I.C. Hence for present purposes of indicating the areas of industry where price agreement prevailed in the mid-1950s, the register can be used as a key to the Minimum List Heading numbers shown in the table below.

THE EXTENT OF PRICE AGREEMENT

Order	*Minimum List Heading numbers*	*Minimum List Heading numbers under which price agreement existed in 1955–56*	*Number of products subject to:* *Effective agreement*	*Less effective agreement*
II	10–14, 19	12, 13, 14, 19	1	4
III	20–24, 29	20–24, 29	9	15
IV	30–36, 39	30, 31, 34, 35, 39	6	8
V	40–44, 49	(Many products subject to maximum price determined by the Iron and Steel Board*)	14†	2†
VI	50–58, 69, 70–75, 79	53, 54, 58, 69, 70, 71, 74, 75, 79	45	23
VII	80–86, 89	85, 86	1	2
VIII	90–95, 99	90, 91, 92, 93, 94, 99	40	20
IX	100–103	100, 101	2	–
X	110–123, 129	110, 112, 113, 114, 117, 120, 121, 122, 123	10	18
XI	130–132	—	–	–
XII	140–143, 147–149	143, 148	–	2
XIII	150–157, 162–164, 168, 169	150, 168	2	–
XIV	170–173, 179	171, 179	–	3
XV	180–183, 186, 189	180, 182, 183, 189	2	5
XVI	190–195, 199	190, 191, 193, 194, 199	4	5

* The activities concerned are specified in the Third Schedule of the Iron and Steel Act, 1953, and include production of pig iron, hot and cold rolled iron and steel products; bright steel bars and hot finished tubes and pipes, and tinplate. The board also has certain powers to determine the prices of steel castings and forgings.

† These refer to non-ferrous metals only.

In this table the last column shows the number of products (which is broadly equivalent to the number of associations) concerned, and is subdivided so as to give an indication of the number of price agreements which were effectively imposed. To take an example, the table shows that Order VI, which covers the engineering, shipbuilding and electrical group of industries, has sixteen Minimum List Headings, nine of which have each at least one price-fixing agreement in the product groups they represent. (The identity of the product groups represented by the Minimum List numbers can be found by looking up these numbers in the Register, pp. 261–312.) Finally, it can be seen that of some sixty-eight products subject to price agreement, forty-five were subject to effective agreements.

In all, about half of the Minimum List Headings into which manufacturing industry is grouped contained at least one price-fixing agreement; some of course had many more; and of the 240 or so products concerned, about half were fairly effectively price controlled.

It is interesting to compare the number of manufacturers' associations found to exist in different industries with the number of products covered by price agreements—most of which are identifiable with one association—in each. A rough comparison is given below.

	Approximate number of associations	*Approximate number of associations through which price agreement was attempted*
Mining and quarrying	19	5
Non-metalliferous mining products	92	24
Chemicals and allied trades	87	14
Metal manufacturing	127	16
Mechanical and electrical engineering	182	68
Vehicles	22	3
Other metal goods	139	60
Precision instruments, etc.	37	2
Textiles	172	28
Leather and fur	17	—
Clothing	63	2
Food, drink and tobacco	120	2
Wood and cork	70	3
Paper and printing	75	7
Miscellaneous manufactures	78	9
	1,300	243

Too much should not be read into this comparison, however. For instance, some of the industry groups contain a higher proportion of consumer goods than others, and in these price enforcement, rather than agreement, may have predominated; the table refers to price fixing only.

For practically all of these 240 or so products there are corresponding associations through which agreements are reached. It should be added that, with minor exceptions, a product was included in the foregoing list only when more than one source of information gave evidence of price agreement. It is partly for this reason that when the P E P list is compared with the suggestions made to the Board of Trade for reference to the Monopolies Commission the two do not coincide. Up to the end of 1955 about sixty products were suggested to the Board of Trade as being covered by arrangements to restrict or prevent price competition. Of these some thirty-five appear also in the P E P list, and about twenty-five do not. This suggests that the P E P figure of 240 errs if anything on the conservative side, and perhaps 300 would be a truer estimate of the number of products whose prices are agreed, mostly through associations.

There remains, of course, the possibility of agreement beyond the aegis of an association. There is little doubt that there are such arrangements, both on a national and a local scale. They are strictly outside the scope of a report dealing with associations as institutions; but their existence confirms the impression that the figure of 250 to 300 price agreements is by no means excessive.

A comparison of the P E P list with the products listed in the Monopolies Commission report on discriminatory trade practices* shows that about forty of the seventy-five listed in that report are covered by both price agreements and discriminatory methods of trading. Approximately half of the remaining thirty products appeared to be subject to collective enforcement of resale prices, and for the rest it is only possible to speculate on the type of discriminatory practice involved and whether or not agreement on prices was also in force.

The products listed under the P E P inquiry also cover for the

* Op. cit. Appendix 2 of that report listed seventy-five products, the supply or processing of which appeared to be relevant to the reference. It was noted that some of the arrangements affected only certain sections of the trade in the products concerned, and others operated only in certain parts of the United Kingdom.

most part those on which Monopolies Commission reports have been published (not all, of course, are relevant to this report), namely, dental goods, cast iron rainwater goods, electric lamps, insulated electric wires and cables, insulin, matches and match-making machinery, imported timber, calico printing, building in the greater London area, semi-manufactures of copper and copper-based alloys, pneumatic tyres, sand and gravel in central Scotland, hard fibre cordage, certain rubber footwear and linoleum. The same applies to those products before the commission on which it had not reported by October 1956.*

So far as the prevalence of price agreements is concerned, then, available evidence suggested that rather less than a quarter of the total number of manufacturers' associations are engaged in this activity to a greater or lesser extent. These, as explained above, are mostly single-product associations.

Attitudes of buyers and members

In the course of the inquiry a certain amount of information was collected on the attitudes of larger concerns both as members of price-fixing associations, and as customers: some as both.

Of some fifty large firms interviewed, twenty-two belonged to price-fixing associations, and of these, twelve were aware of price-fixing associations among their suppliers. A further ten did not belong to any price-fixing associations but were aware of their existence among their suppliers. Firms in the last category were generally critical of such arrangements, especially where price-fixed products formed a high proportion of their total purchases. On the other hand, where the products concerned were a small part of the total purchases it was frequently observed that the trouble involved in attempting to buy on more favourable terms was not worth while. In no instance were firms in touch with associations among their suppliers, except where rebate schemes were in operation.

Those that belonged to price-fixing associations presented a greater variety of attitudes. This group includes two public corporations. Some of the largest concerns, especially in certain

* At this stage, the following reports of the Commission remained to be published: certain electrical and allied machinery and plant; certain industrial and medical gases; standard metal windows and doors; electric valves and cathode ray tubes; tea; chemical fertilisers. Inquiries into electrical street lighting equipment, steel frames for buildings, and electric batteries have been allowed to lapse.

branches of textiles and electrical engineering, are ardent supporters of price agreement on grounds of stability and the furtherance of service competition, and to enable adequate funds to be built up for research, educational and development purposes. Others were lukewarm and a few were obviously at pains to ensure that they contracted out of any restrictive agreements wherever possible, and when they did not, that the arrangements were necessary and as fair as possible to all concerned. In some cases firms were obliged to belong to certain associations in order to get adequate supplies, or outlets for their product, either on the best possible terms or, indeed, at all.

Some of the firms which both belong to pricing associations and are substantial purchasers from members of other pricing associations, do not attempt to break or to circumvent agreements among their suppliers. More often, however, firms attempt to buy on the best possible terms and will deal with non-members, or defaulters, to this end, at the same time supporting similar agreements as sellers. In one instance, the sales director of a firm which belonged to a pricing association as a manufacturer warmly praised the work of the association and the benefits of belonging to it. The firm also purchased some equipment of the same kind as it produced. "But we don't buy from members of that association if we can help it", explained the firm's buyer. "It's a price ring."

PART III

Organisation of Associations

CHAPTER 6

THE LOGIC OF ORGANISATION

THE art of establishing institutions for co-operation in any field is not a simple one, and trade associations present their share of difficulties to initiators and organisers.

Some general characteristics inherent in the nature of these associations must be noted at the beginning, since they constitute inescapable premisses of the situation. In the first place, associations aim to speak and act on behalf of an industry or part of an industry, and they must therefore make some effort to be comprehensive and representative.* Though associations constantly need to express views to other bodies, their scope is not decided primarily by agreed opinions, like a political party; rather their members are united by participation in a common field of activity, like an employees' trade union. Associations are not mere groups of firms with similar views, or assemblages of like-minded manufacturers. Agreement between member-firms may be natural and usual, but it is not there by definition.

Associations consist primarily of firms, not of individual business men, in contrast to operatives' trade unions, which have individual membership. Associations must therefore take account of the commercial welfare of the companies concerned, in respect of the product covered by the association. The differences in business interests, between large firms and small, between prosperous firms and less flourishing ones, and so on, must be reconciled within the association. Unity is therefore not merely a matter of the human factor and personal decisions.

Membership of almost all associations is purely voluntary, in fact as well as in theory. Firms must be persuaded to join and convinced of the value of maintaining their membership. In some associations there may be economic hazards for the outsider, but

* They may not succeed, for there are rival associations in some fields; but all aim to be inclusive.

a dissatisfied member must believe them to be serious if it is to remain in the association, and their force is very rarely compulsive. The majority of associations are very conscious of their voluntary nature, and proceed only with the active consent of their members.

In addition to these basic factors, each industry is confronted with its own special problems. Differences between industries in structure, needs, and capacity for agreement have resulted in a great variety of solutions to these problems of organisation, and it would not be profitable here to examine in detail the constitutional history of any one association. Instead the general situation facing associations will be analysed, and the logic of the forms assumed by them described.

This will be done by first discussing the scope of associations, and then looking at the legal framework in which they must operate. The function of the formal constitutions of associations will then be considered, followed by a discussion in general terms of the maintenance of unity and the centrifugal and centripetal forces in an association. This will lead on, in the chapter on association practice, to an account of the way associations make decisions and determine policy, through their secretariats and governing bodies.

The scope of an association

It is not often nowadays that associations need to be established in industries hitherto completely devoid of organisation. More usually it is a question of widening some existing organisation, or amalgamating various fragmentary bodies, or extending the functions of an association of limited purpose. Nevertheless, certain obstacles must be overcome and certain questions settled before either a new establishment or a reconstruction can succeed.

One of the main questions must be the scope of the industry which it is proposed to attempt to organise. Since a firm may join an unlimited number of associations if it chooses, and government departments may consult with several bodies on any point, boundaries do not have to be precise and frontier problems are not acute. But there is the issue of the definition of the industry—that is, are makers of various similar or ancillary products to be included? In engineering, for example, it is not easy to decide whether manufacture of a particular product falls within the industry or not. Again, it is not obvious whether athletic clothing should be represented by a clothing association or a sports organisation; or whether tractor manufacturers are part of the motor vehicle industry or belong more appropriately to agricultural machinery. If a trade is independently organised it may, of course, affiliate both ways, as the Lawn Tennis Ball Convention is affiliated to the Federation of British Rubber and Allied Manufacturers Associations and the Federation of British Manufacturers of Sports and Games.

Besides matters of the horizontal demarcation of industries, decisions may also be needed about the vertical range of the association. Usually only manufacturers of the product concerned are admissible, but it is possible to include suppliers of raw materials, merchants, importers, wholesalers, retailers, repairers, and a variety of other categories, either as full members or associates. Any association which enforced resale prices must have included distributors as well as manufacturers. Even if it is preferred to restrict the association to manufacturers, it will normally not be practicable to exclude vertical firms with their own distributive outlets; and firms with interests in other products (to whom the association's industry may be less than vital) will have to be included, though one clothing association has excluded firms which have textile production interests.

Usually, therefore, the formal conditions of admission are broad enough. Sometimes there is a membership sub-committee, but normally the council of an association considers applications, principally to ensure that prospective members are bona fide manufacturers within the industry. It is frequently stipulated that members must be British-controlled firms. In some cases, the British Non-Ferrous Metals Federation for example, the consent of the federation is necessary before a firm is admitted to a constituent association.*

The group of firms which initiates an association may be small, but it must secure the adherence of the majority of firms, or at least of the major units, within the first year or so unless the association is to be seriously handicapped and perhaps its purposes frustrated. Though a hundred per cent coverage is not essential,

* Associations dealing with labour matters (the Incorporated Federated Associations of Boot and Shoe Manufacturers, for instance) often require from their members compliance with a national agreement made with the unions.

representation and negotiation are futile if the association cannot offer acceptance of any undertaking reached by a worthwhile proportion of firms, and commercial agreements are valueless if there are large numbers of outside competitors.

Whatever the scope of the association its existence has a legal aspect. The question of legal form does not always receive very active consideration, for it is quite possible for an association to be fully successful as an informal unincorporated organisation; and in fact most remain that. But nevertheless there are other possibilities, and it is important that the consequences of the legal form adopted should be understood.

LEGAL FORMS

Legally, a trade association may be a company, an unincorporated body, or a trade union. Those associations which are companies can be distinguished easily enough, for no body has this status unless it is registered with the Registrar of Companies. But the division between unincorporated bodies and trade unions is not so clear; for though a number of employers' trade unions are registered with the Registrar of Friendly Societies, the status of trade union is not acquired, in law, by virtue of registration, but is inherent in the activities of the organisation. The applicable terms of the Trade Union Acts are that by definition a trade union is

> any combination, whether temporary or permanent, the principal objects of which are, under its constitution . . . the regulation of the relations between . . . masters and masters, or the imposing of restrictive conditions on the conduct of any trade or business. . . .*

A trade association without restrictive activities or one in which restrictive activities are not a principal object, therefore, can choose whether or not to become, by registration, a corporate body within the Companies Acts. An association largely concerned with restrictive activities, however, has no choice of status; it is, whether aware of it or not, an employers' trade union. Its only positive choice is the limited one of whether or not to register (or have certified) this predetermined status.

* s. 16 of the Trade Union Act, 1876, as amended by s. 2, ss. 1 of the Trade Union Act, 1913.

There are complications, however, to this basically simple situation. No association can be both a company and a trade union.* Nevertheless it does appear that some incorporated associations find it possible to undertake restrictive activities of one kind or another.† In the first place, the implication of the Trade Union Acts seems to be that it is the *enforcement* of restrictive conditions that makes an organisation a trade union, not their mere existence. Secondly, it has been decided that the imposition of restrictions which are not its *main* objects does not render an association a trade union.‡ So it seems that associations registered as companies can sponsor, and possibly even enforce, price, discount and other agreements "in restraint of trade", so long as these are subsidiary functions.

Nevertheless associations registered as companies are chary of even making agreements on prices or conditions of sale. For instance, until 1948, a year after its incorporation, the Tyre Manufacturers Conference Ltd., which is not constituted as a price-fixing body, recorded in the minutes of its Car and Giant Group decisions to vary prices as decisions of the group. From that year, however, similar decisions were recorded as decisions of individual members.§ Again, many of the incorporated associations, to avoid any suggestion of restrictive activities, include in their objects a clause specifically excluding any activity which would bring them within the definition of a trade union. In these cases such activities are *ultra vires* and would not be upheld in law.||

To a considerable extent, therefore, a trade association's legal status is determined by the nature of its activities. But in most cases the association will have some range of choice; and it is therefore relevant to set out the implications for the association of being a company, of becoming a registered or certified trade union, or of remaining an informal group.

* Trade Union Act, 1871, s. 5.

† Legally, these include wage negotiation and credit protection, as well as price agreements and so on.

‡ *Performing Rights Society Ltd.* v. *London Theatre of Varieties Ltd.* (1924), A.C. 1; and see *British Association of Glass Bottle Manufacturers Ltd.* v. *Nettlefold* (1911), 27 T.L.R. 527.

§ *Report of the Monopolies and Restrictive Practices Commission on the Supply and Export of Pneumatic Tyres* (H.M.S.O.), 1955, p. 47.

|| *Aberdeen Master Masons' Association Ltd.* v. *Smith* (1908), S.C. 669.

The company

The type of company status almost always adopted by trade associations is that of limitation by guarantee. Each member guarantees to contribute a certain sum in the event of winding-up, but there is no share capital and no profit-making is allowed.* About 180 trade associations among those listed at the end of this report are registered as companies.† Among the very few of these which are private companies limited by share capital, only one, The Knitting Pin Association Ltd., appears to function as a genuine trade association. The clue to the existence of the other two or three may be given by the chief object of the Patent Glazing Manufacturers Association Ltd., which is

> to further the interests in any way which the law allows of the Patent Glazing Conference, and to form a convenient means for investment.

The advantages to a trade association which flow from registration as a company arise from the legal personality it acquires thereby. Thus, though some large associations may become incorporated for prestige reasons, it is common for associations to have more specific cause to choose company status. Though associations are not trading concerns, they may have need to make contracts of a commercial character. Some sponsor exhibitions—the Society of Motor Manufacturers and Traders Ltd., the Society of British Aircraft Constructors Ltd., the Office Appliance and Business Equipment Trade Association and many more. Others, the National Hardware Alliance Ltd., for example, are concerned with trade protection; and some, such as the Federation of Master Cotton Spinners Associations Ltd., with fire, accident and employers' insurance. One of the objects of the Flush Door Manufacturers Association is the establishment of a joint selling organisation. Associations with this type of activity clearly find

* This way of limiting the liability of a company was introduced by the Companies Act, 1862, to allow the incorporation of bodies financed by annual subscription, rather than trading concerns supported by share capital. The liability of each member on the winding-up of the company is limited to the amount of his guarantee (Companies Act, 1948, s. 2); in practice this is usually only £10 or less. A guarantee company without share capital may not divide its profits or assets among members, and if it does it will be treated as if it were limited by share capital (ibid., s. 21). Virtually all associations which are guarantee companies do not have share capital.

† See Appendix B.

incorporation an act of prudence.* It enables them to own property,† to make contracts,‡ and to sue and be sued in their own name. It also makes possible the amendment of the objects of the association without the completely unanimous support otherwise required.

The only disadvantage of company status, to an association which is eligible, appears to be that certain documents must be available for public inspection. Thus the Memorandum and Articles of Association, and annual returns giving the list of directors and the year's accounts must be sent to the Registrar of Companies; and these are available to the public at the Company Search Room. In addition, these documents must give the address of the offices of the association, where a full list of members must be available to any inquirer.§

Some associations may dislike the appendage of the word "Limited" to their title, since it is commonly associated only with trading concerns. This can be dropped by licence of the Board of Trade, on certain conditions: that the association is "formed for the purpose of promoting commerce, art, science, religion, charity"; that it intends to apply its profits and other income to those objects; and that it prohibits the payment of dividends to members.|| A number of associations—the Cocoa, Chocolate and Confectionery Alliance, the Association of Animal Gut Cleaners, the British Chemical Plant Manufacturers Association, and many others—have taken advantage of this provision.

The employers' trade union

Though their legal status as trade unions is not dependent on it, associations may choose to register or become certified as such, with the Registrar of Friendly Societies. Registration is possible if the association satisfies the Registrar that its chief objects are within the statutory definition of a trade union. It gives the organisation the advantages of being able to sue and be sued in its own name, of being able to hold property through trustees with

* Some associations have set up a *separate* incorporated body for these functions —thus the British Iron and Steel Federation established the British Iron and Steel Corporation Ltd.

† Companies Act, 1948, s. 14. For example, their own headquarters.

‡ Ibid., s. 32. For example, contracts of employment with their staff.

§ Companies Act, 1948, s. 107, s. 113, s. 125.

|| Ibid., s. 19.

full continuity,* and of making contracts in its own name.† On the other hand the association is obliged to lodge with the Registrar a copy of the rules and of any amendments, and to make annual returns of accounts and officers to him; and these are available for public inspection. Twenty-three associations within the definition of this report are registered in this way.‡

Certification is a simpler matter. It merely involves satisfying the Registrar about the objects of the association. It does not entail either the privileges or the obligations of registration and its purpose is merely to assure the association and, if necessary, the courts, that it is in fact a trade union. Twenty-nine associations, as defined in this report, have claimed the Registrar's certificate in this way.§

The number of associations which are, in the eyes of the law, trade unions in virtue of a main activity "in restraint of trade" cannot be assessed.

On the whole, these variations do not affect the characteristics of trade unions as special legal entities. Two aspects of this status are of major importance. In the first place, the Trade Disputes Act, 1906, gives unions immunity from liability in tort. This immunity means that any association which injures others by its restrictive activities cannot be sued for conspiracy, defamation or any similar matter, and none of its harmful actions, if *intra vires*, can be questioned in a court of law. The protection of the Act extends only to the combination itself, and not to members or officials; but the wording of the relevant sub-section|| suggests that it even covers torts about to be committed; and that it prevents, therefore, injunctions to restrain associations from committing these acts. It is to ensure that they are entitled to this immunity, of course, that some associations register or take out certificates of their status.

Secondly, the courts will not enforce certain contracts of a trade union. Therefore, associations which are acting in restraint of trade cannot directly enforce agreements between members about conditions on which they transact business, or agreements to pay subscriptions or penalties; nor can they directly enforce

* Trade Union Act, 1871, s. 7.

† *Bonsor* v. *Musicians' Union* (1956), A.C. 104.

‡ See Appendix C. § See Appendix D.

|| Trade Disputes Act, 1906, s. 4, ss. 1. See Scrutton L.J. in *Ware and de Freville Ltd.* v. *Motor Trade Association* (1921), 3 K.B. 40, at p. 75.

agreements to apply their funds to the discharge of a fine, or an agreement with another trade union. Members of an association who break this sort of agreement cannot be sued.*

The unincorporated association

Over 1,000, or the majority of the trade associations covered by this report, are neither companies nor registered or certified trade unions. A fair number of them would be held legally to be trade unions, but it is likely that most do not fall even into this category. It remains, therefore, to point out one or two of the legal features of unincorporated bodies. This class includes all 1,000 unregistered associations, trade unions or not, and indeed the certified trade unions.

These associations have no corporate legal existence. This at first seems to involve them in a number of legal disadvantages and inconveniences. Property must be held for the association by a trust or by individual members. In most circumstances the council—and perhaps the members—of the association will find themselves fully liable for all actions which they have authorised, including any contractual ones. The association cannot sue or be sued in its own name. In theory every member must consent to the association's actions, and to changes in its rules. In practice, these legal disadvantages may not be very serious. Associations do not often own much property; they do not enter into many contracts; they would rather do without the right to sue or be sued, and indemnify the individuals held responsible instead; and members are willing enough to consent to any acts on which a majority of the association decides.

These matters are regarded as serious in some quarters, however, and in the face of the dangers of unlimited liability, associations are urged to become incorporated. But although individuals with legal training are sensible of the disadvantages, these rarely seem substantial to business men. They are more likely to look upon company status as being appropriate to the trading concern, and as leading to control by a board of directors. In fact, of course, these fears do not apply to companies limited by guarantee with properly representative constitutions; but allied with inertia, they may explain why most associations remain informal societies.

* For this reason the British Motor Trade Association, for example, designed its own enforcement procedure, with a stop list as a final sanction.

CONSTITUTIONS

It is evident that, restrictive trade practices apart, the law does not press very closely on the forms assumed by trade associations. It is necessary therefore to look for other moulding forces. A little evidence may be gleaned from constitutional documents. Those associations which are registered as public companies have formal constitutions set out in the Memorandum and Articles of Association, and those which are registered or certified as trade unions have a full constitution in their rules. Other associations do not need such meticulous detail, and a shorter document is usual.

It is not often, of course, that these constitutions are consulted; they do not impinge greatly on the day-to-day working of the association. The objects of the association, for example, are usually stated in the widest terms, and the mention of some activity is no indication that the association actually performs it, or intends to perform it in the foreseeable future. Its mention is merely to enable it to be taken up easily if changing circumstances make its introduction desirable.*

In general the Memorandum and Articles of Association of a registered company must clearly eschew any activity "in restraint of trade", and in fact the Memorandum of an incorporated trade association often includes some such phrase as "not to act as or carry on the business of a trade union". The opposite is the case with registered employers' trade unions. There, functions involving the commercial regulation of the industry are explicitly stated.

For example, one object in the 1933 Rules of the Notts Lace and Net Dressers Association is

> to prevent unfair competition, and price-cutting, and unfair attempts to get work for themselves from the customers of other members.

An object of the National Association of Crankshaft and Cylinder Grinders, in their 1947 Rules, is to

> prevent the operation of unscrupulous traders who prejudice good workmanship, reduce prices below an economic level, violate trade agreements, and adopt trading methods inimical to the trade.

* At least one association, however, the British Refrigeration Association, reports annually on action taken under each object laid down in the constitution.

Associations which are not incorporated, registered or certified in any way sometimes have restrictive objects and sometimes prohibitions of them. Those which have regulatory functions must of course be *de facto* trade unions—for example the British Silk Throwsters Association had as an object:

> To fix and regulate the minimum selling prices of all classes of thrown silk yarns and the conditions of sale so as to eliminate price-cutting.

and it stated that

> The fixing of such prices shall take place on Monday and Wednesday in each week....

On the other hand, the Society of British Soap Makers provides that

> The society shall not promote, encourage or sanction any steps tending to prevent or restrict competition between one member of the society and another, or as between members of the society and non-members, and whether by way of price-fixing, allocation of markets or otherwise.

But, in the main, the formal generalities of a constitution give little practical guidance to the purposes of an association, whether they are set out in legal documents or not. Nevertheless, the process of constitution-making is not without significance, for these documents can ensure a balance of power in the association. In time relative strengths and the criteria used to establish them become habitual, and in the absence of structural change in the industry there is rarely any argument about them. When associations are first being formed, however, and at other critical times, there may be misgivings in some quarters about the consequences of membership. Small firms ask whether the association will be dominated by a few big firms; and large ones do not want to be overruled by a great number of small firms with a low proportion of total output. These and other doubts and suspicions, if they occur, will have to be met in some way. A carefully balanced constitution will often help to do this.

The constitution, therefore, has to take account of facts about the relative importance in an industry of different-sized firms, different regions, and different trades, that are generally only vaguely understood. The formalisation of previously unstated relationships is an inherent quality of the growth of institutions in society; and the key to the significance of many trade association constitutions—particularly those of federations—is that they must recognise the proportionate strengths of sections of industry. And often where nothing is expressed in a written constitution, something of the structure of the industry can be learnt from the actual composition of an association council.

The necessity of unity

There are three possible ways in which these relativities are manifested: in the scale of subscriptions, in voting powers in elections and at general meetings, and in the composition of governing bodies. The size of a firm's subscription* rarely affects its influence in the councils of the association unless it is so large that its withdrawal would materially harm the activities of the association. In any case, loss of industrial comprehensiveness is a more serious consideration with associations. When voting is necessary it is usually on the principle, one firm, one vote. The largest firms are almost invariably elected to governing bodies—partly because their staff can more easily supply the necessary expertise, partly because their firms are recognised as leaders of the industry; but mainly because policies which do not have their support are not effective in the industry. The obvious way to ensure this support is to have them share in policy making.

The composition of the governing body is, in contrast, sometimes a matter for prolonged bargaining. When they are well established, councils and executives do not often take issues to a vote: they try to achieve some agreement and compromise. Nevertheless the various groups of firms will be anxious to make sure their interests are kept in view, and if some part of an industry is under-represented it is likely to suspect that the consensus of opinion on the council does not properly reflect the attitude of the industry. Some method of representation has therefore to be devised that is acceptable to all. The success of the balance of forces thus brought about is not merely a matter of equity, for if firms feel dissatisfied with the trend of association policy they will be inclined to resign. It is therefore vital for an association to be able to rely on its decisions being in accord with the needs of all types

* Sometimes firms' subscription rates are kept secret so that the size of the firms will not be revealed.

of member. Examples of the machinery created for this purpose are given below in the section on governing bodies (pp. 205–208).

It is desirable, too, for an association to construct a constitution that seems fair not only to its members and to potential recruits, but also to outsiders. There are times when responsible tasks need to be done in an industry—control, allocation of supplies, development, and so on. An association that is comprehensive and fairly organised is more likely to be favoured as the appropriate body for the job than partial or biased ones.

Centripetal forces

It is evident that this problem of unity is central to any consideration of trade association organisation. It is not the case, of course, that associations are often on the verge of breaking up; on the contrary, they are mostly secure and well-established. But this shows rather that custom and prudent arrangements have reinforced the original outside forces to hold the association firmly together. It does not mean that there are no potential lines of division. Indeed, it is usual to claim on behalf of associations that they present "united fronts" to other bodies, the implication being that without the association there would be disunity of some sort.

In an essay* on the stresses to be found in federal systems of government, Lord Bryce distinguished the centripetal forces tending to hold a union together, and the centrifugal forces which incline to break it apart. An analysis on similar lines can usefully be made of the various strains to be found in trade associations.

The primary centripetal force in almost all cases is, of course, similarity of interest arising from similarity of product. The range of associations varies tremendously, from organisations like the Association of British Chemical Manufacturers or the British Engineers Association covering whole sectors of industry, to associations catering for producers of one specific product, such as the Aluminium Milk Bottle Cap Manufacturers Association, the Sterilised Catgut Manufacturers Association or the Shoulder Pad Manufacturers Association. But though the width of interest of these bodies may be very different, the principle, that there should be some general likeness of goods produced, remains.

* James Bryce, ***Studies in History and Jurisprudence***, Oxford (Clarendon Press), 1901.

There are several exceptions to this rule: but the achievement of unity on some other principle has usually been more difficult or more limited in purpose. The National Council of Building Material Producers is a federation of forty-one associations concerned with the production of materials and components used by the building industry, and the sole unifying factor is their position as suppliers to the same industry. Its primary work is as a negotiating and advisory body at the highest level, however, and it leaves most association functions to its constituents. The Federation of Rubber and Allied Manufacturers Associations is unified by a raw material and its substitutes, rather than by similar end-products; and again it is mainly confined to general negotiation, with some of its constituents, such as the Tyre Manufacturers Conference, operating largely on their own. The National Hardware Alliance has found the construction of unity difficult owing to the imprecision of product definition and hence of those engaged in the trade.

Apart from these apparent anomalies, however, it is type of product that unites the members of an association, for if products are broadly alike then the raw materials, the processes of production, and market conditions will all probably be alike too. Given these likely similarities, then firms will tend to be affected in the same way by the factors mentioned in the chapter on the reasons for growth*—by labour relations, by economic crises, by international conditions—and by the government intervention discussed in the chapter on the influence of associations.† Since firms are in like case, they can profit by a like response.

So far as the real business interests of firms are concerned, then, the advantages of membership all arise from this fundamental technical similarity. But there may be subsidiary forces at work; by no means so important and only occurring in some cases, yet not without their occasional significance.

A trade association is often a sort of club, which it is good form to join. Many firms with little genuine interest in the work of the association have no thought of resigning. To belong gives a firm a feeling of respectability, of not being a trouble-maker in the industry. Subscriptions are often negligible as far as a firm is concerned, and are paid out of a sort of industrial patriotism. This gregarious feeling may be accompanied by a sense of security

* Chapter 1. † Chapter 3.

derived from membership. Although his firm is not getting anything of value at the moment from the association, a business man may feel that it is there in case of need, and that he ought to help keep it in being as a standby.

There are also social pressures. Some associations include the arrangement of social functions among their objects: there are frequently annual dinners or luncheons, and occasionally associations have standing social committees. Not to be concerned with these affairs is to be something of a nonconformist. Again, where industries are regionally concentrated, an industrialist who remains outside the association is known as a non-member and a non-supporter of collective effort in the community and in the circles in which he lives. Hence, if there are no positive disadvantages, a business man will prefer to be in his association rather than out of it.

In addition to these psychological forces, a few associations have devised direct sanctions.* In many cases, however, these apply to any firm inside or outside the association which ventures to run counter to its agreed principles. The best known of these was the system of the British Motor Trade Association, which imposed sanctions on traders who failed to observe the prices individually prescribed by the various car manufacturers. This power extended to manufacturers themselves, who might have been fined or had their distributive outlets cut off if they had committed a breach of the association's rules. Although no measures were taken against non-members of the B.M.T.A. as such, membership was tremendously advantageous to manufacturers since it gave them access to the industry's established distributive system; and for distributors membership was in practice unavoidable, since manufacturers made such membership a condition of contract whenever they supplied cars.

In general, associations which include a high proportion of an industry's manufacturers and distributors can put very strong pressure to join on the others by the operation of exclusive dealing arrangements. For example, the Association of Manufacturers and Distributors of Garage Equipment has most of the

* Collective enforcement of resale price maintenance has been made illegal by the Restrictive Trade Practices Act, 1956. Other arrangements may become illegal under the processes of the Act, but in those cases where exemption is granted the above analysis will apply.

country's distributors in membership, and since these only buy from members, any manufacturer wishing to use their services must join. Again, the Chemists Federation of Manufacturers, Wholesalers and Retailers of Medical and Pharmaceutical Products controls all sections of the trade and administers the "Chemists' Friends List": no manufacturer can have a product put on the list unless he is a member of the federation, and since the list is used by distributors as a guarantee of quality, membership of the federation is virtually compulsory for every reliable manufacturing firm.

Membership of an association may occasionally give better access to supplies. Thus, only members of the Lancashire Boot, Shoe and Slipper Manufacturers Association can be shareholders in the Valley Supply Company, and thereby obtain more economic access to raw materials for the industry.

During World War II and the period of control following it many firms felt it prudent to be members of associations, since these had contact with the Board of Trade and other central authorities. There was, of course, no preferential treatment on principle for association members, but these usually gained in practice a superior knowledge of possibilities and problems, and were thus able to make a quicker response to a changing situation.

Similarly, some associations deal with labour matters, and are the recognised negotiating body with the trade unions. A firm can stand out from such an association and nevertheless pay the agreed wage-rates; but most find it better to be in, and have some influence on negotiations and use the services of association officials for conciliation purposes.

Finally, there are other minor forces which may serve to hold members in an association. There were cases, for example, where insurance cover against workmen's compensation claims was only given to association members.*

In spite of these various pressures acting to keep firms in membership, it still remains true that associations are essentially voluntary bodies. If membership did not give advantages, associations would not exist: that is their *raison d'être*. Really compulsive powers over firms are found only in vertical associations controlling distribution as well as manufacture—in fact, where

* For example, only to members of the National Association of Drop Forgers and Stampers in the late 1930s.

the association as a collectivity can control a greater range of the total economic process than any individual firm. A company with control right from raw material to consumer could not be coerced by any association.

The centripetal power of an association is also directly dependent on the unity of a nucleus of major units. Membership becomes much less compulsive if there is a considerable proportion of an industry already outside—gravitational pull depends on mass. It is even less necessary if there is a rival body in the field. But this raises the question of centrifugal forces.

Centrifugal forces

In the past, one of the main centrifugal forces has been the strong individualist tradition in many industries such as textiles; and where this was not too strong to prevent the formation of an association it has sometimes hampered the adoption of effective policies. This feeling is not now widespread, and co-operation and association are not regarded as incompatible with private enterprise. There are, of course, a few independent-minded firms which join no organisations at all; but though there is often strong resistance to various practices, such as price-fixing, there is now little root-and-branch opposition to all forms of collaboration.

The forces which now tend on the whole towards the disruption of trade associations can be seen by looking at those cases where complete unity has in fact proved to be impracticable. There are three varieties of these: those industries where there are rival bodies within the same field; those where overall organisations might seem appropriate but have not come together; and those where there are notable absences from membership of the association.

In the china clay industry there are two associations, the British China Clay Producers Federation Ltd., and the China Clay Association.* At one time the federation (which is mainly concerned with representational matters and negotiation with the trade unions) included nearly all the industry; in 1946, however, many firms resigned. The China Clay Association, which deals with marketing problems, now covers more of the industry's output; it developed out of the "China Clay Agreement", established in 1937. Both the National Paint Federation and the Society

* *Board of Trade Working Party Report on China Clay* (H.M.S.O.), 1948, p. 21.

of British Paint Manufacturers Ltd., which split away from the federation in 1945, continue in full activity. In general engineering there are two associations, the British Engineers Association, a long-established association including most of the major concerns in mechanical engineering; and the Engineering Industries Association, set up in 1941 and comprising a very wide range of firms. In hosiery there are the National Hosiery Manufacturers Federation and the smaller British Hosiery Manufacturers Association.

Various attempts to set up an organisation representative of the whole clothing industry have come to nothing. The ironfoundry interests have always stood out from the British Iron and Steel Federation. The glass industry is divided into the Glass Manufacturers Federation, covering containers and domestic glassware, and the Sheet and Plate Glass Manufacturers Association. The cotton industry has the Cotton Board, a statutory body, in the absence of a united trade association.

The third variety is exemplified by the absence of the London Brick Company from the National Federation of Clay Industries, and of the Imperial Tobacco Company from the Federation of Home and Export Tobacco Manufacturers.

The reasons for these divisions are various and each case has its own explanation. But some recurrent lines of disunity can be traced among them. The rival associations tend to divide on size of firm—very roughly, of course; there are numerous large firms, for example, in the Engineering Industries Association, and small ones in the British Engineers Association.* Yet frequently in these cases one of the associations makes specific claims to look after the "small man", indicating at least that there is some distrust between different-sized firms in that industry. It is interesting that among the two general associations, the National Union of Manufacturers makes a similar plea to cater especially for the small and medium-sized business.

The lack of a general organisation may not mean disunity if the natural community of interest between manufacturers of the same product is lacking: in the clothing industry, for instance, the structure of enterprise, the materials used, the labour-force and the demands of the markets are all very different for different

* This is not the only difference; the Engineering Industries Association has a wider scope than the British Engineers Association, including, for example, some electrical firms.

branches, and consequently no common attitude to problems is found over the industry. The lack of unity in this and other industries has meant that there must be several organisations, each covering as broad a sector as possible.

Absence from membership of a dominating firm is not always disastrous for an association, for the absentee may be friendly and co-operative. The motive for non-membership is generally fear of being tied to association policies designed for much smaller concerns. Associations cannot offer many attractions to these very large combines, for they can provide their own services, and have independent access to government departments.

These causes of actual disunity all exist as potential influences inside more successful associations. Small firms tend to distrust large combines in all branches of industry, and when they are in the same association they are often inclined to feel neglected in the running of the association. On the other hand large firms do not want to be overruled, either on policy questions or in the matter of prices, by small businesses with what they sometimes regard as a limited outlook. There is thus an inherent tension which must be minimised as far as possible. Large firms have usually no objection to the principle of one firm one vote in association elections:* if small firms run the associations in some way contrary to their interests, they will resign from it, or threaten to do so. Some large combines, such as I.C.I. or Courtaulds, are at pains to avoid dominating associations, but their wide interests and decisive share of production makes it difficult. Thus the weight of major firms must inevitably be felt in the counsels of an association. On the whole, most of the voluntary work is done by the larger firms, since only their directors and staff can provide the necessary expertise.

It has been noticed in some associations containing a wide range of size of firm, that while the smaller firms are interested in the services provided, export information, technical guidance and so on, the larger units (who provide their own services) are more interested in policy questions. The small firms tend to regard government action as beyond their influence, but the bigger firms try to use the association as a means of making their views known and of bringing pressure to bear.

* Constitutions often provide for a poll, in which voting may be proportionate to size, but these are little used in practice.

In some industries the natural community of interest is sufficient to allow the formation of a general association, but in fact there is little in common between groups within it. Here the general association is either a loose federation with restricted functions, or most of the work devolves on the product sections of the association. The Textile Finishing Trades Association and the Radio Industry Council are examples of such bodies.

There are other possible lines of division which give rise to strains within associations. Though it is true that most associations with regional constituent bodies are so organised because historically they are federations or amalgamations of localised associations, there is still not always complete harmony between different parts of the country within various associations. There are, for example, differences between London and provincial manufacturers to be reconciled in some industries, such as furniture. The newspaper industry has separate associations for the London Press, The Newspaper Proprietors Association, and the provincial papers, The Newspaper Society. On the other hand, in the wool textile industry, although its three sections in Yorkshire, Scotland and the West of England maintain their local patriotism, a central trade association has been successfully established in Bradford.

There may be some disagreement between new firms in an industry and old-established ones; or between conservative and progressive ones. But this does not often go beyond the natural differences of view and of habitual outlook found in any collection of individuals.

Some associations include importers as well as British producers. The Society of Motor Manufacturers and Traders has an importers' section within its organisation, but since conflict of interest on trade matters is obviously bound to arise between these dealers and home manufacturers, the British Manufacturers' Section of the society has established the right to make representations to government departments and so on independently.

Perhaps the chronic disease of trade associations, however, as of trade unions, is apathy. It is not a problem with all associations, but the great majority are troubled by it to some degree. Federal bodies which do not have direct dealings with firms do not have to face the problem, but it may be serious for their constituent associations. There is some tendency for interest to be greater in associations concerned with some form of price regulation: but here as elsewhere there are always some firms who play a purely passive role in the activities of the association. The danger for the association in this is that lack of participation may lead to a lack of appreciation of the work being done and of its importance. Firms cannot value things they do not know; and there is a danger that these firms will regard their association subscription as unnecessary if they should at some time be faced with the need to retrench.

Sometimes, of course, the fact that a secretariat has no contact with a firm shows contentment rather than otherwise; if things are going well there is no need to complain to the association. Certainly many firms are content to be passive followers in association matters, but have no intention of resigning. Yet lack of active interest by a high proportion of members is never a really satisfactory situation, for it must lead eventually to a lack of understanding of the needs and attitude of the industry at large by those representing it.

Association officials and enthusiastic members make considerable efforts to meet the problem, especially in industries where it is serious, such as light clothing and engineering. The Engineering Industries Association is endeavouring to meet the problem by developing personal contacts, increasing the number of visits to firms and improving its monthly bulletin. In the British Engineers Association the secretary has special responsibility for contacting new, prospective and apathetic existing members.

There is always a possible conflict in associations where one group of members are suppliers to others, as is often the case in the Association of British Chemical Manufacturers, the Wool Textile Delegation, the Radio Industry Council, and the British Iron and Steel Federation. The Association of British Chemical Manufacturers excludes all market relationships from discussion within the association, however, and so the division of interest is irrelevant to the association's purposes.

Finally, the purpose which impelled the formation of an association may no longer be operative. Associations formed during times of depression may be deemed unnecessary by their members in more prosperous times; and organisations set up to negotiate with government departments in periods of control may be abandoned when they are relaxed. In fact, however, though the activities of associations change with the needs of the times, there is a strong tendency for the organisations themselves to survive.* Associations set up for representative or restrictive purposes tend to develop centralised common services, and these are recognised as valuable in themselves. Again, the decline of government control and the consequent diminution in that line of activity was followed by an increase of technical and productivity services provided by many associations.

All in all, of course, though the general history of trade associations has been chequered, a large number have survived: the centripetal forces have proved stronger in the event than the centrifugal ones. The problems of organisation have, in fact, been met, and it remains to describe the means whereby they have been solved.

* The Association of Tinned Cream Manufacturers appears to have survived throughout the war and post-war periods, though the manufacture of tinned cream was entirely prohibited.

CHAPTER 7

ORGANISATION IN PRACTICE

THE burden of the last chapter was that there is implicit in the organisation of every association an attempt to maintain its own unity. But associations need more than constitutional agreements; they are functional institutions, and they must have continuing arrangements for discussion and decision. There must be, in each association, some machinery for its own government. The decisions which are required to run an association vary from those of a merely routine character to those which may be vital for the future of the industry. Some can be delegated to employed officials, but the more important ones cannot be taken without extensive consultation throughout the industry.

Apart from the arrangements for deciding association policy, there must also be provision for servicing governing bodies and for giving such assistance to the industry as may be decided upon. Staff is needed to carry out the executive and administrative tasks of associations. Most of those who have any contacts with associations deal with these officials, and for many purposes it is these people who are implied when reference is made to "the association". It is necessary to consider the association as a working unit concerned with day-to-day matters, before examining higher authorities and remoter levels of control.

SECRETARIATS

There are perhaps forms of collaboration in industry which need no secretarial arrangements at all. If groups of manufacturers arrange to meet fairly regularly to discuss price levels or other common problems; or if firms make a practice of consulting each other, or merely keep each other informed, about actions they are taking, then some sort of society may be said to exist. It can fairly be assumed that there is such co-operation in several industries. Where there is price-leadership, for instance, the leader may give early notice to other firms about its intentions; and there are also informal contacts on technical and contract matters.

But these *ad hoc* systems are not within the definition of an association, and for practical purposes any inquiry must be confined to those with at least an acknowledged title, an address, and a subscribing membership. Anything less formal is an agreement rather than an institution, and can scarcely persist except on a local basis or among a fairly small number of firms. These understandings may be economically significant as trade practices; but they are of little consequence as part of the trade association world.

Among associations that can be located with some precision, the most rudimentary type of organisation is that based on the member-firm. In some cases it is agreed that the necessary secretarial work for an association shall be carried out by each of the member-firms, or each member of the governing body, in turn. Or alternatively the administration of the association's affairs may be put permanently into the hands of one of its members. If the work involved is at all substantial the association may make some payment to its member for these services. But with this type of arrangement the organisation required is essentially informal, and matters of consequence are referred to the next meeting of the governing body. The system often finds favour when the association is dormant but is being kept alive in case of future need.

Examples of this type of administration are found in the Taper Pin Manufacturers Association, where Guest Keen and Nettlefolds, Ltd. perform the secretarial duties and the National Ammonia Liquor Association, for whom Imperial Chemical Industries, Ltd., at Billingham act as secretaries. Other associations where this method of operation appears to exist include the Abrasive Industries Association, the National Association of Charcoal Manufacturers, the Milk Can Manufacturers Association, and the Cheddar and Caerphilly Cheesemakers Association.

Firms of accountants and solicitors

When an association wishes its secretarial duties to be carried out by an independent staff, they may be undertaken by a firm of accountants (or, occasionally, of solicitors). These deal with matters from a professional standpoint, and hence all substantial decisions tend to be referred to executive or council meetings. This assures the secretariat of a neutral and impartial status, at some extra cost to the association, perhaps, and possibly with the loss of expert knowledge at the centre, compared with the member-firm style of administration. The method was frequently used, of course, among those associations whose main purpose was the fixing of common prices. Decisions about price levels are rarely arbitrary: some formula which relates them to costs is usually applied. Accountants are therefore necessary for purposes of computation, and, being neutral, they can collate production costs and other information in confidence.

There are certainly many associations run by accountants that do not fix prices—the Office Appliance and Business Equipment Trade Association and the British Tin Box Federation are examples. Some associations which no longer maintain price agreements continue as representative bodies, and are still serviced by accountants. For an association whose activities do not require full-time staff, the services of accountants experienced in the field offer a neutral and convenient method of administration whether their expert professional knowledge is called on or not.

Accordingly, with the widening of the functions of associations, several firms of accountants have developed their own services in many ways, and no longer confine their activities to the minimum secretarial duties. It is true to say, nevertheless, that in the main these accountants do not exercise any degree of discretion. A request or suggestion made to these associations will normally have to wait for some form of consultation with the chairman or governing body for a reply.

It is probable that in addition to the named and formally constituted associations run in this way, there are a fair number of the loosely constituted groups mentioned at the beginning of this section which use the services of firms of accountants. But apart from these private arrangements, accountant-run associations comprise a high proportion of those covering specific products, as distinct from those covering wider fields.

Notable associations administered by accountants include the Federation of Associations of Colliery Equipment Manufacturers, the Mechanical Handling Engineers Association, the British Rivet Association, the Permanent Magnet Association and the Chain Link Fencing Association—all run by Messrs. Peat Marwick Mitchell and Co., who appear to service over sixty associations in all from six offices in different centres of industry. Messrs. Wenham Brothers, with offices in London and Birmingham, have over a dozen named associations, including the Steel Nail

Association and the Boot and Floor Polishes Manufacturers Association.

Messrs. Heathcote and Coleman of Birmingham also administer a number of associations, including the British Tube Association and the British Plastic Hardware Association. Other accountants servicing several associations include Messrs. Kidson and Taylor, of Manchester and London; Messrs. Jones, Crewsdon and Youatt, of Manchester; and Messrs. Thompson McLintock, of Glasgow, Manchester, and London.

There are much rarer cases of solicitors acting as secretaries. The Glasgow firm of solicitors, Biggart, Lumsden and Company, has a long-established connection with employers' and trade associations. At present they administer the British Nautical Instrument Trade Association, the Clyde Ship Repairers Association, and other bodies not strictly within this report's definition.

It is often impossible to be sure in particular cases whether an association is run by accountants or not, if the address does not make it clear and in the absence of direct contact. Nevertheless it is estimated that between 150 and 200 manufacturers' associations, within the definition used in this report, and listed in the register, are serviced by accountants.

Group organisation

Another variety of secretarial arrangement is provided for associations by major chambers of commerce or federations. These bodies have considerable experience in trade association work of all kinds, and can provide efficient services for those associations which do not require an independent headquarters and secretariat of their own.

The practice of these large organisations is to allocate members of their staff to take charge of association work. One person will act as secretary to several associations, and perhaps have other duties besides; the number varies with the amount of business involved in each case. In this way continuity and genuine understanding of the industry can be secured. It is, of course, for the associations themselves to decide how much responsibility is to be given to their secretaries; but they are obviously more likely to have confidence in them if they give continuous attention to their industries and are generally experienced in commercial and industrial matters. These qualities can be best obtained for the smaller association by attachment to large organisations, which employ officials with the required capabilities.

The Federation of British Industries provides administrative services for five associations, and the National Union of Manufacturers for about thirty.* Associations administered by the F.B.I. include the British Industrial Measuring and Control Apparatus Manufacturers Association and the Steel Wool Manufacturers Association. Associations whose offices are situated with those of the N.U.M. in Holborn include the British Baby Carriage Manufacturers Association, the Casein Button Manufacturers Association and the Surgical Instrument Manufacturers Association.†

There are three chambers of commerce which provide administrative services for national associations: those of London, Manchester and Birmingham. The London Chamber of Commerce is responsible for many associations of importers and merchants; but it also administers nearly thirty manufacturers' associations, including the Federation of Home and Export Tobacco Manufacturers Ltd., the British Radio Cabinet Manufacturers Association, and the Toilet Preparations and Perfumery Manufacturers Federation of Great Britain. The Manchester Chamber of Commerce has a major interest in the cotton textile industry. Many of the associations which it runs were wartime growths, designed to ensure supplies of raw materials and the continuance of some production—the Household Textiles Association, for example. The Manchester Chamber also operates the Domestic Textiles Federation,‡ the Furnishing Fabric Federation, the Ticking Group, and several others. Most of the associations at the Birmingham Chamber of Commerce are concerned with the metal-using trades. They include the Steel Wheelbarrow Manufacturers Association, the Stainless Steel Fabricators of Great Britain and the Association of Hand Lifting Tackle Makers, and about ten others.

It is possible for an association which does not wish to depend on another body for its secretarial work to achieve some independence without operating in complete isolation: it can share

* There are, of course, many more associations affiliated to these bodies.

† A full list is given in the official register of the N.U.M., *The Manufacturers' Manual*.

‡ A body with wider interests than the H.T.A.

accommodation and employ staff in common with other associations. In some cases affiliated associations are housed with their federation. The British Valve Manufacturers Association, for example, shares accommodation with the British Engineers Association. Again, with the British Paper and Board Makers Association are found the Building Board Manufacturers Association of Great Britain, Ltd., the Filter Paper Makers Association and others, sharing staff and offices, and the Coated Paper and Board Makers Association with a separate staff but in the same offices. The National Paint Federation serves the Surface Coating Synthetic Resin Manufacturers Association, the Association of Cellulose Lacquer Manufacturers and others.

The British Disinfectant Manufacturers Association, the Association of British Insecticide Manufacturers, the Association of British Sheep and Cattle Dip Manufacturers, the Industrial Pest Control Association, the Animal Medicine Manufacturers Association, the British Colour Makers Association, and the British Barytes Producers Association are all affiliated to and operated by the staff of the Association of British Chemical Manufacturers. At Light Trades House, Sheffield, there is a more complex grouping. Two federations, the Federation of British Hand Tool Manufacturers and the National Federation of Engineers Tools Manufacturers, are housed there, with many of their constituent associations, and also the Sheffield Light Trade Employers Association, which deals with labour matters and covers both groups.

Other associations concerned with similar products are housed together, but not in the shelter of their federations—thus there are a number of rubber product associations which are to be found in the Royal Exchange at Manchester, and not with the federation in London. There are cases of associations, often with some technical similarity or overlapping membership, sharing offices and staff though they are not affiliated or formally allied. The British Chemical Plant Manufacturers Association shares with the Food Machinery Association in this way.

Self-contained secretariats

Perhaps less than half of all manufacturers' associations are administered completely independently; but most of those with combined administrations just considered, and the federations and dominating partners in other groups, have in practice the same flexibility and efficiency of service as the isolated organisation.

Two major aspects of association activity, collective representation and economic regulation, do not need a large staff. It is when the association has extensive common services—when it collects and disseminates statistics, when it organises exhibitions, when it publishes a journal that is more than notes on association affairs, when it has a technical information service—that many officials are required to run it. The size of an association secretariat cannot always be taken as a measure of the impact of that body on the nation's government or economy, but it is rather an indication of the direct assistance which it offers to its member-firms.

If the size of an association's secretariat is determined largely by its common services, its location is decided by its representational functions. The headquarters of most national associations are, therefore, in London. Some regionally concentrated industries such as pottery or non-ferrous metals or textiles have their association centred in the provinces. Two of these, the British Man-made Fibres Federation and the Scotch Whisky Association, also have branches in London.

Association officials

The chief official of an association goes under various titles. "Secretary" is the traditional and still the most frequent name: but, as his authority and functions have grown, the term "director" has come into use. Some associations have both secretary and director,* one dealing with organisation and the other with policy matters. Other associations have chosen other titles. The Engineering Industries Association has a secretary-general; the Society of Motor Manufacturers and Traders has a chief executive; and the Shipbuilding Conference a controller, as well as a director and two secretaries. The term "director" and these other variants imply a higher degree of independence than "secretary": but it would be dangerous to infer the authority of an official in any particular case from his title alone.

The greatest degree of authority exercised by servants of

* For example, the British Chemical Plant Manufacturers Association and the Federation of British Rubber and Allied Manufacturers Associations.

associations is that of independent chairmen. The purpose of such appointments is twofold—to secure someone entirely neutral at the centre of affairs and to put this person in a position of leadership, where he can give his attention to overriding general problems of the industry. It is sometimes felt that a chairman from any member-firm would necessarily be preoccupied with day-to-day problems, and it may be the case that leading representatives are all identified with a particular section of the industry, or with a controversial point of view. In these circumstances, an individual of standing from outside the industry is more easily accepted as an impartial head of the association.

Sir Andrew Duncan's work as independent chairman of the British Iron and Steel Federation in the 1930s is perhaps the best-known instance of such an arrangement; but there are many others, although the practice is not necessarily a permanent one, and associations may revert to the more usual type of chairman from inside the industry. The British Iron and Steel Federation, the British Man-made Fibres Federation, the British Bolt, Nut, Screw and Rivet Federation, and the Metal Window Association Ltd. are among the associations who have this type of officer today.

Directors and secretaries are appointed by the councils or other governing bodies. It was alleged by a sub-committee of the Committee on Trusts in 1919 that Lever Bros. Ltd. had the specific right to nominate a stated number of the executive officers of the United Kingdom Soap Manufacturers Association. This expedient, however, must be regarded as unique for an association with independent headquarters. It is not the practice to recruit officials from the staffs of member-firms. It is not common to find association secretaries or directors who have had business experience in the industries they represent. The main reason for this is that such persons might show partiality for their former associates; but it is true also that the techniques of negotiation and other abilities required for association work are not easily acquired by service in individual firms.

It is usual for association officials to have an industrial background, in other fields than the one they have come to serve. Otherwise the most common qualifications held by chief officials of associations are professional ones in law or accountancy, and there are some with the qualifications of one of the institutes of secretaries. Associations in industries employing more complex technical processes often need officials with an understanding of these matters, and thus scientific degrees or diplomas are required. There are a few officials with academic training in economics or commerce.

But, in the main, associations look for experience in a like field—with other associations, chambers of commerce or in the Civil Service. Though there may be difficulties where technical knowledge is necessary, there is a good deal of recruitment of senior officials from the lower ranks of other associations. Manchester Chamber of Commerce, for example, seems to have trained a number of the present secretaries and directors of associations. The effect of this recognition that special organisational skill is required has been the development of a new profession.

Hitherto, inside knowledge of industry has been confined to business men, but it is now possible, for a few officials at least, to acquire a close understanding of an industry without being connected with any particular enterprise.

In the late 1930s there was formed, for social purposes, a Secretaries Club. This club now has about two hundred members, all secretaries, assistant secretaries or accountants connected with national trade associations. Meetings are held monthly in London for lunch, when there is usually a guest speaker from industry or commerce.

In addition to controlling the day-to-day administration of the services which the association provides for its members, the director or secretary usually plays a part in the determination of wider policy. Associations find they need to employ high-quality staff not only for their general advantage but also in order to meet government departments and other bodies with officials of equivalent calibre. But the discretion allowed to these officials varies considerably from association to association. Some directors work with the minimum of reference to governing bodies, and have considerable influence on the determination of policy. Others seem expected to consult their chairman or even their executive on every point that departs at all from routine.

A desire to avoid any suspicion of "industrial bureaucracy" is one motive for restricting the authority of paid officials. There is a feeling that ultimate decisions should be taken, for good or ill, by business men involved in the fortunes of the industry. Associations are voluntary organisations, and firms do not want to lose control of matters which may be of vital concern; hence they prefer associations to be closely supervised by elected officers rather than dominated by permanent officials.

In spite of this mistrust there is a tendency for the relative status of permanent officials to increase in the counsels of associations. Character and experience make an individual official's opinion highly respected; and an experienced director or secretary may have a better knowledge of the facts and a more detached outlook than the newly elected officers from firms. Gradually, therefore, both the area of an official's discretion and his influence on questions which go before elected officers are likely to increase. Even so, the director of an association who has a policy of his own may easily alienate part of the association—eventually perhaps all of it.

Another factor which tends to augment the influence of officials is that they make contact, in the course of their work, with the individuals in Government and other bodies who are closely concerned with the industry. It is the official who knows in practice how to get things done on behalf of the industry and who has mastered the technique of representation. In a way, therefore, directors and secretaries can achieve a position analogous to that of the senior civil servant. Although they can never have the decisive voice in any matter, their advice can have the strongest influence.

The establishment of personal contacts with officials in the ministries, in professional and technical bodies, and in trade associations in adjacent industries is one of the most important duties of any director or secretary. Although these relationships begin, no doubt, as formal negotiations, eventually it becomes possible to take matters in a more conversational way. Normally the senior official of a major national association is on friendly terms with the assistant secretary in the production department responsible for the industry, and he probably knows also the relevant under-secretaries and deputy secretaries. Association officials are also likely to be acquainted with principals and the more senior executive officers.

In addition to outside contacts it is also the business of an association official to get to know his members. In so far as they serve on committees and councils this is no problem; but it is likely that the bulk of firms will not be in touch with the association except by correspondence—and that often of a routine nature. Most association secretaries and directors, therefore, make efforts to visit the offices and works of their member-firms. This not only enables them to meet the less prominent business men in the association, but also to acquire an enhanced sense of reality in considering the industry's problems. Nevertheless it is a general opinion among officials that they do not see enough of these ordinary members; the pressure of work is such that there is always something more urgent to do than visit a firm.

The other staff of trade associations either have similar qualifications to the senior officials, or have specialist professional or technical knowledge. Sometimes they give general assistance, but usually they take charge of some particular aspect or service of the association. Numbers normally vary with the extent of the common services provided, but there are ways of avoiding an increase in the number of regular staff. Some associations employ outside contractors or temporary workers for particular jobs. Press publicity can obviously be handled by an advertising agency in the normal way. The Apparel and Fashion Industry's Association has fashion displays and similar projects organised by outsiders; and the exhibitions of many industries are arranged by associations in conjunction with firms of exhibition promoters. The Federation of Rubber and Allied Manufacturers Associations is an example of an association which makes a practice of employing temporary staff to undertake special tasks. Another method is for much of the secretarial and organisational work to be done by elected officers in their firms, as in the Federation of British Carpet Manufacturers and the Employers Federation of Cane and Willow Workers Associations.

Headquarters staffing: some examples

The following instances serve to illustrate how a major national association may staff its headquarters. One association with a very large staff is the Cement and Concrete Association, which has over two hundred. These include qualified engineers, architects, research workers, technical assistants, public relations officers and general office staff. They are under the control of the director, who is assisted by the technical director, the director of information and the secretary. In addition to the headquarters in London, there is a research station at Wexham Springs, near Slough, and a branch office in Edinburgh.

The British Iron and Steel Federation has about three hundred employees, headed by an independent chairman, four directors and a secretary. The research director is also head of the British Iron and Steel Research Association. Most of the staff are employed at Steel House in London, but area training officers have offices in the provinces.

The Joint Iron Council and the Wool Textile Delegation illustrate the interlacing of organisations at the official level. The Joint Iron Council, the Council of Ironfoundry Associations and the Council of Iron Producers share accommodation and are controlled by the same director. A number of the staff work on a "common service" basis, but most serve one or other of the associations; these include (for the Council of Ironfoundry Associations) a press and information officer and a training officer. The Wool Textile Delegation and the Wool (and Allied) Textile Employers Council—a body responsible for labour and productivity matters in Yorkshire—have the same secretary, are housed in the same building and share some of the same staff. They control the Wool Industry Bureau of Statistics, a recruitment, education and training department and a work study centre; and altogether about thirty-three people are employed. The Wool Export Group, though co-operating closely, has a separate organisation.

The British Electrical and Allied Manufacturers Association has a staff of approximately 180 employees located at its headquarters in London, and at a branch office at Ascot. The organisation is headed by the director, export director and the secretary, who are the three principal executive officers. In addition there are various heads of departments whose prime duties cover such services as standardisation, legal advice, statistics and publicity. The staff also includes section secretaries who are responsible for the work of the sections, which are organised by generic classes of products, for example, domestic electric appliances and small switch and fuse gear.

The senior staff, such as the directors, secretary, legal adviser and the chief accountant, are men of professional qualifications who have had many years' experience in the industry. Many of the section secretaries are also qualified engineers and members of professional institutions.

Owing to the nature of its constitution, the B.E.A.M.A. as such cannot deal with prices. The trade groups are therefore organised independently, and the B.E.A.M.A. provides them with accommodation and secretarial services on a strictly business basis. In addition the association provides secretarial staff for kindred associations, such as the National Association of Lift Makers, the British Synchronous Clock Conference, the Electric Light Fittings Association and the Association of Short-circuit Testing Authorities (Inc.).

GOVERNING BODIES

Whatever its activities and whatever administrative arrangements it may establish, a trade association must have a governing committee in charge of its affairs. A catalogue of the formal constitutions of these bodies would scarcely be illuminating; but, as argued in the section on constitutions (pp. 177–179), they often provide the key to the unity, and hence the effectiveness, of the association. It is therefore useful to examine some general questions concerning their composition, and to give illustrations of the machinery of government in various associations.

Presidents and chairmen

Nearly all large associations have provision in their constitutions for the election of honorary officers of some sort, and the majority of them have filled these positions. Honorary presidents and honorary vice-presidents are normally former office bearers of the association who have retired from active work, and whose service to the association or eminence in the industry it is desired to honour. They are no doubt consulted on matters of importance, but play little part in the current operation of the association.

Chairmen, and those presidents other than honorary ones,* are active and important figures. They are usually elected by the association at the annual meeting. In a minority of cases they are chosen by the elected councils. Often they serve as deputy chairmen, vice-chairmen and so on before or after their term of office.

The most interesting distinction is perhaps that between those chairmen (whether elected annually or not) who serve for long periods and those whose term is only for one, two, or three years. Rotation of office is much more common: the reasons are clear

* The term "chairman" will be used to include active presidents.

enough. Firms do not want the association to be dominated by one personality, and they seek to prevent the emergence of "Grand Old Men" in controlling positions. Moreover, eminent business men do not want to be burdened with heavy association duties for the remainder of their lives. Rotation of the chairmanship tends to be preferred, therefore, in any association which is busy enough to make serious claims on the time of its chairman. The contrary practice is found even in very active associations, where there is a distinguished and respected figure at the head of affairs, permanently acceptable to all members. This has happened, for example, in the Rayon Weaving Association, the Association of British Wood Wool Manufacturers, and the Engineering Industries Association. When such a person retires, the association may thereafter rotate the office. This happened recently when the founder of the British Industrial Measuring and Control Apparatus Manufacturers Association retired.

Pressure of work and the fact that these posts are increasingly held by busy executive directors, arising from the increased activity of associations, is making rotation of the chairmanship much more usual. The chairman of an association keeps in close touch with the secretariat during his term of office. Normally he is aware from day to day of what is happening at headquarters. Many chairmen make a practice of visiting the director or secretary regularly—some have their own office there—and where this is not possible there is constant communication by telephone or letter. In fact, the bulk of the non-routine decisions necessary for running the association are taken by the chairmen and chief official in collaboration.

Evidence seems to show that chairmen spend an appreciable part of their working time on association affairs. In addition to frequent consultation with the administrative staff, a chairman attends all council and executive meetings, and often those of many committees. He also takes part in important negotiations with other bodies. These activities are liable to take, in some cases, up to two or more days a week of a chairman's time, and one day a week is no more than average. Few important national associations demand less service of their presiding officers.

Almost all associations give their chairman authority to act in cases of emergency. Beyond these very rare occasions, however, most chairmen can deal with matters which are better attended to promptly and which can be decided within the lines of accepted policy. This not only minimises delay, but also avoids a plethora of items on the agenda of the council or executive. Within policy limits, considerable discretion is allowed by tradition to the presiding officers of the British Non-ferrous Metals Federation, the Society of Motor Manufacturers and Traders, the Society of British Gas Industries, the British Paper and Board Makers Association (Incorporated), and several others.

In order to ease still further the decision-making process, a few associations have set up small advisory committees, with whom a chairman may consult informally and at short notice. These usually consist of the association's senior honorary office-bearers, and rarely exceed three or four members. Such a body is the Chairman's Committee of the Cake and Biscuit Alliance Ltd., a nucleus of four members of the council. The Wool Textile Delegation has no committee, but it is the custom of the chairman to seek a second opinion of the vice-chairman when necessary.

The Federation of British Manufacturers of Sports and Games and the Federation of British Rubber and Allied Manufacturers Associations also have small president's advisory committees. These bodies do not merely serve as consultative groups, however, but hold preliminary discussions on the long-range policies of their federations, although they do not finally decide such policies.

Size of councils and executives

The main organ of government in trade associations is a representative committee, usually called the council. Apart from the overriding authority of general meetings, such a body has the power to make all decisions necessary to the running of the association. There is frequently a smaller executive whose authority is derived from the council.

Councils vary considerably in size. The Society of Motor Manufacturers and Traders has a council with over ninety members, and the Cotton Spinners and Manufacturers Association a central committee with about a hundred members. The British Paper and Board Makers Association (Incorporated) has a council of seventy-nine members, and the National Hardware Alliance has between eighty and a hundred. Then there are several associations with councils numbering about sixty—the Shipbuilding Conference (seventy), the Federation of Master Cotton Spinners

Associations (sixty-five), the British Iron and Steel Federation (about sixty), the Incorporated Federated Associations of Boot and Shoe Manufacturers (about sixty) and the Federation of British Rubber and Allied Manufacturers Associations (fifty-five).

The majority of major associations, however, have councils of a size somewhere between the forty-six of the Wool Textile Delegation or the forty-two of the British Plastics Federation, and the twenty of the Association of British Chemical Manufacturers and the Federation of British Manufacturers of Sports and Games. Smaller governing bodies include the sixteen members of the Radio Industry Council and the seventeen of the National Council of the Engineering Industries Association.

With so wide a range it is clear that the type of discussion must be different in the large councils from that in the smaller ones. The larger bodies tend to review decisions of a secretariat or executive committee, and to consider comparatively pre-digested material—for example, confirming or rejecting plans worked out by committees. Their role is that of supreme control of the association's activities on behalf of its members. The smaller ones are also in supreme control, but they can take a more constructive part, suggesting and deciding lines of action themselves.

In some cases one body is sufficient. The British Man-made Fibres Federation, with a council of thirty-five members, has found it possible to dispense with its standing committee (which had twenty-five members) and operate satisfactorily with a single authority. Other associations—the Association of British Chemical Manufacturers, the Federation of British Manufacturers of Sports and Games, the Wholesale Clothing Manufacturers Federation, for instance—have always worked with one governing body.

But usually there is a smaller executive committee, meeting monthly, as well as the full council, which meets quarterly in most cases. The executive committee of the Association of British Pharmaceutical Industry has only four members;* but it is more common for these committees to have between eight and twenty members. These bodies exercise a more detailed control than a large council, though acting always by its authority and under its general supervision.

In general, then, the size of an association's council affects its

* With the right to co-opt others.

function within the organisation, and determines whether an executive is necessary or not. An exception is the Radio Industry Council which, with sixteen individual members, also has an executive with eight.

In looking for the factors affecting the size of governing body decided upon, however, it is necessary to look at the structure of the industry and the scope of the association. Associations which are federations of local organisations—the Federation of Master Cotton Spinners, the Cotton Spinners and Manufacturers Association, the Incorporated Federated Associations of Boot and Shoe Manufacturers, the National Paint Federation—need to have all their constituents represented on their governing councils. These are therefore large. The Society of Motor Manufacturers and Traders needs to have representatives of its seventeen sections on the council. If the caravan manufacturers and the hire-purchase finance section are each to have a member, then in order to reflect their relative importance fairly, the car manufacturers need to have fourteen, commercial vehicle makers eleven, and so on. Similarly, the council of the British Iron and Steel Federation, which is appointed by the ten member-conferences, needs to be properly representative of about thirty product-associations of differing importance.

In contrast, smaller and less sectionalised associations have smaller governing bodies. The Federation of Calico Printers has a single executive of seventeen members, the British Industrial Measuring and Control Apparatus Manufacturers Association a committee of eight, and the British Pressure Cookers Manufacturers Association a council with five members.

Composition of councils and executives

The need to represent many interests on a governing body may cause that body to be large, but size alone does not solve the problem. No matter how many members a council may have, some relationship of representation to industrial importance must be arranged. This topic is discussed in the chapter on the logic of organisation (pp. 177–179). Some examples of the methods adopted for the election and composition of governing councils are given here.

Wherever an association is divided into sections or groups the question of direct or indirect election arises. The councils of federal associations are chosen almost invariably by the constituent associations; and where trade sections are not strong the firms elect the central council directly. But between these cases there are a number of associations which, though not federal in principle. have governing bodies composed of the officers of trade groups or sections. Thus eighteen out of twenty-five members of the council of the Society of British Gas Industries are chairmen of its sections. The chairmen of the groups within the Federation of British Manufacturers of Sports and Games constitute a majority of its council. In the Apparel and Fashion Industry's Association the council is nominated by the eight garment sections. The general council of the British Leather Federation includes the chairman and honorary secretary of each of its four sections, one other member of each section and the chairman of each subsection and district section. In the British Plastics Federation, chairmen of groups are *ex-officio* members of the council.

The central point of interest in the composition of these governing bodies, however, is not the directness or otherwise of election, but the devices adopted to ensure adequate reflection of the industry's varied interests.

The size of firm is obviously important here. The National Paint Federation organises its council elections in such a way that the numerical majority of small firms has approximately one-half the members, while the less numerous but equally important large firms have the other half.* Half the places on the council of the Cocoa, Chocolate and Confectionery Alliance are allocated to chocolate manufacturers, and these are chosen by groups of firms of different sizes, the five biggest firms having five representatives.

Secondly, there is a need for geographical balance. The Incorporated Federated Associations of Boot and Shoe Manufacturers weights the representation of its regional associations by the number of their member-firms. The British Furniture Manufacturers Federated Associations have tried to ensure that the provincial manufacturers have not been outweighted by the more numerous London firms.

Thirdly, there are numerous product and process groupings, sometimes of considerable complexity. The arrangements of the

* The small firms, which employ one-half of the total employee strength of all members of the federation, elect their representatives through the local association; those of large firms are elected on a national basis.

Society of Motor Manufacturers and Traders have already been mentioned. The Cake and Biscuit Alliance has a council of fixed composition—nine members from the British Cake and Biscuit Association, six from the National Association of Biscuit Manufacturers, and one each from the Co-operative Wholesale Society Ltd., the Co-operative Union, J. Lyons & Co. Ltd., the members of the Northern Ireland Wafer Biscuit Association Ltd., and the Associated Oatcake Manufacturers.*

The council of the British Non-ferrous Metals Federation has twenty-eight members, four of its member-associations providing four members each, and the others two. The British Cycle and Motor Cycle Industries Association Ltd. has on its council six representatives of bicycle manufacturers, six of motor cycle manufacturers, six of manufacturers of proprietary articles, two of tyre manufacturers, and three of factors. On the council of the National Federation of Clay Industries the thirty-six members are elected in their trade sections; the brick section, for example, has sixteen members and the tile section two.

The British Iron and Steel Federation has a council of about sixty members. Of these twenty-one represent the British Steel Producers Conference, and seven the Light Rolled Steel Products Conference. Six other conferences have three or four representatives, and two have two. About six additional councilmen are co-opted. The apportionment of places is decided by the executive committee.

The executive committee of the Glass Manufacturers Federation has eight representatives of glass container manufacturers and seven of other glass manufacturers. It is interesting to note that this division does not correspond to the five newly-created membership sections of the federation, based on products. The Shipbuilding Conference aims to make its executive board representative of the various interests of members with regard to both their geographical distribution and to the class of ship produced.

Perhaps the most interesting ways of constituting governing bodies are found in those large associations which have both individual firms as members and also member-associations. This situation prevails in the Federation of British Industries and in the National Union of Manufacturers. Among industry associations

* Two representatives of the Ministry of Food have not sat since April 1954.

it occurs in the British Engineers Association. This has a council of about forty members; there is one from each of the seventeen affiliated associations, and the rest are elected by individual member-firms. Since some firms—perhaps a hundred—are members of both the British Engineers Association itself and of its sectional associations they can thus have a twofold influence; but in practice any bias this introduces is negligible.

The arrangements in the Textile Finishing Trades Association are also worthy of note. This federal association has two executive committees, one for its Labour Group (with seven member-associations) and one for its Commercial and Industrial Group (with four). Two member-associations, which are concerned with both aspects, are represented on the two groups. There is a General Purposes Committee which covers both groups.

Authority of councils

Most associations grant their councils a general commission to take charge of all the affairs of the organisation. Only in a few cases are there restrictions on their powers. In the National Paint Federation and the Cocoa, Chocolate and Confectionery Alliance, for example, any change in subscription rates must be referred to a general meeting. The general committee of the Federation of Master Cotton Spinners Associations has wide powers, but it is laid down that any general action involving a strike, lockout, short time or organised lessening of production shall not be taken unless two-thirds of the committee are in agreement and unless the proposed action has been confirmed in writing by firms owning eighty per cent of the spindleage in membership.

In the main, however, the only limitation on a council's actions are those arising from its position as an elected body which must retain the confidence of member-firms. As explained in the section on the maintenance of unity (pp. 177–188), a council not only needs majority support but must also work with the consent of any minority that may exist. The sort of authority needed for this is enhanced by the practice of choosing top-class personnel to serve on councils. The British Iron and Steel Federation stipulates, for instance, that its councilmen must be directly engaged in a senior position in the industry. In most cases council members are elected as individuals, and must serve in person; where member-firms are nominated it is always possible for the duties to pass from, say, the managing director to the works manager or the sales manager, and so on. This may be no disadvantage from the firm's point of view: but to other association members it might seem that the elected firm no longer regarded association matters as of the first importance, and it would also tend to lower the prestige of the council in the industry.

The need of the association for the services of the heads of firms may be lessened where the association contains multi-product firms, for there are advantages in having the head of the department or branch of a business which is most interested in the association, rather than his ultimate controller. On the whole, though, an association can be most confident that it is playing a part of real consequence in an industry if the leaders of that industry attend personally to association affairs; and it can play that part with maximum effectiveness only if it does secure their participation.

The British Engineers Association takes the view that the policies of an industrial association should be determined solely by those with a stake in the industry; and to ensure that this principle is maintained it provides that the representatives of its seventeen sectional associations on the council must themselves be manufacturers connected with a member-firm, and not association staff. The representatives of member-associations on the Wool Textile Delegation also are manufacturers: but they are supplemented by fourteen senior officials of constituent associations, as secretary members with restricted rights. In this way overriding control is kept in the hands of business men, but the experience of officials, especially important in a federal association, is brought directly and continuously into the counsels of the delegation.

Committees

The work of elected councils and executives can be lightened by delegation to committees. It is in this way that the holders of the less senior positions in member-firms take part in the operations of the association. Committees, of course, are appointed by the councils and report to them.

Small associations often have only one or two permanent committees at the most, though the large ones may have a dozen or more. A finance, or a finance and general purposes committee, is usual, but beyond that titles and functions vary. As explained in the chapter on common services (pp. 112–152), an association frequently sets up a committee to supervise the working of a particular service.

Committees dealing with technical matters are common: either a single technical committee, as in the Federation of British Rubber and Allied Manufacturers Associations, the Society of Motor Manufacturers and Traders and the British Engineers Association; or a whole series of committees, such as are found in the Society of British Aircraft Constructors. The British Plastics Federation has a main technical committee, and each of its product groups also has a number of technical committees. Other topics frequently found suitable for committee action are transport, raw material supplies, and co-ordination with a research organisation or the British Standards Institution. Export committees are also common, often having originated as independent export groups.

Frequently association committees are *ad hoc*, set up to deal with some particular issue such as purchase tax, trade effluents, fuel efficiency, or a Monopolies Commission inquiry. Even committees with a more durable air are apt to prove temporary as a subject becomes a routine matter for the secretariat, and other and more urgent issues arise.

Sections and groups

Most associations have some division of their membership into trade or product groups. This is less necessary, of course, in small associations with a comparatively narrow scope. But even in the British Industrial Measuring and Control Apparatus Manufacturers Association, which has thirty-six members, the makers of water meters meet separately to discuss problems which are only of concern to them. Some federal associations work so closely together that they are little different from sectionalised associations —where, for example, the constituent associations are serviced by the federation. One or two have both sections and constituent associations. In the Food Machinery Association there are nine sections, each dealing with equipment for a particular trade; three of these sections, however, are constituted as distinct associations—the Bakery Equipment Manufacturers Society, the Mineral Water Engineers Association, and the Dairy Engineers Association, though all are serviced entirely by the F.M.A. secretariat. In a few cases there are two tiers. Thus, the groups of the Society of Motor Manufacturers and Traders are essentially sub-divisions of its seventeen trade sections; and in the British Plastics Federation five of the six groups are divided into sections.

Much of the work of trade associations is done by these sections and groups, and in the normal way they have complete autonomy in their activities, and elect their own committees. Nevertheless they are not independent bodies, and the association must be held together. This raises two issues.

In the first place, the usual rule for the working of section committees is for them to have complete freedom to act as they think fit, unless any contemplated action will affect other members, when decisions must be submitted to the executive or council of the association. Occasionally arrangements are specified by which a central council keeps an eye on what is afoot. In the Association of British Chemical Manufacturers all group minutes are submitted to the council for formal acceptance. In the Apparel and Fashion Industry's Association all decisions of the eight garment sections are reported to the council, which can overrule them if contrary to overriding policy. The sections of the Glass Manufacturers Federation cannot make representations to outside bodies, or bind the federation by their decisions.

Secondly, there is usually some rigidity in sectional organisation, compared with the ease of establishment and disbanding of general functional committees. Sections and groups are deeply embedded in the structure of the industry, and the established arrangements are difficult to revise. Groups within the British Plastics Federation may not be abolished without their own consent unless the membership has fallen below six. The eighteen sections of the Society of British Gas Industries were established and can only be dissolved in an annual general meeting of the society. The groups of the Cocoa, Chocolate and Confectionery Alliance provide an instance of sub-divisions established by the articles of association, which would need to be changed if any group were dissolved. On the other hand, some associations have maintained a stronger central control. The sections of the Glass Manufacturers Federation have been authorised by its executive committee, and can be dissolved by it if three-quarters of its members support the resolution. The sections of the Wholesale Clothing Manufacturers Federation are set up by and dissolved by the executive council, and the council of the Federation of British Manufacturers of Sports and Games has similar powers over its groups.

Though groups and sections on a trade or product basis are by far the most usual arrangement, there are one or two examples of provincial organisations being set up. The Federation of British Industries and the National Union of Manufacturers have well-developed regional organisations based on various provincial industrial centres. The Engineering Industries Association has divided its members among eight regions, each with its own committee; and these regions have the right to constitute area groups, thirty-five of which now exist. There are also occasional groupings of regional, Scottish or Welsh members in associations with the usual product sections; thus the Scottish members of the Association of British Pharmaceutical Industry have a group of their own, dealing chiefly with matters of local interest.

General meetings

The members of trade associations exercise control over the policies of their organisations by electing the governing bodies, not by meeting and making decisions themselves. Nevertheless in the majority of associations there is some form of general meeting. In those associations which are registered as companies there must be, of course, an annual general meeting when the year's accounts and report are considered, and new officers are elected. But, as with other companies, these are often formal occasions, and all business is transacted quickly and without discussion.

There are many associations who hold yearly gatherings of a more substantial character, sometimes lasting two or three days, either connected with the necessary annual general meeting in the case of incorporated associations, or specially arranged by other associations. The Joint Iron Council holds an annual convention where any member-firm of the Council of Ironfoundry Associations or the Council of Iron Producers can be represented. The primary business of this meeting is to consider the report of the Joint Iron Council, and there is thus opportunity for general discussion of all matters affecting the industry and its associations. General meetings of the members of the Association of British Pharmaceutical Industry are held twice a year and are important and active occasions when there is full discussion of the association's affairs. But there are also many associations which, though they do not do so much as these two, arrange lunch or dinner, with a guest speaker likely to interest their members, so that the annual meeting is more than an empty formality.

One interesting, and possibly unique, exception to all this occurs in the British Industrial Measuring and Control Apparatus Manufacturers Association. Here the number of members is small enough to enable general meetings to be held every two months, alternating with meetings of the governing committee. The frequency of these meetings, especially in relation to those of the committee, enables member-firms to exercise continuous control over association business in a way that is not practicable in larger organisations.

FINANCE

In order to provide some idea of the scale of association finance, a brief survey of their accounts is first given here. Problems on the revenue side, mainly concerned with subscriptions, are then considered; and finally there are notes on the usual forms of association expenditure.

Examination of the accounts of trade associations cannot give a full picture of their membership or activities, but it can provide particular facts and help to correct mistaken impressions. Accounts usually do not show, for example, what proportion of an association's income comes from its different types of member; but they do indicate any ancillary revenue there may be, apart from members' subscriptions. Again, in the majority of cases it is not possible to trace the cost of particular activities; but often some idea of expenditure on, say, publicity can be picked out.

Figures are rarely available, of course, except for those associations which are registered as companies, or are registered trade unions. These are obliged to furnish annual accounts which are available to the public at the Company Search Room of the Board of Trade and the Registry of Friendly Societies respectively. The information used in this section is therefore derived from a minority of cases, but it is unlikely that the general impression that these give is seriously misleading.

The incorporated association with the highest income appears to be the Society of Motor Manufacturers and Traders, whose total income in 1954 was £330,694. Of this, £178,483 was derived from the surplus on exhibitions with which the society was concerned. On the other hand, £147,732 was passed on to other bodies, including £80,000 to the Motor Industry Research Association.

The British Electrical and Allied Manufacturers Association had an income in 1953–54 of £215,044. Of this, £120,533 came in contributions from other associations and £64,160 in direct subscriptions from firms; and £28,144 of the total was passed on to other bodies. The Cement and Concrete Association's income of £255,483 in 1954–55 was almost entirely (£251,432) from firms' subscriptions, and only £10,673 went in subscriptions and donations to other bodies.

Another association with a very large income is the Federation of Master Cotton Spinners Associations Ltd. This is largely owing to its accident insurance scheme, which covers member-firms against third-party risks and common-law claims by employees who may be injured. Thus, though the federation's total income in 1954 was over £212,000, as much as £86,000 consisted of a reserve against accident claims carried over from earlier years. There is no separate fund for this department, and claims of more than £70,000 had to be met; hence the amount raised by levy was some £120,000, though the general expenses of the federation were only £45,000.

Some information is available about the income of the British Iron and Steel Federation, which appears to be substantial. In 1953 it was stated that the federation derived about £800,000 from the proceeds of a levy of one shilling per ton on steel produced.* It is understood that this levy is now at a lower rate. There is no information about the income of the Brewers Society, but with this possible exception it does not seem likely that there are any associations with annual incomes exceeding £100,000 except the five already mentioned. Associations with high income figures, but below this top range, include the Society of British Aircraft Constructors (£71,373 in 1954), the British Non-ferrous Metals Federation (£67,000 in 1954–55), the Incorporated Federated Associations of Boot and Shoe Manufacturers (£50,663 in 1954–55), and the Association of British Chemical Manufacturers (£48,246 in 1954–55).

Below these, association incomes vary with the range and type

* House of Commons Debates, 10 March 1953, Col. 1239–40.

of their activities. Federal bodies covering wide sectors of industry do not necessarily need high incomes—the National Council of Building Material Producers has about £6,000 and the Radio Industry Council £19,000. The income of the Federation of British Rubber and Allied Manufacturers Associations at about £13,000 a year is considerably less than that of one of its affiliated associations, the Tyre Manufacturers Conference (£56,000 in 1954). The National Paint Federation received about £25,000 in 1954–55 and its rival, the Society of British Paint Manufacturers Ltd., about £11,000.

Association incomes can be very low. The activities of some of them appear to require little money. The Artificial Flower Manufacturers Association had an income of just under £400 in 1954–55; but the Flush Door Manufacturers Association Ltd. in 1954 received only £22, of which £10 10s. was paid out as a subscription to the British Standards Institution. The British Wire Netting Manufacturers Association Ltd. had in 1953–54 an income of £1 13s.

The incomes of associations registered as trade unions are not usually high. The £30,449 received by the Radio and Electronic Component Manufacturers Federation seems to be the largest. The Apparel and Fashion Industry's Association received £12,117 in 1952; the National Employers Association of Vehicle Builders £21,424 in 1954; and the Chemists Federation £9,264 in 1954. But incomes under £2,000 per annum are not uncommon in this class of association.

There is little need for trade associations to hold any considerable capital assets: they may own their own offices, and some have investments or other accumulated reserves. The Society of Motor Manufacturers and Traders had assets worth £431,281 in 1954, largely investments. Other incorporated associations with large assets include the Cement and Concrete Association (£356,247 in 1955), the Society of British Aircraft Constructors (£264,160 in 1954) and the Federation of Master Cotton Spinners Associations Ltd. (£233,237 in 1954).

Subscriptions

For almost all associations the only important source of income is the subscriptions they receive from members. A few associations have provisions which enable the regular subscriptions to be supplemented by special levies. These have occasionally been invoked, perhaps to finance publicity campaigns.

The simplest principle on which subscriptions or levies can be based is that of the flat rate for all members. In the National Union of Manufacturers all firms, however large, pay fifteen guineas a year.* Until 1956 a flat-rate payment was also made in the Apparel and Fashion Industry's Association. The Zinc Pigment Development Association and several small-firm associations like the National Association of Master Monumental Masons are others which have flat-rate subscriptions. Where all firms in an association are much the same size, the arrangement may be adopted on grounds of simplicity and convenience. It may be preferred also by small firms, who feel that if large firms pay more they may tend to control the association, since "he who pays the piper calls the tune". It may be urged, however, that large firms must have a major share in determining association policy, whatever they pay; and that since the flat rate must be one the smallest firms can pay, the effect of this arrangement on the total income of an association is crippling.

Some criterion of size is therefore usually adopted, and firms pay subscriptions on the scale which this indicates. But the choice of criterion is not always easy. There are three desiderata:

i. it should be fair—that is, it should reflect firms' interest in the industry;
ii. it should be determinate—firms should be able to measure easily and precisely their position on the scale;
iii. it should not involve the revelation of any information which firms wish to keep private.

The circumstances of different industries lead associations to make different attempts at meeting these requirements.

Among the most frequently used scales are those based on the number of employees. They are used in the Federation of British Industries, in the National Paint Federation, in the Cake and Biscuit Alliance and in the Wholesale Clothing Manufacturers Federation. In many cases, however, it is not easy to make this method determinate, for in multi-product firms the numbers actually concerned with a particular product may not be known.

* A rebate of £5 for firms employing less than twenty-five people has been instituted.

Some associations specify "operatives" engaged on actual production, for instance the National Federation of Clay Industries and the Federation of British Rubber and Allied Manufacturers Associations. Others avoid a count of numbers, and use the amount of wages paid as the necessary measure. The British Electrical and Allied Manufacturers Association, the Textile Finishing Trades Association, the Federation of British Manufacturers of Sports and Games and the British Non-Ferrous Metals Federation all use wages as a basis for deciding subscriptions.

Then there are various measures of capacity and of production. The Federation of Master Cotton Spinners Associations raises its comparatively large income by means of a levy on the members of its constituent associations, based on spindles installed and capable of running. The subscriptions to the Rayon Weaving Association are based on loomage. In the British Paper and Board Manufacturers Association they are based partly on the length of machine wire and partly on the firm's Schedule 'A' tax assessment. In the Shipbuilding Conference members' subscriptions vary according to their output; in the Cement and Concrete Association according to the tonnage sold by members on the home market.

The need for a criterion about which information is readily available has led some associations to rely on measurements of capital. Engineering Industries Association subscriptions are paid on the basis of issued share capital. In the Association of British Chemical Manufacturers they are measured by the employed capital of the member-firm.

Perhaps among the fairest of the systems available are those using turnover as a basis, as is done by the Federation of Calico Printers and the Society of British Gas Industries. Unfortunately this item is the one which firms are least willing to disclose, even in strict confidence to the secretariat of their association. The Cocoa, Chocolate and Confectionery Alliance uses turnover as a measure of variations in subscriptions paid by ordinary members, but in 1955 it was still using 1952 as a base year, partly in order to avoid a too frequent revelation of confidential statistics. Net value of output might be an even fairer criterion, but it is even more difficult to ascertain.

Some associations with a numerically small membership fix subscriptions by agreement among members rather than by employing any system of measurement. The National Council of Building Material Producers does this, for example, since its only members are associations in a wide variety of industries. The Zinc Development Association at one time had a scale based on the amount of zinc which members exported to the United Kingdom, but this led to wide variations in the association's income from year to year and agreed payments were substituted.

There are some other unclassifiable arrangements. In the Typewriter (and Allied) Trades Federation the members each pay a standard amount, graded roughly according to the turnover appropriate to their class—associates, retailers, importers or manufacturers. In the British Iron and Steel Federation levies are raised from the various conferences in proportion to the representation of the conference on the federation's council, this representation being determined by the executive committee. In addition, as already mentioned above, there is a levy on steel production, and in practice the payments of firms vary with their output.

There can be little profitable generalisation about the actual amount of subscriptions. In the smaller associations many firms only pay two or three guineas a year; in contrast the British Electrical and Allied Manufacturers Association has a maximum of £3,500 per annum, and the Glass Manufacturers Federation one of £1,300 annually. But not all the major associations have firms subscribing amounts comparable to these: the highest payment in the British Engineers Association is £134 a year, for firms paying over £1,500,000 annually in wages.

Other income

A few associations have sources of income in addition to the prescribed payments of members. Exhibition revenues are perhaps the most notable of these. The Society of Motor Manufacturers and Traders in 1954 derived a surplus of £139,420 from the International Motor Exhibition, £31,390 from the Commercial Motor Exhibition, and £7,673 from the Smithfield Show, compared with a total of £142,299 received in subscriptions and entrance fees. The Radio Industry Council derived £4,450 from the National Radio Show in 1953; it is the custom to apply such revenue to the following year's Show. In 1954 the Society of British Aircraft Constructors carried a surplus of £21,875 from the Farnborough Flying Display and Exhibition to its general reserve. There are other instances where some regular income accrues from exhibitions—for example, in the Office Appliance and Business Equipment Trades Association—but the amount cannot be accurately distinguished.

Apart from this possible major contribution, associations usually have various minor supplements to their income. The Cocoa, Chocolate and Confectionery Alliance, for example, with a subscription income of about £15,000 in 1954, adds to it from the letting of rooms, from the Alliance Journal and other sources to make about £20,000 in all. The British Engineers Association had £1,532 in 1954 from the sales of the B.E.A. Handbook (out of a total income of £19,207). The Zinc Development Association organises conferences on a self-financing basis, and if these are included the total income and expenditure of the Z.D.A. is increased by some £10,000. Associations frequently have some small income from investments, and those who provide services for other associations are credited with the payments for them. In general, however, it is safe to assume that the income side of any association's accounts is dominated by the subscriptions of its members.

Expenditure

Associations are non-profitmaking bodies, and hence they endeavour to achieve equality of expenditure and income. Any excess income may be a serious inconvenience, for it might make the association liable to taxation. At all events, a surplus which emerges at the end of an association's financial year is carried forward and not distributed to members.

In associations mainly concerned with representation of the industry or with economic regulation, the main expenses are the salaries and wages of staff. In addition there may be rent or rates for office premises, and the usual office running costs—lighting, heating, telephone, stationery, printing, and so on. These are the minimal expenses, though of course, as stated in the first part of this chapter, an association may pay a larger body to provide these services.

In addition, there are items which, though not universal, are very common. These include subscriptions to bodies such as the British Standards Institution, the Federation of British Industries, the British Employers Confederation, professional bodies and various international chambers of commerce. In those industries where there is a research association roughly conterminous with it, a trade association may collect and pass on the necessary money to support the research, though this is by no means always the case, and often the financial arrangements of research associations are quite separate.

Mr Duncan Sandys, then Minister of Supply, stated in the House of Commons in 1953* that the levy of the British Iron and Steel Federation (1s. per ton in 1952) was spent in the following proportions:

Salaries, rents and administration . .	3½d.
Statistical compilation and publication .	1½d.
Scrap drive publicity	1d.
Training scheme organisation . .	¾d.
Reserve for capital expenditure . .	2½d.
External relations	¼d.
Taxation	2½d.

The expenses arising from publicity work of one kind or another are usually high, whether it is a question of printing and publication by the association itself, or of buying space for advertisements. Exhibitions may bring in revenue eventually, but they are certainly costly in the first place.

There are, if all these things are considered, too many differences and anomalies in association finance to make simple generalisations about it completely valid; but to say that, in the main, it is a question of administrative work being paid for by members' subscriptions is not very far short of the truth.

Statutory industrial levies

The question of compulsory levies in industry is not strictly part of the subject of association finance, but it is a topic with which associations have been concerned and which may concern them again in the future.

Section nine of the Industrial Organisation and Development Act, 1947, provides that charges may be imposed in industries where there is no development council for any of three purposes: scientific research, promotion of export trade, or the improvement of design. The Act also stipulates that there must already be

* House of Commons Debates, 10 March, 1953, Col. 1239–40.

a body capable of carrying out the proposed work, or one must be brought into being. It is not clear whether trade associations would be regarded as suitable bodies themselves, since they are voluntary and rarely include a hundred per cent of firms in an industry. It is certainly possible, however, for an association to take the initiative in securing a levy and in having a satisfactory body set up to provide the required service.

In the wool industry advantage has been taken of the enactment to set up a statutory levy for research purposes calculated to produce about £150,000 per annum. The levy is administered by the Wool Textile Research Council, representing research bodies as well as trade associations. Wool export promotion is supported by a similar levy. For a time there was also a levy under this Act in the lace industry.

FEDERATION AND CO-ORDINATION

Previous sections have made clear the considerable degree of co-operation between associations. These paragraphs merely discuss one or two organisational aspects of the more formal types of collaboration.

As is apparent from the section on secretariats, day-to-day contact between associations is very much the concern of the paid officials. Even beyond these routine matters, however, there is a tendency for directors and secretaries of associations to take an increasing share of the external representation of the association. Though industrialists from firms still carry out most of the important representational work themselves, there is some tendency for associations to nominate their senior paid official as their representative (or one of their representatives) on joint committees, on federal bodies, on the Grand Council of the F.B.I. or on the Executive Council of the N.U.M. A few associations try to resist this trend, but the practical advantages of the employment of senior staff in these capacities usually seem to outweigh any dislike of representation by paid officials. Directors and secretaries can follow closely the activities of these wider organisations, read their papers and attend their meetings regularly, and if they have the confidence of their associations there seems no reason why they should not serve in these positions.

The federal principle

In spite of the difference of principle, the difference in working between some federations and some unitary associations with highly developed sections or groups is not great. In the section on governing bodies it has been explained that groups have varying amounts of operational independence. In theory the constituent associations of a federation have complete autonomy, and any co-ordination or supervision from the centre is a completely voluntary arrangement. This is true in practice also where the member-associations have considerable organisations of their own. But where secretarial arrangements are shared and there is much overlapping membership among firms, the difference between a federation and a group system may not be very significant.

The theoretical position, however, may be not without interest. Professor K. C. Wheare* has insisted that, at government level, the true federal principle is that of co-ordinate powers: the authority of both central and regional governments is supreme in its own sphere, and neither has supervisory or controlling powers over the matters reserved to the other. In terms of trade associations this principle would imply that genuine federation occurs when constituent associations deal exclusively with matters related to their region, product or process, and the federation itself deals with general matters concerning the whole industry. Any claim by the federation to supervise its constituent's actions where they might affect other members, or for any other reason, would be a step to closer unity—to what Professor Wheare would consider a system of devolution rather than a federation. But if the federation had no specific authority to act even on matters of wide concern except by the consent of its various member-associations, then there would be only confederation, and not real federation. The voluntary nature of federations, as in other associations, makes for constant inclination in this direction, and bodies like the National Hardware Alliance, the Textile Finishing Trades Association and the Radio Industry Council are probably best regarded as confederations. It is nevertheless not too misleading to classify the Wool Textile Delegation, the British Man-made Fibres Federation and the Wholesale Clothing Manufacturers Federation among the genuine federations. Bodies like the British Iron and Steel Federation, which has some control over the membership

* K. C. Wheare, *Federal Government* (Oxford University Press), 1946.

of its conferences, and the British Non-ferrous Metals Federation, which can request modifications of the constitutions of its member-associations, as well as supervise the admission of new member-firms, incline to something more than pure federation.*

There are few differences in theory between the position of the constituent associations in federations of product associations, and in federations of regional ones. But in practice regional bodies rarely operate at all at national level—they do not deal much with Whitehall, for example, or undertake national publicity—whereas product or process associations may well carry out a considerable amount of negotiation with ministries, or arrange nation-wide advertising of their product. The co-ordinate or parallel nature of activities is more noticeable, therefore, in product federations than in geographical ones, where a hierarchy of authority tends to appear.

In the main, federations work through their constituent associations, and in some cases direct contact with firms is negligible. The development of common services at federal level, however, makes for increased contact, especially where a constituent association has only a small secretariat. When technical matters are under consideration, too, a federal body may need the assistance of experts only to be found in the firms.

Organisation of the F.B.I.

The scope of the Federation of British Industries and of the National Union of Manufacturers has already been discussed in the chapter on the structure of associations in industry (pp. 45–56), and their activities described in the introduction to Part II. Some notes on their organisation are given here.†

The secretariat of the F.B.I. at its headquarters in Tothill Street, Westminster, includes specialists in many fields. It numbers about 160, of whom forty work in the Overseas Department. It is headed by the Director-General and is divided into five departments—those of the general secretary, the overseas director, the economic director, the technical director, and the home services

* The British Non-ferrous Metals Federation has, in 1956, admitted firms to direct membership.

† For fuller accounts, see *F.B.I.—What it is and What it does*, a pamphlet published by the F.B.I.; and S. E. Finer, "The Federation of British Industries", in *Political Studies*, February 1956. The annual *F.B.I. Register* is a standard reference book.

and information director. In addition the F.B.I. has a regional organisation in ten areas of Great Britain with a staff of fifty and about 140 overseas representatives and correspondents. In practice, much of the work of the F.B.I. is done by senior office-bearers and other committee members from firms.

The federation operates under Royal Charter, granted seven years after its foundation, which lays down its constitution. The governing body of the federation is the Grand Council, which is elected triennially and meets monthly. This comprises the president and past presidents—perhaps ten or a dozen individuals; about 300 representatives nominated by trade associations in membership (at least one each, and a second for those whose member-firms employ over 100,000 workers); about 150 representatives of individual firms, who are grouped into electoral panels for voting purposes; and one representative appointed for each of the fourteen federation districts by the regional councils. At all times the representation of trade associations must be twice that of individual firms. Chairmen of standing committees are *ex officio* members of the Grand Council.

The President of the F.B.I., who has invariably been a leading industrialist, usually serves for a very active two years. He has the help of a President's Advisory Committee, consisting of the five immediate past presidents, on matters of approach and presentation. This body nominates a deputy president with the approval of the Grand Council, and he is commonly elected president at the annual general meeting in the next year, and re-elected in the succeeding year.

There are many other committees; and it is through them that most F.B.I. policy is first formulated. Their membership is to some extent dictated by the subject with which a particular committee deals. Those that require to tap the experience of individual industries are mainly composed of representatives of member-associations; others consist of experts drawn from individual firms.

There are also ten regional councils elected by member-firms in the region and having a local office and small staff. Their function is to deal with local issues, to keep the centre and the regions in close touch, and through their representatives on the Grand Council and its committees to contribute to the formation of policy at the national level.

The wide range of F.B.I. activity depends on considerable financial support from its members. Its annual income is of the order of £300,000. The larger proportion comes not from the trade associations, which pay a comparatively small flat-rate subscription (£133 6s. 8d. in 1956) but from the individual firms, which pay on a graduated scale based on numbers employed (varying from £15 to £275 per annum in 1956). Overseas work is responsible for a large proportion of expenditure. The bulk is on staff, followed by running costs, premises and publications.

Organisation of the N.U.M.

The National Union of Manufacturers,* which was founded in 1915, has its headquarters in the City in Holborn Viaduct. The London and Home Counties Branch, one of the ten regional organisations, also has its offices in the same building. There are also branch organisations in nine other important industrial areas in Great Britain with headquarters at Birmingham, Leeds, Manchester, Newcastle, Nottingham, Sheffield, Cardiff and Glasgow. The central staff is headed by a director, a deputy-director and a secretary, and includes officials providing the expert assistance and industrial advisory services.

The National Union is governed by an executive council, which meets about once a month. The officers and fifteen members of the council are elected at the annual general meeting. The remaining members are nominated by the branches, in proportion to their membership, and by the affiliated associations. Nominations from the branches are made by the council or committee of each branch, which in its turn consists partly of elected members and partly of nominees of the area committees subsidiary to the branch. All policy decisions are made by these elected representatives, often on proposals originating from the area or branch committees. Much of the work of the N.U.M. is done by its seven standing committees—on Commonwealth trade, export assistance, finance, free enterprise, legislation, taxation, and transport. The rate of subscription is fifteen guineas a year for all members, with a rebate of £5 for firms employing less than twenty-five people.

* The N.U.M. publishes a pamphlet, *National Union of Manufacturers: Why it exists, how it works*, and an annual directory, *The Manufacturers' Manual*, which give fuller information.

Inter-association committees

When matters arise which affect more than one association they usually find it best to co-operate on an entirely *ad hoc* basis or through the F.B.I. or N.U.M. There are, however, a few inter-association committees of a long-standing character. Perhaps the most notable of these is the engineering committee formed by the British Engineers Association, the British Electrical and Allied Manufacturers Association, the Society of Motor Manufacturers and Traders and the Society of British Aircraft Constructors. Another instance is provided by the Conference Joint Council in which the office-bearers of the Shipbuilding Conference, the Dry Dock Owners and Repairers Central Council, and the National Association of Marine Engine Builders meet.

The international interests of many industries lead to co-operation between associations on an international level. These activities may need financial support, and will involve representation by the association's elected officers or paid officials. In this way the British Electrical and Allied Manufacturers Association supports the World Power Conference, the Cocoa, Chocolate and Confectionery Alliance supports the International Office of Cocoa and Chocolate and the International Sugar Confectionery Manufacturers Association, and so on.

PART IV

The Attitude of Member-Firms

CHAPTER 8

THE USE MADE OF TRADE ASSOCIATIONS BY SMALL FIRMS

IN the preceding parts of this report the structure, organisation and activities of trade associations have been examined from the vantage point of the associations themselves and, also, from the angle of the experience of the principal public bodies with which they come into contact.

The purpose of the two chapters which follow is to complete the picture by adding information about the role of trade associations obtained from the remaining source—the firms which are members of them. The material brought together in these chapters represents the results of a sample survey of several hundred small firms—each employing fewer than two hundred operatives—as well as fifty large and very large firms in a great number of industries.

The principal aim of the survey was to find out what use is made by member-firms of the services provided for their benefit by trade associations and, also, the extent to which firms take a direct part in the affairs of the organisations to which they belong. Another object was to ascertain the degree of membership of trade associations, especially among medium and small firms. The material is presented in two parts dealing with small and large firms respectively. All the data was obtained in the course of personal interviews with the managing director or other senior executive of the firms included in the survey.

The sample

In constructing the sample of small firms, the following four criteria of selection were used in different combinations.

First the predominant size of the firms in various industries was established. Under this head three main categories were identified:

small-firm industries—which are those in which firms with less than two hundred operatives produce more than 50 per cent of the total output by value; large-firm industries where firms with over five hundred operatives produce more than 50 per cent of the total output by value; and the remainder which are not dominated by either.

Secondly, some industries were chosen because they manufacture consumer goods and others were included because they are clearly capital goods producing industries.

The third factor considered was that of the proportion of total sales exported. Trades exporting more than 15 per cent of total sales by value were designated as "high" exporters.

The fourth criterion employed in choosing industries for the sample concerns the rate of expansion of different trades measured in terms of the increase in the labour-force between 1935 and 1948 as given in the last fully published census of production of the Board of Trade. Seven of the fifteen trades selected show an increase of over 30 per cent in the labour force between the two dates and this was considered to be a rate of expansion above the average for the whole of British industry. In some of the trades chosen there has either been no increase in the labour force at all or it has actually declined.

The total sample used for the survey was 882 firms each employing fewer than two hundred operatives (that is, not counting managerial and clerical workers) spread over fifteen trades as defined in the Standard Industrial Classification and located in sixteen industrial centres in Great Britain.

How many firms co-operated in the survey?

For a variety of reasons no contact at all was established with 64 firms. These include 12 cases where the interviewer was referred to an office outside the interviewing area and 7 where the address related to a wholesaler. At the remaining 45 addresses the interviewers found that the firms had either moved out of the district or closed down altogether. The effective sample, therefore, consisted of 818 firms. At 192 of these addresses the interviewers could not obtain interviews and this left a total of 626 firms which actually co-operated in the survey. Table 1 gives an analysis of co-operation by individual trades. The analysis reveals that the response rate for the sample as a whole was 71 per cent. If the

64 cases where an interview was either impossible, or where it could only be obtained by travelling outside the interviewing area, are excluded the response rate becomes about 76 per cent.

TABLE I

ANALYSIS OF CO-OPERATION AND TRADE ASSOCIATION MEMBERSHIP

	Co-operating firms					
Trade	*Members of associations*	*Non-members*	*Total*	*Refusals*†	*No contact*‡	*Grand total*
China and earthenware .	26 (65%)*	14	40	14	7	61
Iron foundries . .	27 (84%)	5	32	24	6	62
Non-ferrous metals .	29 (70%)	12	41	21	2	64
Machine tools . .	26 (67%)	13	39	17	2	58
Mechanical engineering .	29 (66%)	15	44	17	3	64
Electrical engineering .	22 (55%)	18	40	14	2	56
Cutlery	37 (77%)	11	48	9	4	61
Jewellery and plate .	45 (88%)	6	51	8	–	59
Cotton weaving . .	27 (90%)	3	30	6	4	40
Woollen and worsted .	44 (80%)	11	55	8	2	65
Cocoa, chocolate and sugar confectionery .	31 (97%)	1	32	11	4	47
Boot and shoe . .	40 (81%)	9	49	8	6	63
Furniture and upholstery .	36 (83%)	7	43	9	10	62
Cardboard box, carton and fibre board packings	35 (79%)	9	44	9	3	56
Plastic goods and fancy articles . . .	19 (50%)	19	38	17	9	64
	473 (76%)§	153	626	192	64	882

How many firms are members of trade associations?

Table 1 also gives an analysis of the proportion of trade association members to non-members among the 626 co-operating firms in the fifteen chosen trades. The survey reveals a range of membership ratios extending from 50 per cent in the plastic goods and fancy articles industry to 97 per cent in the cocoa, chocolate

* i.e. 65 per cent of the co-operating firms in this industry were members of at least one trade association.

† Including 11 cases where refusal given with explanation that director was away.

‡ Includes 12 cases where interviewer was referred to an office outside the interviewing area, and 7 where the address related to a wholesaler, etc. At the remaining 45 addresses either the firm had moved away or closed down.

§ This figure, although numerically identical with the response rate mentioned before, must not be confused with it.

and sugar confectionery trade. Taking the co-operating part of the sample as a whole, 76 per cent are members of at least one manufacturer's trade association.

Number of trade associations to which the firms belong

In a number of industries, as has been shown in the chapter on the structure of associations in British industry, there are several trade associations which are organised to cover either the same product or the same group of manufacturers. In addition there are the multi-product and federal bodies. Where this is the case (and for other reasons also) a firm may be a member of more than one trade association. The survey shows that of the 473 firms which are members of associations, 255 belong to only one, 153 are members of two associations, 46 have membership in three bodies, 12 belong to four associations, 4 firms are members of at least five associations and 3 belong to six or more associations. Table 2 gives the number of associations and shows their distribution between the fifteen trades.

TABLE 2

NUMBER OF ASSOCIATIONS LISTED

	No. of firms who are members of:						
Trade	*1*	*2*	*3*	*4*	*5*	*6**	*Total*
China and earthenware	14	11	1	–	–	–	26
Iron foundries	5	12	7	2	1	–	27
Non-ferrous metals	18	10	–	–	–	1	29
Machine tools	10	8	7	1	–	–	26
Mechanical engineering	16	8	4	1	–	–	29
Electrical engineering	11	6	2	2	1	–	22
Cutlery	24	9	2	–	1	1	37
Jewellery and plate	35	10	–	–	–	–	45
Cotton weaving	6	15	6	–	–	–	27
Woollen and worsted	23	15	4	1	1	–	44
Cocoa, chocolate and sugar confectionery	19	8	4	–	–	–	31
Boot and shoe	19	16	3	2	–	–	40
Furniture and upholstery	25	9	2	–	–	–	36
Cardboard box, carton and fibre board packings	17	11	3	3	–	1	35
Plastic goods and fancy articles	13	5	1	–	–	–	19
	255	153	46	12	4	3	473

* Includes 2 cases where more than 10 associations were given.

These figures are subject to a number of qualifications. In compiling the table those associations which are obviously research associations and employers' associations have been excluded whenever they were noticed, but it has not been possible to exclude consistently all associations lying outside the terms of reference. Moreover, the treatment of the question has varied somewhat according to the informant. To give an example, one member of the British Wool Federation will have mentioned only this association and is therefore down on the table as belonging to only one, while another will have mentioned not only the federation, but also the Wool Textile Delegation, to which it is affiliated, and so the firm has been entered in the table as belonging to two associations. This qualification applies to other trades as well.

In a survey of this kind it is not possible to make definite inferences about particular associations from the opinions of a comparatively small number of their members. In the main, therefore, the analysis has been related to the industries only. A rough indication of the associations mentioned by the firms interviewed in each trade is given below, but statements elsewhere in this section referring to a particular industry should not be assumed to apply specifically to these organisations.

In the china and earthenware industry the associations most frequently mentioned in regard to membership by the firms in the sample were the British Pottery Manufacturers Federation, Potters Millers Association, and English China Manufacturers Association.

Most of the iron foundries interviewed belonged to the Council of Iron Foundry Associations through one or more of the product associations. In the non-ferrous metals industry the Light Metal Founders Association, Zinc Alloy Die Casters Association, Association of Bronze and Brass Founders, and the British Non-Ferrous Metals Federation and its constituent associations were mentioned more than once.

In the machine tools industry a number of firms belonged to the Engineering Industries Association, National Federation of Engineers Tool Manufacturers, Machine Tool Trades Association, and the Gauge and Tool Makers Association Ltd. In electrical engineering the British Electrical and Allied Manufacturers Association, Permanent Magnet Association, and Engineering

Industries Association were mentioned. A very wide variety of product associations was encountered in the mechanical engineering trade. Not enough firms belonged to any one association to give any sort of compressed list.

Among cutlery firms the Sheffield Cutlery Manufacturers Association was mentioned most frequently. In the jewellery and plate trade most firms were members of the British Jewellers Association.

The Cotton Spinners and Manufacturers Association and the Rayon Weaving Association were listed by a sizeable number of firms in the cotton weaving industry.

A high proportion of the woollen and worsted manufacturers belonged to the constituent associations of the Wool Textile Delegation. The Worsted Spinners Federation, Bradford and District Manufacturers Federation, and Bradford and District Master Spinners Federation—both of these local associations are affiliated to the Woollen and Worsted Trades Federation—were mentioned several times.

In the cocoa, chocolate and confectionery trade the Cocoa, Chocolate and Confectionery Alliance Ltd. predominates.

Boot and shoe manufacturers usually belong to local associations, and through them to the Incorporated Federated Associations of Boot and Shoe Manufacturers of Great Britain and Ireland.

Furniture makers frequently were members of the British Furniture Manufacturers Federated Associations by virtue of their membership in local bodies.

Several firms in the sample grouped under the heading cardboard box, carton and fibre board packings, belonged to the National Federation of Packing Case Manufacturers. Many different product associations as well as several local ones were also mentioned.

Many of the firms making plastic goods and fancy articles were found to be members of the British Plastics Federation, and some belonged to the Casein Button Manufacturers Association.

When did the firms join their associations?

In the course of each interview the firm was asked to indicate the approximate date when it first joined the trade association in which it is most interested. The results show that of the 473 firms belonging to at least one trade association, 56 had joined before World War I, but the vast majority became members only in the World War II and post-war period. The detailed results are given below:

Date of joining	*Number of firms*
Before 1906	15
1906–1915	41
1916–1925	44
1926–1935	61
1936–1945	140
1946 and later	117
Others*	17
Don't know	38
TOTAL	473

This list, of course, does not disclose anything about the causes or the occasion of joining; high membership figures in later years are partly due to the formation of new associations and the establishment of new firms.

The survey, moreover, revealed that 48 of the firms in the sample which are at present members of a trade association at one time belonged to a different association. In 19 of these cases the firm found that its interests were adequately covered by another association to which it already belonged; in 11 instances there was an amalgamation of associations; 7 firms found they were no longer in the trade covered by the association, and in 5 cases disagreement between the firm and the association was the reason for withdrawal. By far the greatest number of these changes and resignations took place after 1946—32 of the 48 firms ceased to be members of one of the trade associations to which they had belonged after that date.

Direct participation in association affairs

One of the questions asked of each member-firm was whether it takes any direct part in the affairs of its association or associations, as the case may be, by having a representative on the governing body and/or on a committee of the association. The results are

* Others includes answers such as "When it was first formed", etc.

given below in Table 3. 348 firms (73 per cent) had no representative whatever on any governing body or committee of the associations to which they belong; 76 (16 per cent) were represented on a committee and 28 (6 per cent) had a representative on the governing body. Only 21 (4 per cent) firms were represented on both the governing body and at least one committee of their respective associations.

TABLE 3

PARTICIPATION IN ASSOCIATION AFFAIRS

Trade	*No participation*	*On a committee only*	*On governing body only*	*On both*
China and earthenware .	13	9	3	1
Iron foundries . . .	22	1	1	3
Non-ferrous metals . .	23	3	3	–
Machine tools . . .	22	3	1	–
Mechanical engineering .	25	4	–	–
Electrical engineering .	18	3	–	1
Cutlery	31	5	–	1
Jewellery and plate . .	33	9	1	2
Cotton weaving . .	19	6	1	1
Woollen and worsted .	29	8	5	2
Cocoa, chocolate and sugar confectionery . .	25	5	1	–
Boot and shoe . .	28	6	3	3
Furniture and upholstery .	27	4	2	3
Cardboard box, carton and fibre board packings .	17	10	5	3
Plastic goods and fancy articles . . .	16	–	2	1
	348	76	28	21

In view of the large number of these small firms compared with the number of possible places on councils and committees, the figure of 27 per cent cannot be considered prima facie a low degree of participation.

Services used by firms

In order to discover the range of trade association services known to member-firms, and also the extent to which firms make use of these services, each co-operating firm was asked, first, to indicate which of twenty-three separate services, listed on a card

TABLE 4

SERVICES USED BY SMALL FIRMS

	China and earthenware	*Iron foundries*	*Non-ferrous metals*	*Machine tools*	*Mechanical engineering*	*Electrical engineering*	*Cutlery*	*Jewellery and plate*	*Cotton weaving*	*Woollen and worsted*	*Cocoa, chocolate and sugar confectionery*	*Boot and shoe*	*Furniture and upholstery*	*Cardboard box, carton and fibre board packings*	*Plastic goods and fancy articles*	TOTAL
Representation on behalf of industry to:						*Number of firms finding service to be of use*										
British government departments	14	7	9	5	7	3	11	11	7	8	11	9	5	10	4	121
Overseas government departments	7	2	1	2	4	2	9	5	2	8	6	7	2	3	2	62
Nationalised industries	11	6	2	1	1	1	4	1	5	5	2	2	3	2	1	47
Local authorities	9	1	1	2	1	1	4	2	3	4	4	4	2	1	1	40
British Standards Institution	4	12	8	6	5	5	4	–	3	10	6	11	12	11	5	102
Other organisations	9	5	4	1	3	1	2	5	3	6	8	7	8	2	–	64
Services provided for members as a whole:																
Exhibitions	5	3	7	6	6	4	8	10	3	5	2	8	12	1	3	83
Joint advertising	2	3	6	2	–	–	2	1	2	2	2	4	5	–	3	34
Public relations through press officer	2	1	2	3	–	1	1	2	2	3	3	6	8	1	2	37
Library facilities	1	1	3	2	2	4	2	2	1	2	3	2	3	1	2	31
Circulation of business inquiries	16	5	6	6	9	7	13	25	5	6	8	16	16	7	11	156
Circulation of market information	17	7	10	9	10	6	12	13	4	12	13	22	16	5	8	164
Standard costing	5	14	8	3	2	1	1	1	3	9	–	6	6	2	3	64
Technical information	7	8	12	5	5	5	15	13	8	11	8	16	10	7	6	136
Standard contracts and terms of sale	6	4	8	3	1	6	2	2	10	12	3	5	6	2	2	72
Information on costs and prices	10	15	10	4	7	2	1	5	7	9	13	15	8	6	5	117
Agreement on discounts	11	4	8	4	2	5	1	1	5	8	8	6	12	3	4	82
Nomination of wholesalers, etc.	7	3	3	2	1	3	2	2	1	2	6	1	2	1	–	36
Services to individual members on request:																
Legal	4	3	4	4	3	2	3	19	6	4	2	6	3	3	–	66
Credit status	2	–	8	2	2	2	–	29	–	5	4	8	5	1	2	70
Travel	–	–	3	2	2	–	–	–	–	2	–	2	1	–	–	12
Interpreting government regulations	11	6	11	6	9	3	5	17	6	10	14	16	13	9	6	142
Export information	14	2	7	5	8	4	13	25	4	12	13	17	8	4	6	142
Total firms using one or more listed services	20	26	24	21	20	17	29	39	19	31	24	36	30	30	16	382
Firms using no listed services	4	1	5	4	9	5	8	6	8	11	7	3	6	3	3	83
Did not know how many services they used	2	–	–	1	–	–	–	–	–	2*	–	1	–	2	–	8

* Includes one firm who said "Association provides all services required."

and handed to the informant, were used by it; and secondly, which services were not used by the firm, although the firm was aware that they were provided by the association. The full results of this part of the survey are given in Tables 4 and 5.

Only 83 firms, or just over 17 per cent of the firms in the sample which are members of trade associations, answered that they do not use any of the services listed in Table 4; 382 of the 473 firms which belong to one or more trade associations reported that they used at least one of the listed services and, in fact, most of them make use of a considerable number of them.

Of the services provided by trade associations, those listed as "Circulation of market information", including trade statistics, and "Circulation of business inquiries" are used most often by member-firms. A very large number of firms in the sample—142 of the 382 using at least one of the services provided—said that they sought the individual help of their associations in connection with export problems and the application of government regulations. Technical information supplied by associations is used by 136 of the 382 firms, that is, 35 per cent. Not many firms apparently seek the help of their association to arrange travel or to use the library facilities, although a sizeable number of them report that they are provided.

Table 4 reveals that for the sample as a whole the variation in the percentage of firms in each trade using the same service is not very great. There are only one or two notable exceptions. The service listed as the provision of information concerning the credit status of other firms is used, for obvious reasons, by many more member-firms in the jewellery and plate industry (29 out of 39) than in any of the other fourteen trades included in the sample. Again, many more firms in the jewellery and plate industry make use of the legal services provided for individual members than any of the other industries.

Looking at the results of this section of the survey from the angle of the individual industries, rather than the separate services listed in the table, an interesting picture emerges. In some industries the incidence of the use made by member-firms of the services provided by trade associations is much higher than in others. The incidence rate is highest in the china and earthenware industry and lowest in the cardboard box, carton and fibre board packings trade. On the average just over nine services were found to be of use by those firms in the former industry which avail themselves of the facilities provided. The equivalent figure for the latter industry is just over three services for each user. The average for the sample as a whole is just over five services per user-firm. Industries with an incidence rate above this are non-ferrous metals, cocoa, chocolate and sugar confectionery, boot and shoe, and furniture and upholstery.

The firms were also asked which of the services provided by trade associations they found most valuable. The services which were mentioned most frequently were: representation on behalf of the industry in question to British government departments (21 mentions), the provision of technical information (22 mentions), and information on costs and prices (21 mentions). Some services, not unexpectedly, were hardly mentioned at all. They were: public relations through press officers (not one mention), representation on behalf of the whole industry to the nationalised industries and local authorities (2 mentions each), joint advertising (2 mentions), library facilities (3 mentions). A considerable number of firms mentioned the annual dinner or other social activities as one of the main ways in which they maintain contact with their associations.

Publications

Keeping members informed about what is happening in the economy as a whole, and more particularly how this affects their own industries, is one of the principal functions of trade associations. To this end most trade associations put out a variety of publications. For the purpose of this survey publications were classified under four headings and the firms were asked which of these are regularly published by their association or associations; and whether they receive them. The results are given below in Table 5.

Firms were also asked the question whether the associations to which they belong provide any services they did not use. A considerable number of firms—353—replied that they were aware of the existence of such services, but the very wide range of them mentioned in almost all trades gives rise to the suspicion that the firms had an optimistic idea of what is actually available. Nor could the answers take account of the quality of the services thought to be available.

TABLE 5

ASSOCIATION PUBLICATIONS RECEIVED BY MEMBER-FIRMS

Trade	*Members of trade associations*	*Journal or bulletin*	*Directory or buyers' guide*	*Statistical summary*	*Abstracts*
		Number of publications received			
China and earthenware	26	10	4	15	9
Iron foundries	27	15	6	13	13
Non-ferrous metals	29	18	10	17	13
Machine tools	26	17	9	11	11
Mechanical engineering	29	20	7	11	10
Electrical engineering	22	19	6	9	8
Cutlery	37	30	4	26	14
Jewellery and plate	45	42	28	18	15
Cotton weaving	27	22	3	14	10
Woollen and worsted	44	33	3	14	9
Cocoa, chocolate and sugar confectionery	31	28	4	19	12
Boot and shoe	40	30	6	8	8
Furniture and upholstery	36	32	4	15	10
Cardboard box, carton and fibre board packings	35	9	1	4	2
Plastic goods and fancy articles	19	12	9	2	7
	473	337	104	196	151

Furthermore, there were only 49 firms which stated that they required services which are not at present provided by their associations. These include standard costing, technical information, and information on credit status.

Answering the question whether the firm regularly gives statistical and other information to its association, 185 of the 473 firms which belong to trade associations reported that they do. The number of employees on the pay-roll, home and export sales, and total output of the undertaking is the information most frequently supplied to the associations. Very few firms in the sample said they furnish information on costs and prices to their associations, and technical information was mentioned by only two firms.

Non-member firms

In the sample of 626 co-operating firms it was found that 153, or about 24 per cent, of the enterprises were not members of any trade association at the time of the inquiry.* But 43 of these firms had once been members, leaving 110 which had never belonged to any trade association. Of the 43 firms which resigned their membership, 33 did so after World War II. Asked to state the reason for their withdrawal, 22 firms said the association was no longer of any use to the firm†; 5 said that they had had disagreements over rules and policy with their associations and had resigned; 5 reported that the association to which they had belonged had wound up; and 4 said they are no longer in the trade covered by the association to which they had belonged and that they had not joined any other association since leaving it.

Probing into the reasons why 110 of the small firms in the sample had never joined any trade association, it emerged that 26 of them thought that the trade association to which they could belong would be of no use to the firm; 20 held aloof because they thought their firm was too small to make its voice heard effectively; 10 said there was no appropriate trade association which they could join; 7 firms refused to join because they objected to the price-fixing activities of the associations to which they could belong.

All the non-member firms which had never belonged to an association were also asked the hypothetical question: "In what circumstances, if any, would you join a manufacturers' trade association?" Forty-one replied outright that they could conceive of no circumstances whatsoever; 14 said they would join if the firm's circumstances changed, that is, if it expanded; 12 firms put the onus on the association, saying they would join if the organisation changed its aims and activities; and 8 firms said they would become members if only they could find an appropriate association. This corresponds with the answer to another question which specifically asked the non-member firms whether they thought a new association was needed in their respective industries. Seven gave an affirmative answer to that question.

* Out of these non-members, 80 were aware of the existence of an association appropriate to their products.

† Most of these firms probably left because government controls were abolished.

CHAPTER 9

THE POSITION OF LARGE FIRMS

THE following notes on the experience of trade associations of a number of large manufacturing firms, including several of the biggest and best-known concerns in the country, are intended as companion material for the survey into the use made of trade associations by small firms reported in Chapter 8.

Some fifty concerns were seen in the course of the inquiry. Although there was no detailed questionnaire and no attempt at a statistical sample, the firms were in fact spread over the whole field of manufacturing industry. No large sector of industry was neglected and none given greater attention than its importance justified. By no means all the firms interviewed were giants, but all were considerably larger than those included in the sample for the small firms survey. The material which is given here, therefore, though not based on extensive statistics, represents impressions gained after much careful investigation.

Membership of trade associations

All but five* of the fifty firms which provided information for this inquiry were members of at least one trade association, other than the F.B.I., within the definition used in this report. The vast majority belonged to many more than one.

Depending on the range of a firm's manufacturing activities and ancillary interests, as well as on the age and nature of its industry, membership of trade associations was found to vary widely. Firms in the motor car, aircraft, and plastics industry belonged to one or two associations only, whereas for a concern of the size and diversity of operations of Unilever Ltd. the figure was close on thirty. The manufacturing interests of the Co-operative Wholesale Society are so various that the organisation has joined between seventy and eighty industrial trade associations

* One of these left its trade association, which is the main organisation for its industry, only recently. Two have never been members. The remaining two are American-owned firms which share the anti-trust assumptions of their parent companies. Since they believe the associations in their industries to be concerned with restrictive practices they have stayed outside.

at the national level as well as an equally substantial number of local bodies. For similar reasons, Imperial Chemical Industries Ltd. belongs to about eighty trade associations.

Although the firm which makes many products is more actively concerned with associations in some sections of its work than in others, the degree of its participation and the value placed upon the various associations does not always depend on the size of the company's interest. One firm, operating in a specialised field of the engineering industry, has become a member of several of the trade associations of its principal customers because there is no existing organisation which is central to its own interests. Another motive for joining these bodies is the desire to show support for an organisation containing many customers and to maintain contact with them on matters of production, such as standardisation, and on agreements about conditions of sale, guarantees and so on.

Benefits of membership

Not all large firms, although they are in full membership, take a genuine and close interest in the work of their associations. Those which are members of a score of associations must be selective in their attention; even so, some large firms do not regard association activities as important enough to influence the planning of their own commercial policies. In some cases, associations are joined for reasons of solidarity and good will rather than relied on in any significant way.

This often means that association matters are allocated to a particular individual within a firm, instead of being treated collectively at the managing board level. Such an arrangement may denote general satisfaction with the work the associations are doing; but it may also indicate that the firm is not looking for a further contribution to its prosperity from the development of the associations' activities. Indeed, for large firms the benefits of membership are often difficult to define. For instance, some of the services provided by associations for their members may be quite inadequate to the needs of a large company and such services are already provided by the individual firms themselves. But in a number of cases even the largest firms find the statistical and information services of their associations exceedingly useful. A firm of heavy engineering plant manufacturers have analysed the value to them of various association publications. They find that good presentation is very important, and that there is a tendency to duplication—not of technical news, but of general commercial matter. Firms which are members of only one or two associations would not, of course, notice this duplication.

In the course of the inquiry it was found that several important firms had joined particular trade associations for a very specific and commercially vital reason. In one case the firm had found it essential to join because the association operates an exclusive dealing scheme—distributors of the product did not buy from non-member manufacturers. In another case the firm was a member of a certain trade association only because the management thought that it would not obtain a fair allocation of exhibition space in any other way.

A number of companies have become full or associate members of associations in order to be able to take part in the deliberations of specialist committees dealing with standardisation and other technical matters. On the whole it was found that large firms lay greater stress than the smaller manufacturers on the representational side of trade association activities than on the other services provided. This applies not only to relations with government departments but also to those with the British Standards Institution, the public corporations, and other trade associations. In spite of this interest a large and important concern is not entirely dependent on its association for influence with the government. The large firm already mentioned which recently resigned from its association is now consulted separately and has a representative on a departmental advisory committee alongside the spokesman of the association. Another firm, easily the most important in its industry, claimed to be consulted individually by the government department concerned before the association itself was approached.

The managing director of one of the firms interviewed said that his firm belonged to a certain association solely in order to obtain early knowledge of proposed legislation. The same director had kept a note of the distribution of his time on association matters for the year 1950. He was the honorary treasurer of the main association in his industry at the time. Out of a total of about 2,000 working hours, 150 were spent on the work of this organisation, 60 hours were devoted to F.B.I. meetings, 30 to management and technical bodies, and 10 to the affairs of the other industrial trade associations which the firm had joined for the reason stated above. In all, over 10 per cent of his working time was occupied by attending meetings and conferences connected with association affairs.

The managing director of a firm in the confectionery industry said he devoted nearly a day a week to the affairs of the Cocoa, Chocolate and Confectionery Alliance. Although no other executives were able to supply comparable figures, several gave the impression that such amounts of time were by no means uncommon.

It was found that the decision to join an association in the case of a multi-product firm is frequently made by the person most vitally interested, subject to approval by the company's secretary or managing director and final affirmation by the board of directors. In concerns of this type the level of representation is normally the head of a department, although if matters become crucial to the company the level of representation is upgraded.

No matter how much time was involved, and whatever the chosen level of representation, almost all the large firms interviewed in the inquiry were—if members of any association—represented on their governing bodies and main committees. For a concern of any size, therefore, membership of an association means not merely access to services, but also active participation in its work.

The position of relatively large undertakings can best be illustrated further by considering some examples. No very large concern, of course, entirely resembles others in its relations with associations, any more than it does in other respects: but the two accounts given here show some of the motives involved.

Unilever Ltd.

Unilever Ltd. and its associated companies provide an example of the large multi-product organisation which belongs to many trade associations. The companies form the second largest unit in British industry, measured by size of assets (£246 million in 1954–55) or income (£48 million in 1954–55),* and are found in

* "Assets" are total net assets, "income" is total gross income. See *A Classified List of Large Companies engaged in British Industry* (National Institute of Economic and Social Research), 1955.

a variety of industries, mainly in the "Food" and "Chemicals and Allied Trades" sectors of the Standard Industrial Classification.

The organisation is a member of between forty and fifty associations of various types. Only about thirty of these fall within the definition used in the report, the others being regional bodies, or comprised of importers and so on.

The reason for Unilever's membership of any association is almost invariably to be found in the main objects of the association rather than in any incidental benefits that may be available. In a considerable number of cases the primary motive for Unilever's participation has been the need for regular contacts between an industry and the Government, either in general or on a particular matter such as the safeguarding of raw material supplies. This is naturally allied to the desire for discussions with other producers on broad policy matters and the exchange of ideas and information. There are, of course, specific reasons for joining particular associations—the improvement of quality in some instances, participation in exhibitions in another, and the establishment of standard conditions of sale in others. Associations where subsidiary benefits are important to the company include the Society of Motor Manufacturers and Traders—joined mainly out of interest in trade statistics—and the British Tin Box Federation, which arranged for the sale of the firm's tin scrap.

The company has maintained a cautious attitude towards price fixing or other economic regulation of trade by associations. It has accepted the necessity of such measures only in exceptional circumstances, and where arrangements existed it preferred recommendation to enforcement by rules. Nevertheless Unilever is a member of several associations which have attempted some degree of commercial regulation—the United Kingdom Glycerine Producers Association Ltd.* for example. The company has welcomed the publication of association agreements, and supports the principle of public safeguards in these matters.

The directors and senior executives of Unilever play an active part in many of the associations to which the company belongs. They represent the firm on the governing bodies of the Society of British Soap Makers, the Margarine Manufacturers Association

* Glycerine is a by-product of soap, and hence the volume produced is independent of the demand for it. The association attempted to secure its economic disposal by stabilising the market and developing new uses.

and associations in other industries in which Unilever Ltd. is especially prominent. But in about half of the thirty or so associations of which the firm is a member there was no representation on the governing committee in 1955.

The Co-operative Wholesale Society Ltd.

The C.W.S. is by no means a typical industrial undertaking, for it possesses many features which mark it out from the usual form of enterprise. It began as a wholesale agency; nevertheless, within ten years of its foundation in 1864 it had acquired a biscuit works and a boot and shoe factory, and it has since continued to develop its manufacturing interests. It now has a considerable share of the national output of many products, and its two hundred manufacturing establishments cover a range of products more diverse than those of any other industrial undertaking. Total sales of these units amounted to some £122 million in 1955, and nearly 40,000 workers were employed in C.W.S. production.

At first it might seem that the C.W.S. had little to gain from trade associations. The distinctive principles on which the C.W.S. is based lead it to take a consistently hostile view of restrictive practices in industry. Some private businesses have maintained a similar hostility, but none has carried it out so rigorously over so wide a field. Moreover, the co-operative movement has its own resources for collective services, and although each retail society is autonomous in its buying policies, the manufacturing side normally enjoys considerable goodwill from the retail societies. In spite of these exceptional factors, however, the various manufacturing units of the C.W.S. have found advantage in joining about eighty trade associations of the type discussed in this report.*

Only a minority of these associations have been at all concerned with restraint of trade, and in these cases the C.W.S. has almost invariably tried to contract out of whatever arrangements were set up. The motives which have impelled managers of C.W.S. establishments to join associations, therefore, illustrate the more

* Within the co-operative movement there are associations of societies to deal specifically with matters relating to individual trades—for example, the Meat Trade Association. These are purely internal to the co-operative organisation, and are not considered in this section or elsewhere in the report.

positive and less defensive contributions which associations can make to the prosperity of an undertaking. One of the main benefits which C.W.S. staff hope to gain from membership is contact with other manufacturers in the trades concerned, and hence a knowledge of general developments in the industries. Coupled with this is a desire for access to various types of detailed information, through association publications or their committees, on technical questions, production statistics, the interpretation of government regulations and so on.

There is also a wish to share in the representational activities of various associations. In some cases the C.W.S. is a large enough producer for its views to have major importance in an industry, but in any case C.W.S. manufacturers generally wish to support the industry whenever there is any need to press its requirements. Membership of one association or another has enabled the C.W.S. to play a part in negotiations on the drafting of British standards, and of government regulations on food standards; to have access to information from research associations; to obtain better supplies of raw materials in the slipper industry; to use recommended forms of contract in some industries; to enjoy comprehensive joint marine insurance on shipments of goatskins from abroad for the glacé kid industry; and to gain many similar benefits.

As a large employer the C.W.S. is a party to many national wage agreements, a number of which are negotiated by trade associations to which the society belongs. The C.W.S. is predominantly concerned with supplies to the home market, and is thus only occasionally concerned with information about overseas markets.

The C.W.S. has representatives on the governing bodies of several associations, including, in 1955, the Association of British and Dominion Condensed Milk Manufacturers; the Association of British Manufacturers of Spray Process Milk Powder; the Cake and Biscuit Alliance; the Cocoa, Chocolate and Confectionery Alliance; the Food Manufacturers Federation; the Incorporated National Association of British and Irish Millers; and the Society of British Soap Makers.

The Scottish Co-operative Wholesale Society Ltd. is similar in principles and organisation to its English counterpart. It is a member of some forty trade associations within the definition used in the report, and also of some associations confined to

Scottish members not included in the register at the end of this report. As would be expected, contact and information, and a share in the representation of the industry, are again the paramount motives for joining.

Experience of other large organisations.

Among the large organisations which are members of industrial associations, one or two public corporations are to be found. Although these bodies are practically monopolies in respect of their major products, they have by-products or ancillary interests which make association membership of interest to them.

The National Coal Board is a member of the British Coking Industry Association as the owner of a considerable proportion of the country's coke-ovens, though it is also the monopoly supplier of raw material to the industry. It is also a member of associations in road tar, creosote, and tar distilling which have regulated the prices of these products; of a number of local brick-making associations in various parts of the country, and hence of the National Federation of Clay Industries; of the National Benzole and Allied Products Association; and of the British Sulphate of Ammonia Federation Ltd. Apart from the benzole association the N.C.B. inherited membership of these bodies from its predecessors. It continues participation to facilitate contact with other producers, to gather technical and other information and in some cases to assist in maintaining the stability of the industry. The Gas Council is also a member of various associations, including the British Tar Confederation. Associations outside the definition used here which are supported include the British Electrical Development Association, to which the Central Electricity Authority belongs, and the International Air Transport Association, whose members include the air corporations.

Both the C.W.S. and Unilever Ltd. were examples of concerns reluctant to join in schemes of economic regulation; but there are, of course, large firms which are convinced of the value and necessity of such schemes. A large undertaking in the electrical industry was a member of over forty trade groups which controlled prices. The great benefit derived from this system, it believed, was stability, and with it, secure employment, planned production and opportunity for development. Not only were existing price arrangements defended, but there have been suggestions from some large firms that others would be beneficial, in cotton weaving, for example, and in a specialised engineering trade.

The number of associations which a large firm decides to join may have been diminished by a hostile attitude to trade regulation, but it depends mainly, of course, on the range of products manufactured. Imperial Chemical Industries Ltd. are members of about eighty associations of various types, but other large companies with less diverse ranges of products have joined many fewer. Courtaulds Ltd., for example, were members of less than a dozen associations, for the most part in the man-made fibres industry. Car firms usually had few association interests beyond the Society of Motor Manufacturers and Traders and its counterpart, the British Motor Trade Association. Aircraft producers usually found that the Society of British Aircraft Constructors was sufficient for their needs.

Among very large firms there is some disposition to support associations whose services they do not really find essential because they feel that this meets with approval in the trade; they regard it as a public-spirited act. For this sort of reason a soft-drinks firm joined local publicans' associations, and a pottery firm accepted commercial regulation which it thought disadvantageous to its potential expansion because it believed that the elimination of small competitors would meet with general disapproval.

In general, it may be said that most large firms join associations primarily in order to share in their representational work and to discuss general industrial policy with their competitors. They are not entirely uninterested in the services available, for in some cases these cannot be provided by any single firm—total output figures for an industry could not be collected, for example—and in other cases they would be much more expensive. There can be little doubt, however, that on balance many large firms contribute, in voluntary work and in expert knowledge, a good deal more than they receive in direct benefit from their associations.

CONCLUSIONS

INDUSTRIAL trade associations are institutions of considerable achievement, but their potentialities are even greater. This report has described associations as they were up to and during the middle 1950s. The most striking fact to emerge in this account is the variety of the services offered and tasks performed. But it is equally noticeable that only a few associations undertake all the activities of which some are capable. A great deal is being done, but, in the main, industry has not so far explored the full possibilities of improving efficiency by co-operating through associations. Now that official policy towards the controversial aspects of collective action has taken legislative shape, the time is appropriate for a reassessment in official, business and academic circles of the prospects inherent in associations. They are among the primary groupings of economic society, and, as such, their significance merits a much greater degree of attention than has been customary from the public and from industry itself. Given the existence of thirty or forty major associations covering complete industries, and more than a thousand others, in varying degrees vigorous and loyally supported, what can they contribute in the future to the nation's economy and what impact can they make on its polity?

Economic aspects

When national associations first began to appear in considerable numbers, about the beginning of the present century, contemporary observers tended to regard them as one of the stages along the route towards industrial amalgamation and the growth of very large monopolistic units. Events have proved otherwise. It would be more accurate to argue that the amalgamation of independent firms has been retarded rather than accelerated by the existence of associations. Their chief significance in fact lies in their capacity to bring autonomous concerns into co-operative activity.

The forces that have established associations as an integral part of the structure of modern industry are fundamentally the same as those that have stimulated the development of other groups in many spheres of human activity. The growth in the specialisation and complexity of the economy has created countless groups whose aim is to protect and promote common interests, in social and political relationships as well as in the processes of production and distribution. Associations differ from most other groups not in their motives, nor in the methods by which they seek to protect their interests, but in the fact that their political and economic impact is too important to be ignored. Governments have been aware of this ever since World War I, but only in wartime have they found themselves able to accept the existence and activities of associations without misgivings.

Policy has varied over the years according to the economic circumstances of the time. During World War I associations were encouraged and brought into co-operation with Government. The post-war years and the Profiteering Act brought them into discredit, but by the early 1930s, when the need for industrial reorganisation became apparent, they again developed in a more benevolent official climate. World War II brought associations into close co-operation with Government once more and left them considerably greater in number and stronger in representation. After 1945, government attitudes towards co-operative activity in industry developed on two fronts. The Working Parties and the Industrial Organisation and Development Act (under which development councils were set up) was official recognition of the advantages to be gained through co-operative action in industry and an attempt to encourage constructive activity. The setting up of the Monopolies and Restrictive Practices Commission marked the first serious attempt to cope with the restraints on competition existing in many industries.

For various reasons, which were touched on in Chapter 1, the Industrial Organisation and Development Act failed in its main purpose. Policy towards restraints on competition, however, has been carried a stage further with the Restrictive Trade Practices Act, 1956, under which the protective devices developed by industry and trade will be subject to public scrutiny and judgment.

The passing of this Act marks the beginning of a new phase in the history of British trade associations. At first, many associations will be directly affected, since they have been sponsoring agreements which will eventually have to be registered, called up for consideration and perhaps prohibited. In time, as this process is worked out, attention both within industry and outside it will be increasingly turned to other aspects of association activities.

If the new Restrictive Practices Court takes the hostile view of agreements that must be expected in the atmosphere which the reports of the Monopolies Commission have created, then a high proportion of restrictionist associations may be unable to find means of satisfying the Court that their agreements are in the public interest. They will therefore have to abandon them. Indeed, in some quarters it is expected that when the general attitude of the Court becomes clear many associations will not even seek exemption but will give up their restrictive arrangements forthwith. At all events, this type of activity will diminish.

Nevertheless, the fact that associations are less likely to be instruments for carrying out these practices does not mean that they will lose interest in them. The arrangements had their origin, in the main, in the concern of manufacturers for the prosperity of their industries, and there is no reason to suppose that their fears of trade recession have been completely removed. They will continue to discuss the commercial position of their industries through their associations, as they have always done. It remains the primary business of a trade association to concern itself with the prosperity of its industry, and although the new Act makes economic self-regulation more difficult to adopt, it does not entirely abolish it, and it leaves open other methods of serving the industry. If an industry finds itself in difficulties its leaders will seek remedies, and no doubt will often appeal to the Government to give tariff protection or to the new Restrictive Practices Court to permit a scheme for the control of competition. That is to say, there will be a change of emphasis from direct action by associations to representation.

The decline in restrictive practices caused by government policy must eventually bring about changes in structure. There can be little doubt that at present price-fixing or discriminatory trading is the *raison d'être* of many associations, and if it is removed there will be little purpose in continuing their existence. Certainly, most restrictive associations have other functions—at the least they undertake occasional representative work. Again, associations do not die easily, and often a body formed for one purpose continues in pursuit of other objects. In spite of these qualifications, many of the smaller product associations are likely to be wound up if they are no longer available for the economic regulation of trade.

Readjustment might well be effected by the strengthening of the type of association with a wider coverage.

Turning now to that part of industrial association life which remains unaffected by the new legislation, it is worth looking more closely at the influences that are likely to shape its future role.

Although it is virtually impossible to generalise over so wide a field, the most noticeable feature of association work during the past twenty years, especially since 1945, is the wider scope of their activities, chiefly in constructive as distinct from defensive functions. It is true that there are many small single-product associations which are merely ticking over, waiting for some occasion requiring collective representation, and probably for long periods providing little more than occasional social functions. But large numbers of associations, and not only the major industrial ones, have extended their common service activities considerably during recent years, and, as shown in Chapter 4, now provide an impressive number for their members.

Many of the services performed by associations can only be provided through co-operative action: exhibitions, the collection of industry statistics, and the systematic collection and exchange of both economic and technical information are obvious examples. Others could probably be carried out by the largest concerns but would be quite beyond the reach of the majority, and are in any case most economically run as a centralised service. Examples include the provision of overseas market information, participation in the work of the British Standards Institution and similar bodies, education and training, library and abstracts services, and many others. In short, by organised exchange of information and the provision of expert services, the active trade association can secure for its members most of the economies of large-scale organisation without creating large-scale units of ownership. Even to the large firm the association offers many advantages as a specialist body concerned with the problems of a particular product or industry, for large firms are now increasingly concerned with a wide range of products.

It would be idle to pretend that the majority of associations are yet beyond the early stages of development as common service agencies. There are notable exceptions; but only a relatively small number are at present exploiting such fields as standard costing, raw material requirements, the collection and dissemination of market information and original statistics, education and training, quality control and the development of new techniques of management. It is not suggested, of course, that every association should undertake ambitious schemes of this sort. However, the operations of the 1956 Act may possibly clear the ground by removing from many small associations what has hitherto been the chief reason for their existence, and (as a by-product) by encouraging others to consider more carefully which functions they can perform most effectively at their particular level of organisation.

There is, then, a tendency on the part of the most progressive associations to undertake a wider variety of services, and it is in these instances that firms regard their membership as a real aid to the conduct of their business. Yet in far too many cases firms are only dimly aware of their associations and remain members through inertia rather than active interest. This is true of most firms belonging to the less active associations, and tends to be found among the smaller firms in all associations. It would not be too wide of the mark to argue that the extent to which smaller and medium-sized firms know and use the services provided is one of the best measures of the associations' effectiveness as common service agencies. Many could do much more both to indicate to members and non-members the work they are doing, and to provide services which would justify and maintain their interest. Firms, for their part, could do more to ensure that their associations are vigorous and useful by making suggestions about the services they would find most helpful, by ensuring that the work of associations is given more general and higher-level attention in their own organisation, and where necessary providing financial support. At present the tendency is for too many concerns to regard associations primarily as defence mechanisms rather than agencies capable of providing or helping to organise services of positive value to everyday business.

The staffing and organisation of associations also offer scope for improvement. In a few instances, where member-firms themselves are prepared to give considerable time and effort to association business, it is possible to have a live organisation with a small staff; but as a general rule the quality and range of an association's work is a direct reflection of the calibre and number of the staff permanently engaged on its affairs. It is noticeable that in the majority of cases the most progressive associations are those where the director or secretary has a considerable degree of discretion in organising the work of the association.

The question of organisation, in relation to the type of work that can be done at different levels, has already been mentioned. Many of the smaller product associations are already linked, usually through federal bodies; but large numbers still appear to exist in isolation even where there is a more broadly-based body to which they could be affiliated, and through which they could help to organise services which for one reason or another they cannot provide on their own. Federations, confederations and joint committees can represent interests based either on product or process, or on common markets. They can either bring together an industry that is fairly clearly defined, as in the case of rubber, or one such as building where component makers are represented in respect of their building interests, although most of their products have little in common. Membership of such bodies can greatly extend the range of activities of a single-product association, while leaving it free to look after matters more specific to its own members.

It would help the representational side of their work if more associations established regularity of contact with the production departments of the Government, so that administrators gathered a general idea of an industry's development, and industry in turn became aware of the Government's outlook on affairs. At present there is a tendency for all except the largest associations to wait for some problem to arise before making contact with a department.

Similarly, most associations might seek wider understanding of their industries among Members of Parliament. This is not a question of briefing advocates in the House (probably after a case has been turned down in a department), for this is only rarely worth while. But it is important to try to make sure that Members, or groups of Members, are well informed about various industries. In the long run, regular information and regular contact is likely to be more fruitful than the setting-up of lobbies which try to deflect a Government from its intentions.

The political impact

So far this discussion of associations' development, and of possible means of improving their services to industry, has taken no account of the external influences that are likely to shape their future. It could hardly be contended nowadays that the Government's interest in the institutions of industry is limited to retarding the extent to which they operate practices in restraint of competition. Restrictive practices apart, the Government can no more afford to ignore the economic and political impact of industrial associations than it can that of the trade unions.

In general, the place of interest groups in the political system of a country is not yet widely understood, and it is the subject of some disagreement.* Yet the chapter on representation and other parts of this report show that this side of the work of associations is of major importance and is so regarded both by industry and by government departments.

By means of consultation and discussion with trade associations, government departments can keep themselves informed about events and about opinion in industry; they can test the attitude of various industries to official policies and proposals; and they can obtain information and advice about details and technical matters, on which a department must itself be ill-informed. In the absence of a representative trade association, a ministry can only turn to leading firms or to individual experts when it needs to consult an industry. But these may not be typical nor reliably informed, whereas an association's views will be the result of regular discussion and a constitutional process of decision. The Government can therefore rely on their authority; and it can also depend on fairly-negotiated agreements being accepted. In short, associations enable a Government to know where it stands with industry in general, and with particular industries on particular issues. Without them, administrators would be groping in the dark for up-to-date knowledge of industry and for understanding of its attitudes.

Associations are essential, then, in an administrative sense. Critics may still say that this is only a matter of convenience and is outweighed by some sinister influence exerted on national policies. It is argued that they only represent partial or particular interests, and in so far as they succeed in pressing their views they cause government decisions to be biased against the general interest.

* Much has been written in the United States; for example, see David Truman, *The Governmental Process* (Knopf & Co.), 1951. In Britain studies are beginning to appear, including W. J. M. Mackenzie, "Pressure Groups: the conceptual framework", *Political Studies*, October 1955; and S. E. Finer, "The Political Power of Private Capital", *Sociological Review*, December 1955 and July 1956.

This is largely a misjudgment of the situation. In the first place, associations are mainly concerned with matters of detail, with administrative questions or with amendments and modifications to legislation. They are active at a level in between broad legislative policy and the administration of particular cases. For example, if a raw material were scarce an association's strongest influence would lie not in deciding whether it should be rationed or not, nor yet in considering individual applications, but in drawing up the general principles of allocation. Individual associations rarely have the power to determine the broad lines of government or party policy. If associations should take action on wider matters, it is likely to be both lawful and publicly conducted; and though in these circumstances the activities of a large association could be of national consequence there are no grounds for regarding such action as unconstitutional.

Secondly, trade associations are not the only interest groups concerned with industrial matters. The trade unions also have well-organised and frequent access to the ministries, and just as pervasive an influence on general policy. Professional and technical organisations and other bodies are also consulted on relevant topics. Whatever the declared or undeniable party sympathies of the members of these interest groups, they prefer to conduct their activities away from the party arena because they want to have continuous influence, to be consulted by all sides, and to achieve recognised authority.

What the situation requires is not that the Government should discount or discourage the attentions of interest groups—on the contrary, it should welcome them; but it should on major issues reserve its own judgment. The influence of trade associations, as of other interest groups, is strongest where the Government has no clear-cut policy of its own. It is an illusion to suppose that there is some general public interest apart from the interest of the various sections of the community; but it is vital to remember that some sectional interests are badly organised and highly inarticulate—often, for instance, those of the final consumer. It is the responsibility of the Government and administration, therefore, to make up its own mind about industrial policy, and in doing so, to show especial concern for those interests which are less strongly organised.

Public policy

When Mr. Lloyd George ascribed a fall in the revenue in 1908–9 to "a year of exceptionally bad trade" he did not assume any responsibility for this state of affairs; today a Chancellor of the Exchequer must attempt a policy which will ensure that trade is not bad. Hence, the Chancellor, and his colleagues and his critics, are concerned to know what is happening in industry, and if dissatisfied they propose measures of reform. And if Government takes this interest in industry, then it is natural that industrialists should take an interest in Government. The mechanics of maintaining stability and promoting flexibility of resources in the economy are far from being fully understood; but it is not rash to prophesy that attempts to achieve these aims will bring the Government into closer contact with industry, and it is equally certain that more will be asked of associations, by both sides, as channels of communication between them.

The community is no less concerned with the efficient use of resources. It may be an exaggeration to assert that in political and industrial circles there is a clearly formulated view of private industry as a form of trusteeship for the community; yet certainly it is true that for many years past there has been a growing awareness of the public responsibilities of private industry, and, more recently, that one of these responsibilities is to be as efficient as possible. During recent years official interest in the constructive activities of associations has perhaps been obscured to the public by the preoccupation, through the Monopolies and the Restrictive Trade Practices Acts, with market control by industrial groups. That is the negative side of official interest—the prevention of certain types of activity. With the growth of government responsibility for the welfare of the economy as a whole, attention is likely to turn increasingly to the positive contributions which associations can make to the efficiency of their industries.

This would not, of course, be an entirely new and unexpected development. The Labour Government, fortified by the reports of many of the Working Parties, tried to establish statutory development councils in various industries. The Conservative Governments followed something of the same principle in forming the Iron and Steel Board, a supervisory body, and from another angle have continued the task of reforming association activities by bringing those deemed restrictive under public scrutiny.

Clearly there are misgivings about the adequacy of associations, and it is important to consider the grounds for these doubts and to estimate how far they are justified. An explanation of much of the uneasiness about manufacturers' associations can be found in some of their basic characteristics.

In the first place, since the unit of membership is the firm and not the individual, associations are subject to the business policies of the various firms. They represent the interests of the industry as it already exists; growing enterprises have, in general, no more influence than static ones, and progressive firms do not necessarily carry more weight than more cautious ones. Associations are not in any way agencies for modifying the structure of their industries or for impelling them into particular lines of action. Those who believe that such action is needed in some industries therefore look elsewhere; they turn to bodies such as development councils not governed by firms, but controlled by chosen industrialists, trade unionists, economic experts, and so on.

Secondly, trade associations are voluntary organisations. In any industry there usually are a few non-members, and there is no way of retaining the membership of any firm that wishes to leave. This means that an association's policy and activities must command the support of the bulk of its member-firms, and in fact some of them deliberately avoid taking up matters that are likely to cause controversy within the industry. This may make them admirably representative and democratic institutions, but it does not always foster vigorous leadership. Critics of associations therefore hold that organisations with compulsory membership (which can operate by majority rule rather than all-round agreement), or independent agencies, would be more successful in promoting industrial change.

Thirdly, as associations develop collective activities some centralisation of power is inevitable. Moreover, by thus acting in concert on more and more matters their strength *vis-à-vis* other groups in the community is increased. It is argued that this type of change must always be a matter of public concern.

How far are misgivings justified? Can the modern trade association be regarded as a satisfactory institution not only for its members but for the public interest at large?

Complaints that trade associations represent only the owners of industry, or only capital and not labour, or only producers and not consumers, and so forth, are surely misconceived. Associations exist to serve the common interests of firms in the free enterprise sector of the economy. The policies of firms are subject to a variety of external influences, but final decisions lie with directors and not with employees, customers or technical experts. The representative bodies of the various industries could scarcely be constituted in any other way, if they are to speak authoritatively for those who are responsible for the major decisions in these industries.

Similarly, it is unrealistic in most cases to expect a non-voluntary body to command the allegiance or sympathy of its industry indefinitely. Such organisations (for example, the Cotton Board and the Furniture Development Council) do exist and are supported, but their popularity is rarely so well assured as that of ordinary associations, whose policies are closely controlled by their members and from which a firm can resign at will. Not surprisingly, business men like to feel firmly in control of their representatives. Moreover, once agreement is reached in a voluntary organisation action can be swift and effective, because support for it is freely given and there is no reluctant minority.

In a free society with a mixed economy, therefore, independent trade associations are irreplaceable institutions. What is less easy to guarantee is that they always fulfil all their potentialities. Conditions vary so much between industries that it is impossible for the outsider to say in detail whether an association is doing all it might or not: yet—as suggested here—there is little doubt that associations are only at the beginning of their positive contributions to industrial efficiency.

As the potentialities of collective action in industry develop it is likely that public concern will become increasingly evident. The centralisation of power which may go with greater activity should therefore be ordered and responsible. It would not be premature for associations themselves to consider now whether a more assured, publicly acknowledged status would not be desirable. At present they take a variety of legal forms and there is no recognised framework for them to assume. The creation of a new legal entity with a system of registration would provide a more informative picture of the activities, representativeness, and general scope of associations and of their value to their industries. Development on these lines would provide a basis for assessing the adequacy of their contribution to economic efficiency.

It has been argued above that since only voluntary and independent associations can be assured of the allegiance of their industries, their widespread replacement or close regulation would do more harm than good. Nevertheless, it must be recognised that the primary job of associations is to promote the welfare of their own industries, and that, for business men, the movement towards collective action in industry is a means of furthering the prosperity of their firms and enhancing the efficiency of private enterprise. The activities of associations are therefore principally of value to their members and the trades in which they operate, and through them to the economy as a whole.

But the need for economic progress is urgent, and it is of the greatest importance that the work of trade associations should be of the highest standard. The general view emerging from this study is that trade associations are performing a useful function, but that their usefulness could be greatly increased. Since in the nature of things there exists a tendency to self-satisfaction and complacency in association circles, there is need to stimulate them in various ways to ensure that their full potentialities are developed. Pressure should come from members rather than from outside, and business men should regard the efficiency of their association as a matter just as essential as the efficiency of their firm.

Associations should not only be efficient—they should also be seen to be so. Like other industrial institutions, they attract the attention of many people besides their own members, and must always expect to be subject to outside scrutiny. The nature of this scrutiny depends on the general arrangements made for relations between Government and industry, and these are beyond the province of this report. But associations would find their status and reputation enhanced if they were able to satisfy not only their member-firms but all those, whether in the Government, the administration or elsewhere, who are concerned in any way with general economic welfare.

These conclusions began with the suggestion that there are prospects of a widespread reassessment, in industry and outside it, of the part that associations can play in the national life. Those types of association activity, such as price-fixing and discriminatory trading, which most directly affect the consumer have now been brought under public control. This must benefit the standing of associations, both by bringing about a more balanced estimation of their work, and by inducing some of them to adopt a more positive and less defensive conception of service to their industries. The situation offers an opportunity and a challenge, and trade associations should welcome it as such.

Register

TRADE ASSOCIATIONS IN MANUFACTURING INDUSTRY

THIS register lists all known associations in manufacturing industry and, where obtainable, the location of their headquarters. Only organisations which fall within the definition used in the report have been included; this has meant the exclusion of Chambers of Commerce, local or regional associations, bodies whose predominant purpose is negotiation with labour, export groups, and associations consisting exclusively of importers or distributors. Where the association of a regional industry operates as a national body—for example, the North Wales Slate Quarries Association—it has been included. Some of the associations given, of course, undertake labour negotiations among their other functions, and associations including manufacturers as well as distributors have not been left out.

Associations whose interests extend over more than one field are listed under each appropriate heading; for example, the Truck and Ladder Manufacturers Association is to be found both under Carts, Perambulators, etc., and under Miscellaneous Wood and Cork Manufactures.

The Federation of British Industries, the National Union of Manufacturers and the National Council of Building Material Producers have too great a range of interests to be conveniently classified, but their member-associations have been indicated as follows:

* Affiliated to the Federation of British Industries.

** Affiliated to the National Union of Manufacturers.

† Represented on the National Council of Building Material Producers.

The legal status of some associations is indicated as follows:

C Registered as a public company.

RTU Registered as an employers' trade union.

CTU Certified to be an employers' trade union.

The register follows the Standard Industrial Classification. This consists of twenty-four Orders, or major industrial groups, and 163 Minimum List Headings, with sub-divisions. (Gaps left in the sequence of numbering are to permit additions to the list.) Main headings, capitalised, are numbered in roman numerals to follow Orders II–XVI, which cover manufacturing industry. Minimum List Headings and sub-divisions are given in bold type, and arabic numerals are used here as in the Standard Industrial Classification. Where associations cover more than one part of industry, cross references to the Minimum List Headings and their sub-divisions are given in brackets.

Associations grouped together usually share the same office address. Space does not permit the inclusion of the full address. The constituent associations of some federal bodies have been indicated where convenient, but these lists are rarely complete since some constituents can only be classified under other headings. In many cases it has not been practicable to indicate a federation's constituents at all.

The register has been made as full and accurate as possible, but the structure of associations in industry is constantly changing, and, since no fully effective means of keeping up to date is available, some errors and omissions no doubt remain. Details refer to the middle 1950s, before the operation of the Restrictive Trade Practices Act, 1956.

II—MINING AND QUARRYING

10. COAL MINING

Federation of Small Mines of Great Britain, Wigan

11. IRON ORE MINING AND QUARRYING

* National Council of Associated Iron Ore Producers, Kettering

12. STONE QUARRYING AND MINING

* Federated Quarry Owners of Great Britain
c Limestone Federation
both London
National Federation of Freestone Quarry Owners, Southport, Lancs.
Scottish Freestone Quarry Masters Association, Locharbriggs, Dumfries
* British Granite and Whinstone Federation, London
British Stone Federation, London

13. SLATE QUARRYING AND MINING

† North Wales Slate Quarries Association, Bangor
English Slate Quarries Association, London

14. CLAY, SAND, GRAVEL AND CHALK PITS

*† Ballast, Sand and Allied Trades Association, London
Chalk Quarrying Association, London
c* British Ball Clay Producers Federation Ltd., Newton Abbott, Devon
Silica and Moulding Sands Association
c*† National Federation of Clay Industries (*also* 20)
both London
* China Clay Association, St. Austell, Cornwall
c* British China Clay Producers Federation Ltd., St. Austell, Cornwall

19. OTHER MINING AND QUARRYING

2. Salt mines, brine pits, salt works

British Salt Federation, Liverpool

4. Other non-metalliferous mining and quarrying

British Fluospar Producers Association, Sheffield

III—NON-METALLIFEROUS MINING PRODUCTS

20. BRICKS AND FIRECLAY GOODS

c*† National Federation of Clay Industries, London (*also* 14)

1. Refractory goods

National Silica Brickmakers Association, London
Magnesite and Chrome Brickmakers Association, Sheffield
Refractories Association of Great Britain, Sheffield
Refractory Users Federation, London
Scottish Firebrick Association, Glasgow
Fire Clay Grate Back Association, London

2. Non-refractory goods

c† British Sanitary Fireclay Association, Leeds.
** National Association of Roofing Tile Manufacturers, Birmingham (*also* 21.2)
Clay Block Association, London
*† Midland Federation of Brick and Tile Manufacturers, Birmingham
Salt Glazed Conduit Association, London
† National Salt Glazed Pipe Manufacturers Association, London
CTU Stock Brick Manufacturers Association, London
C Pressed Brick Makers Association Ltd., London
c† Sand Lime Brick Manufacturers Association Ltd., London
British Engineering Brick Association, Birmingham
Scottish Fireclay Pipe Association, Glasgow
National Clayware Federation, Bridgwater, Somerset

** National Horticultural Pottery Manufacturers Association, London
British Stoneware Manufacturers Association (*also* 21.2)
National Federation of General Stoneware Manufacturers (*also* 21.2)
both Derby

21. CHINA AND EARTHENWARE

* British Pottery Manufacturers Federation
includes

1. Electrical ware

British Electro-ceramics Manufacturers Association

2. Other china and earthenware

† British Sanitary Earthenware Manufacturers Association
British Teapot Manufacturers Association
Chemists' Sundries Association
Conference of Earthenware Manufacturers
English China Manufacturers Association
Export Earthenware Manufacturers Association
Fine China and Earthenware Manufacturers Association
Floor Quarry Association
General Earthenware (Home and Export) Manufacturers Association
† Glazed and Floor Tile Manufacturers Association
Home Trade Earthenware Association
Ornamental Pottery Manufacturers Association
all Stoke-on-Trent
** National Association of Roofing Tile Manufacturers, Birmingham (*also* 20.2)
Staffordshire Potteries (Hotel Ware) Manufacturers Association, Hanley
London Potters Association, London
British Stoneware Manufacturers Association (*also* 20.2)
National Federation of General Stoneware Manufacturers (*also* 20.2)
both Derby
Tile Fireplace Makers Association, London (*also* 29.2)
Potters Millers Association, Burslem
Terra Cotta Association 1937, London

22. GLASS

* ** Glass Manufacturers Federation (*also* 100.2)
c British Chemical Ware Manufacturers Association Ltd.
British Lamp-blown Scientific Glassware Manufacturers Association
all London
National Federation of Constructional Glass Associations
Glass Benders Association
* Plate Glass Association
all London

*† Sheet and Plate Glass Manufacturers Association, St. Helens
Association of Glass Container Manufacturers, Leeds
C British Laboratory Ware Association Ltd., London
C Glass Textile Association Ltd., Manchester (*also* 129.3)
**† Patent Glazing Conference, London
Stourbridge Glass Manufacturers Association, Stourbridge
Lampshade Manufacturers Association, London (*also* 183.3)

24. CEMENT

CTU *† Cement Makers Federation
C Cement and Concrete Association
both London
Association of Manufacturers of Cement Waterproofers and Allied Products, London

29. OTHER NON-METALLIFEROUS MINING MANUFACTURES

1. Abrasives

Abrasive Industries Association, Stafford
Emery and Coated Abrasives Manufacturers Association, London
Diamond Abrasive Association, Welwyn Garden City
British Grit Association, Airdrie, Lanarkshire

2. Cast stone and cast concrete products

RTU British Cast Concrete Federation, London
Federation of Clinker Block Manufacturers, Surbiton, Surrey
C Reinforced Concrete Association, London
Cast Stone and Concrete Federation, London
British Ready Mixed Concrete Association, Feltham, Middlesex
Tile Fireplace Makers Association, London (*also* 21.2)
CTU Associated Paving Manufacturers
Scottish Pre-cast Concrete Manufacturers Association, Falkirk

3. Other

† Asbestos Cement Manufacturers Association, Birmingham
*† British Whiting Federation, London
† Gypsum Building Products Association, London
Southern Lime Association, London
C Mica Trade Association, London
CTU National Association of Putty Manufacturers, London
National Federation of Terrazzo Mosaic Specialists, London
National Pitched Roofing Council, London

c Association of Vermiculite Exfoliators Ltd., London
Magnesia-Asbestos-Glass Insulation Manufacturers Council, Coulsdon, Surrey
† Structural Insulation Association, London
Basic Slag Producers Association, London
British Slag Macadam Federation, Leeds
** Federation of Coated Macadam Industries, London
British Slag Federation, London
c Foamed Slag Producers Federation Ltd., London
Slag Wool Association, London
Road Bitumen Association
c Asphalt Roads Association Ltd.
both London
Cold Asphalt Association, London
c National Association of Master Asphalters Ltd., London
Natural Asphalt Mine Owners and Manufacturers Council, London
Decorative Marble Federation, London
RTU National Association of Master Monumental Masons, London
Scottish Master Monumental Sculptors Association
CTU Wholesale Memorial Manufacturers Association, London

IV—CHEMICALS AND ALLIED TRADES

30. COKE OVENS AND BY-PRODUCT WORKS

* British Coking Industry Association, London
British Tar Confederation
British Road Tar Association
Association of Tar Distillers
includes
Naphthalene Producers Committee
Pitch Supply Association
all London
c British Sulphate of Ammonia Federation Ltd., London
c Low Temperature Coal Distillers Association of Great Britain Ltd., London
National Ammonia Liquor Association, Billingham, Co. Durham (*also* 31.4)
National Association of Charcoal Manufacturers, Worksop, Notts.
c British Tarpaviers Association
c Road Emulsion Association Ltd.
both London
c Creosote Producers Association Ltd., London (*also* 36)

31. CHEMICALS AND DYES

c* Association of British Chemical Manufacturers, London

1. Dyes and dyestuffs

CTU British Colour Makers Association (*also* 34 *and* 168.3)

2. Fertilisers, disinfectants, etc.

British Disinfectant Manufacturers Association
Association of British Insecticide Manufacturers
Association of British Sheep and Cattle Dip Manufacturers
Industrial Pest Control Association
all London

c* Fertilizer Manufacturers Association Ltd.
c Horticultural Fertilizer Association Ltd.
c Superphosphate Manufacturers Association Ltd.
all London

c Association of British Organic Fertilizers Ltd., London

3. Synthetic resins and plastics materials

c* British Plastics Federation, London (*also* 199.1)
Casein Plastic Association, London (*also* 199.1)

4. Other chemicals

British Barytes Producers Association, London
c National Sulphuric Acid Association Ltd., London
Cresylic Acid Producers Association
Phenol Producers Association
c British Acetylene Association, London
c British Sulphate of Copper Association Ltd., London
British Tanning Extract Manufacturers Association, London
c Fire Extinguisher Trades Association, Ashford, Middlesex (*also* 99.8)
National Ammonia Liquor Association, Billingham, Co. Durham (*also* 30)
Soda Crystal Manufacturers Federation, London
Sulphonators Association, Manchester
* White Spirit Association, London

32. PHARMACEUTICAL PREPARATIONS, TOILET PREPARATIONS, PERFUMERY

1. Pharmaceutical preparations

* Association of British Pharmaceutical Industry, London
Animal Medicine Manufacturers Association, London
RTU Chemists' Federation of Manufacturers, Wholesalers, and Retailers of Medical and Pharmaceutical Products, London

Association of Wholesale Druggists and Manufacturers of Medical Preparations, London
Medical and Surgical Plaster Makers Conference, Leicester (*also* 122.2)
c* Proprietary Association of Great Britain
Proprietary Articles Trade Association
both London

2. Toilet preparations and perfumery

c Toilet Preparations Federation Ltd.
British Aromatic Compound Manufacturers Association
Dentifrice Manufacturers Association
all London
Cosmetic and Toilet Preparations Trade Association

33. EXPLOSIVES AND FIREWORKS

British Pyrotechnists Association, Leicester

34. PAINT AND VARNISH

c*† National Federation of Associated Paint Colour and Varnish Manufacturers of the United Kingdom (known as the National Paint Federation)
Surface Coating Synthetic Resin Manufacturers Association
Association of Cellulose Lacquer Manufacturers
all London
c* Society of British Paint Manufacturers Ltd.
Association of Ship's Composition Manufacturers
both London
Zinc Pigment Association, London (*also* 49.4)
** British Artists' Colours Manufacturers Association, London
British Iron-Oxide (Synthetic) Manufacturers Group, Rugeley, Staffs.
Enamel Association, London
c** Paint Manufacturers and Allied Trades Association Ltd., London
CTU Paint Materials Trade Association, Surbiton, Surrey
CTU United Kingdom White Lead Convention, London
Vitreous Enamellers Association, Birmingham
*† White Lead and Lead Oxide Convention, London
British Colour Makers Association (*also* 31.1 *and* 168.3)

35. SOAP, CANDLES, GLYCERINE, POLISHES, INK AND MATCHES

1. Soap, candles, glycerine

Society of British Soap Makers, London
** Soap Makers Association, London
c United Kingdom Glycerine Producers Association Ltd., London

2. Polishes, ink and matches

Boot and Floor Polishes Manufacturers Association, London
* Federation of British Printing Ink Manufacturers, London
** Ink and Adhesive Manufacturers Association, London (*also* 39.4)
Society of British Match Manufacturers, London

36. MINERAL OIL REFINING

Benzole and Allied Products Association
National Benzole Association
both London
c Creosote Producers Association Ltd., London (*also* 30)
Lighter Fuel Trade Association, London
White Oils Association, London

39. OTHER OILS, GREASES, GLUE, ETC.

1. Lubricating oils and greases

c National Lubricating Oils and Greases Federation, London
c Motor Accessories Manufacturers Association, London (*also* 83)

2. Oil seed crushing and refining of vegetable and marine oils

National Linseed Oil Processors Association, Hull
National Seed Crushers Association, London

3. Animal oils and greases and fish liver oils

Edible Oil Association, London
c Raw Fat Melters Association of Great Britain, Manchester (*also* 162.6)

4. Glue, gum, paste, etc.

Adhesive Insulating Tape Manufacturers Committee, Manchester (*also* 121.3)
** Adhesive Tape Manufacturers Association, Welwyn Garden City, Herts. (*also* 121.3)
** Adhesive Manufacturers Association
** Ink and Adhesive Manufacturers Association (*also* 35.2)
** British Dextrine Manufacturers Association
all London
British Rubber and Resin Adhesive Manufacturers Association, Leicester (*also* 190.2)
c Federation of Bone Users and Allied Trades Ltd.
c* Federation of Gelatine and Glue Manufacturers Ltd.
both London
Casein Glue Manufacturers Association, Southampton

V.—METAL MANUFACTURE

40. BLAST FURNACES

*† British Iron and Steel Federation, London (*also* 41)
* Joint Iron Council (*also* 42)
Council of Iron Producers
Foundry Pig Iron Producers Association
all London
* Pig Iron Producers Conference
includes
* Basic Pig Iron Producers Association
* National Association of Hematite Pig Iron Makers
all Birmingham
Scottish Ironmasters Association, Glasgow

41. IRON AND STEEL MELTING, ROLLING, ETC., not elsewhere specified

*† British Iron and Steel Federation, London (*also* 40)

2. Iron puddling and wrought iron, etc.

Federated Forgemasters Association, Sheffield
British Wrought Iron Association, Glasgow
* Heavy Forgings and Railway Tyres, Axles, Solid Wheels and Disc Wheel Centres Conference, Sheffield (*also* 85)
includes
* National Forgemasters Association, Sheffield (*also* 92)
* Railway, Tyre and Axle Manufacturers Association, Sheffield (*also* 85)
Cylinder and Refined Iron Association, Birmingham
British Spheroidal Graphite Iron Producers Association, London

3 and 4. Steel manufacture (with or without melting)

Members of the British Iron and Steel Federation:
* British Steel Producers Conference, London
includes
* British Sheet Bar Association
* Rail Makers Association
both London
North-East Coast Heavy Steel Association
Midlands and Welsh Heavy Steel Association
Scottish Heavy Steel Association
* Forging Ingot Makers Association, Sheffield
* National Billet Association
* Tube Steel Association
both Sheffield

* Scottish Steelmakers Association, Glasgow
* South Wales Siemens Steel Association, Swansea
* Crucible and High Speed Steel Conference
includes
* Crucible and Tool Steel Association
* High Speed Steel Association
Alloy and Stainless Steel Conference
includes
* Alloy Steels Association
includes
Alloy Steel Black Bar Association
Alloy Steel Bright Bar Association
* Stainless Steel Manufacturers Association
all Sheffield
* Light Rolled Steel Products Conference
includes
* Cold Rolled Steel Strip Association
* National Association for Rolled and Re-rolled Steel Products
all London
* Bright Steel Bar Association
* Steel Arch and Light Rail Association
both London
* Sheet Makers Conference, London (*also* 43)
* Tinplate Conference (1925), Swansea (*also* 43)
* Wire Rod Conference, Sheffield (*also* 93)
Other iron and steel associations:
* British Steelfounders Association, Sheffield
Cold Rolled Sections Association, Birmingham (*also* 49)
Railing Association, London
Scottish Steel Founders Association, Glasgow
Sheffield Stainless Steel Manufacturers Association, Sheffield (*also* 90.2)
Silver Steel Association, Sheffield

42. IRON FOUNDRIES

* Joint Iron Council (*also* 40)
* ** Council of Ironfoundry Associations
both London
* British Ironfounders Association, Glasgow and London
Ironfounders National Confederation, Birmingham
National Ironfounding Employers Federation, London

1. Cast iron pipes and fittings

† Gutter Bracket Manufacturers Association, Birmingham
Gutter Manufacturers Association, Birmingham

Cast Iron Pipe Association, London
Greensand Pipe Founders Association, Glasgow

2. Cast iron stoves and grates

c† Cast Iron Heating Boiler and Radiator Manufacturers Association, London (*also* 53)
c Range Boilermakers Association Ltd., Rotherham

3. Cisterns, baths and other sanitary fittings

British Bath Manufacturers Association Ltd., Glasgow
Flushing Cistern Makers Association, Dudley, Worcs. (*also* 94.3)
Metal Sink Manufacturers Association, London

4. Engineers' castings (excluding malleable castings)

Association of Automobile and Allied High Duty Ironfounders, Birmingham

5. Malleable iron castings

National Association of Malleable Ironfounders, Walsall, Staffs.

6. Other iron casting

Cast Iron Chair Association, Middlesborough, Yorks.
Cast Iron Segment Association, London
Cast Iron Axlebox Association
National Ingot Mould Association
both Sheffield
Clog Iron Manufacturers Association

43. SHEETS AND TINPLATE

* Sheet Makers Conference, London (*also* 41.3 *and* .4)
* Tinplate Conference (1925), Swansea (*also* 41.3 *and* .4)
c* Sheet Metal Industries Association Ltd., London
British Steel Boiler Plate Makers Association, Glasgow
Steel Sheet Piling Association

44. IRON AND STEEL TUBES

* British Hot Finished Tube Conference
includes
* Gas List Tube and Fittings Association, Birmingham
General Hot Finished Tube Association, London
Large Tube Association, Birmingham
† British Malleable Tube Fitting Association, London
Association of Steel Conduit Manufacturers, Birmingham
British Tube Association, Birmingham
Cased Tube Association, Birmingham
Collapsible Tube Manufacturers Association, London

Conduit Fittings Manufacturers Association, Birmingham
* Panel of Precision Tube Manufacturers, Birmingham

49. NON-FERROUS METALS SMELTING, ROLLING, ETC.

* British Non-ferrous Metals Federation, Birmingham
Cold Rolled Sections Association, Birmingham (*also* 41.3 *and* .4)
Scottish Non-ferrous Metals Association, Glasgow
British Non-ferrous Smelters Association, London

1. Copper and brass

c Copper Development Association, Radlett, Herts.
Members of the British Non-ferrous Metals Federation:
Non-Electrical Copper Association
* High Conductivity Copper Association
both London
* Cold Rolled Brass and Copper Association, Birmingham
Rolling for Hire Brass and Copper Association, Birmingham
* Extruded Brass and Copper Alloy Association, Birmingham
Cadmium Copper Association, London
*† Brass and Copper Tube Association, Birmingham
* Condenser Plate Association
* Manufactured Copper Association, Birmingham
c Associated Brass and Copper Manufacturers of Great Britain Ltd., Birmingham
† Copper Ball Manufacturers Association, Birmingham
Copper Tube Fittings Manufacturers Association, Birmingham
Rod Rollers Association, London (*also* 71)
Stamped Brassfoundry Association, Birmingham
† Scottish Association of Manufacturing Coppersmiths, Glasgow
Association of Bronze and Brass Founders, Birmingham
British Bronze and Brass Ingot Manufacturers Association, London
RTU * ** National Brassfoundry Association, Birmingham

2. Aluminium and magnesium

c Aluminium Development Association, London
*† Aluminium Industry Council, Birmingham
* Association of British Aluminium and Gold Bronze Powder (Flake) Manufacturers, London
British Aluminium Foil Rollers Association, London
Magnesium Industry Council, Birmingham
Federation of Light Metal Smelters
Alliance of Light Alloy Refiners
both London
Light Metal Founders Association, Birmingham
Wrought Light Alloys Association, Birmingham

3. Lead

c Lead Development Association
**† Lead Sheet and Pipe Manufacturers Federation
United Kingdom Lead Manufacturers Association
all London
c British Lead Manufacturers Association Ltd., London
British Compo and Tin Coated Lead Manufacturers Association

4. Zinc

† Zinc Development Association
includes
Hot Dip Galvanisers Association (*also* 99.7)
* Zinc Alloy Die Casters Association
Zinc Pigment Association (*also* 34)
all London
* Zinc Rollers Association, Birmingham

5. Other

British Hard Metal Association, Sheffield
British Tinfoil Manufacturers Association, London
Nickel Iron Association, Sheffield
* Nickel Silver Association, Birmingham
Solder Makers Association, London

VI—ENGINEERING, SHIPBUILDING AND ELECTRICAL GOODS

50. SHIPBUILDING AND SHIP REPAIRING

* Shipbuilding Conference
Dry Dock Owners and Repairers Central Council
both London
CTU Ship and Boat Builders National Federation, London
Fishing Boat Builders Association, Aberdeen

51. MARINE ENGINEERING

National Association of Marine Engine Builders, London

52. AGRICULTURAL MACHINERY (EXCEPT TRACTORS)

* Agricultural Engineers Association, London
* Agricultural Machine Parts Association, Sheffield
Association of Bee Keeping Appliance Manufacturers, Gloucester
c Dairy Appliances Manufacturers and Distributors Association, London (*also* 69.12)
Milking Machine Manufacturers Association, London
Scottish Agricultural Machinery Association, Edinburgh

53. BOILERS AND BOILERHOUSE PLANT

Association of Boiler Setters, Chimney and Furnace Constructors, London
Association of Shell Boilermakers
Association of Vertical Boiler Manufacturers
both Manchester
c† Cast Iron Heating Boiler and Radiator Manufacturers Association Ltd., London (*also* 42)
Combustion Engineering Association, London (*also* 55)
Copper Cylinder and Boiler Manufacturers Association, Manchester
c Range Boilermakers Association Ltd., Rotherham
Scottish Association of Manufacturing Coppersmiths, Glasgow
Society of Furnace Builders, Sheffield
Stoker and Furnacemakers Association, London
Underfeed Stokermakers Association, London
* Water-Tube Boilermakers Association, London
Associated Condenser Makers

54. MACHINE TOOLS AND ENGINEERS' SMALL TOOLS

c* Machine Tool Trades Association Inc., London
Engineers and Allied Hand Tool Makers Association, Wolverhampton (*also* 90.1)
* British Hacksaw Makers Association
* Machine Knife and Allied Trades Association
National Federation of Engineers' Tool Manufacturers (*also* 90.1)
Saw Manufacturers Association (*also* 90.1)
* Sheffield Engineers' (Small) Tools Manufacturers Association
Milling Cutter and Reamer Trades Association
all Sheffield

55. STATIONARY ENGINES

1. Internal combustion engines

c* British Internal Combustion Engine Manufacturers Association, London
Combustion Engineering Association, London (*also* 53)
Diesel Engine Users Association, London

2. Steam reciprocating engines, etc.

Superheater Manufacturers Association, Manchester

56. TEXTILE MACHINERY AND ACCESSORIES

Textile Machinery and Accessory Manufacturers Association, Manchester
* Bobbin Manufacturers Association (*also* 179.3)
English Wire Heald Manufacturers Association
* Loom Makers Association
Shuttle Manufacturers Association of Great Britain
all Manchester

Reed and Heald Association
Reed Manufacturers Association
both Birmingham
British Knitting Machine Builders Association, Leicester
Dobby, Lag and Pug Manufacturers Association
* Employers Federation of Card Clothing Manufacturers, Bradford
RTU Lace Machine Builders and Allied Trades Association, Nottingham
Irish Power Loom Manufacturers Association, Belfast
Scottish Bobbin and Shuttle Manufacturers Association, Dundee
Textile Combmaking Employers Federation, Bradford

57. ORDNANCE AND SMALL ARMS

1 and 2. Government and private factories

C Gun Makers Association (Inc. 1912) Ltd., Birmingham

58. CONSTRUCTIONAL ENGINEERING

British Constructional Steelwork Association, London

69. OTHER NON-ELECTRICAL ENGINEERING

C* British Engineers Association Inc., London
Engineering Industries Association, London
C Machinery Users Association Inc., London
Engineering Equipment Users Association, London

1. Office machinery

C* Office Appliance and Business Equipment Trades Association, London
RTU Typewriter (and Allied) Trades Federation of Great Britain and Ireland, London
RTU British Typewriter Manufacturers Association, Nottingham

2. Ball and roller bearings

* Ball and Roller Bearings Manufacturers Association, London

3. Mining machinery

* Federation of Associations of Colliery Equipment Manufacturers
includes
Council of Underground Machinery Manufacturers
Coal Preparation Plant Association
Skip Plant Association
Winding Engine Association
all Sheffield

4. Heating and ventilating apparatus

Unit Heater Manufacturers Association, London
c British Oil Burner Manufacturers Association, London
Oil Burning Apparatus Association, Birmingham
Petroleum Lamp and Stove Trades Association of the United Kingdom, Birmingham
c Fan Manufacturers Association Ltd., London (*also* 79.2)
Fans and Ancillary Equipment Industrial and Export Group, London (*also* 79.2)
Association of Heating, Ventilating and Domestic Engineering Employers, London
Invisible Panel Warming Association, London

5. Gas meters

Gas Meter Makers Conference, Carshalton Beeches, Surrey

6. Scales and weighing machinery

** National Federation of Scale and Weighing Machine Manufacturers
c** London Association of Scale and Weighing Machine Manufacturers (Inc.) both London

7. Cranes, lifts, conveyers, etc.

Aerial Ropeways Association, London
* Association of Crane Makers, London
Association of Hand Lifting Tackle Makers, Birmingham
Dredger Association, London
Excavator Makers Association, Newcastle-on-Tyne
* Mechanical Handling Engineers Association, London
* National Association of Lift Makers, London

8. Printing and bookbinding machinery

c* Association of British Manufacturers of Printers Machinery, London
Association of Dandyroll Makers and Mould Makers, London

9. Refrigerating machinery

* British Refrigeration Association, London

10. Pumps and pumping machinery

British Pump Manufacturers Association, London
Petrol Pump Manufacturers Association, London
Petrol Measuring Pump Manufacturers Association

11. Transmission chains

Machine Made Chain Manufacturers Association, Cradley Heath, Staffs. (*also* 92.3)
Precision Chain Industrial and Export Group, Manchester

12. Other non-electrical engineering

c* Food Machinery Association
includes
c Bakery Equipment Manufacturers Society
Mineral Water Engineers Association
c Dairy Engineers Association
c* British Chemical Plant Manufacturers Association, London
British Sugar Machinery Manufacturers Association, Glasgow
** Joint Council of Associations of Catering Apparatus Manufacturers
c** Catering Equipment Manufacturers Association
both London
Dairy and Ice Cream Equipment Association, London
c Dairy Appliances Manufacturers and Distributors Assn., London (*also* 52)
Association of Road Traffic Sign Makers, London (*also* 79.2)
Coin Operated Machine Association
Association of Manufacturers and Distributors of Garage Equipment, London
British Brush Machinery Manufacturers Association, Portsmouth
British Compressed Air Society, London
** British Lawnmower Makers Federation, London
c British Power Press Manufacturers Association, London
British Valve Manufacturers Association, London
Concrete Mixer Manufacturers Association, London
* Contractors' Plant Association, London
c Council of British Manufacturers of Petroleum Equipment, London
* Federation of Manufacturers of Contractors' Plant, London
c Foundry Trades Equipment and Supplies Association Ltd.
* Hydraulic Association
both London
Model Engineering Trade Association, London (*also* 193.1)
RTU National Association of Crankshaft and Cylinder Grinders, Bristol
RTU National Association of Restaurant Engineers, London
Paper Machinery Makers Association, London
Sewage Plant Manufacturers Association, London
* Society of British Gas Industries, London
Society of Laundry Engineers and Allied Trades, London
Spray Equipment Manufacturers Association, London
* Steel Works Plant Association, London
* Tank and Industrial Plant Association, London
Water Purification Plant Group, London

70. ELECTRICAL MACHINERY

C British Electrical and Allied Manufacturers Association (Inc.), London
C British Electrical Development Association Inc., London
CTU Electrical Fair Trading Council, London
Association of Electrical Machinery Trades, London
Associated Plant Manufacturers, London
CTU Association of Manufacturers of Small Switch and Fuse Gear, London
Association of Dynamo and Motor Manufacturers
Associated Switch Gear Manufacturers
Associated Transformer Makers
all Ascot, Berkshire
Meter Manufacturers Association, London
Summation Meter Manufacturers Association, Manchester

71. ELECTRICAL WIRES AND CABLES

CTU* Cable Makers Association
includes
Mains Cable Manufacturers Association
Mains Cable Manufacturers Association (Super Tension)
Rubber and Thermoplastic Cable Manufacturers Association
Telephone Cablemakers Association
* Covered Conductors Association
Rod Rollers Association (*also* 49.1)
all London
Independent Cable Makers Association
Association of Plastic Cable Makers
both London
CTU Association of Manufacturers of Electric Wiring Accessories, London
Electrical Steel Conduit Manufacturers Association, Birmingham

72. TELEGRAPH AND TELEPHONE APPARATUS

1 and 2. Government and other

Telephone Manufacturers Committee, London
C* Telecommunication Engineering and Manufacturing Association, London

73. WIRELESS APPARATUS (EXCEPT VALVES) AND GRAMOPHONES

C* Radio Industry Council
includes
* British Radio Equipment Manufacturers Association
both London
* Radio Communication and Electronic Engineering Association, London
RTU* Radio and Electronic Component Manufacturers Federation, London

Amusement Trades Association, London (*also* 79.2)

c Association of Musical Instrument Industries Ltd., East Finchley, Middlesex (*also* 103)

Electronic Manufacturers Association, London

74. WIRELESS VALVES AND ELECTRIC LAMPS

CTU* British Radio Valve Manufacturers Association, London

* Electric Lamp Manufacturers Association, London

c Electric Lamp Manufacturers Association of Great Britain Ltd., London (predecessor of Electric Lamp Manufacturers Association)

Cold Cathode Tubular Lighting Association

Independent Lamp Manufacturers Association

both London

Electric Discharge Lamp Auxiliaries Council, London

CTU Electric Light Fittings Association, London

CTU Electric Sign Manufacturers Association, London

Miners Electric Lamp Manufacturers Association, London

National Association of Manufacturers of Electric Lighting Equipment

75. BATTERIES AND ACCUMULATORS

1. Primary

* Association of Radio Battery Manufacturers, London

Primary Cell Manufacturers Conference, Woolwich

2. Secondary

Accumulator Makers Association

British Starter Battery Association

Portable Accumulator Makers Association

all London

Society of Electrical Accumulator Manufacturers, London

79. OTHER ELECTRICAL GOODS

2. Other than equipment for motor vehicles, etc.

Associated Ceiling and Table Fan Manufacturers

Associated Manufacturers of Domestic Electrical Appliances

Associated Manufacturers of Domestic Electric Cookers

all are sections of B.E.A.M.A., London

Amusement Trades Association, London (*also* 73)

c Association of Road Traffic Sign Makers Ltd., London (*also* 69.12)

British Electric Fence Unit Manufacturers Association, Letchworth, Herts.

c Electric Vehicle Association of Great Britain, London

Electric Water Heater Manufacturers Association, London
c Electro-Medical Trade Association Ltd., London
Fans and Ancillary Equipment Industrial and Export Group, London (*also* 69.4)
c Fan Manufacturers Association Ltd., London (*also* 69.4)
c Hearing Aid Manufacturers Association, London
CTU National Federated Electrical Association, London
Road Signal Manufacturers Association, London
Scottish Electrical Manufacturers and Factors Association
Washing Machine Makers Association, Accrington, Lancs.
X-Ray Manufacturers Association, London
Permanent Magnet Association, Sheffield

VII—VEHICLES

80. MANUFACTURE OF MOTOR VEHICLES AND CYCLES

c* Society of Motor Manufacturers and Traders Ltd., London
CTU British Motor Trade Association, London
c* British Cycle and Motor Cycle Industries Association Ltd.
CTU Cycle Trade Union
both Coventry
British Transport Vehicle Manufacturers Association, London
CTU Carrier Tricycle Association
c National Caravan Council Ltd., London
National Federation of Vehicle Trades, London
c National Traction Engine and Tractor Association Inc., London
c Scottish Motor Trade Association

82. MANUFACTURE AND REPAIR OF AIRCRAFT

c* Society of British Aircraft Constructors Ltd., London

83. MANUFACTURE OF PARTS AND ACCESSORIES FOR MOTOR VEHICLES AND AIRCRAFT

* Aircraft Bolt and Nut Manufacturers Association, Birmingham (*also* 91)
British Gear Manufacturers Association, London
c Motor Accessories Manufacturers Association Ltd. (*also* 39.1)

85. LOCOMOTIVE MANUFACTURE

Locomotive and Allied Manufacturers Association, London
* Heavy Forgings and Railway Tyres, Axles, Solid Wheels and Disc Wheel Centres Conference, Sheffield (*also* 41.2)
* Railway Tyre and Axle Manufacturers Association, Sheffield (*also* 41.2)

86. MANUFACTURE OF RAILWAY CARRIAGES AND WAGONS AND TRAMS

1. Railway

Railway Brakes and Signals Industrial and Export Group, London
* Railway Carriage and Wagon Building Association
CTU* Wagon Repairing Association
both London

2. Other

Industrial Truck Manufacturers Association, London
Pit Tub and Mine Car Manufacturers Association, Sheffield

89. CARTS, PERAMBULATORS, ETC.

** Truck and Ladder Manufacturers Association (*also* 179.3)
** British Baby Carriage Manufacturers Association
both London
Steel Wheelbarrow Manufacturers Association, Birmingham

VIII—METAL GOODS NOT ELSEWHERE SPECIFIED

90. TOOLS AND CUTLERY

C National Hardware Alliance Ltd., London (*also* 94)

1. Tools and Implements

Federation of British Hand Tool Manufacturers, Sheffield
includes
Association of United Kingdom Plier Manufacturers, Warrington
Engineers and Allied Hand Tool Makers Association, Wolverhampton (*also* 54)
Cut Thread Screwing Tool Manufacturers Association
* File Manufacturers Association
* Garden Shear Association
Hard Edge Flexible Back Band Saw Association
* Heavy Edge Tool and Allied Trades Association
* Light Edge Tool and Allied Trades Association
Saw Trade Association
* Scythe Sickle and Hook Manufacturers Association
* Sheep Shear Manufacturers Association
Welded and Brazed High Speed Tool Trade Association
Twist Drill Trades Association

National Federation of Engineers' Tools Manufacturers (*also* 54)
includes
Saw Manufacturers Association (*also* 54)
Saw Trade Association
all Sheffield
British Diamond Die Federation, London
Edge Tool Manufacturers Association, Derby
c* Gauge and Tool Makers Association Ltd., London
Portable Electric Tool Manufacturers Association, London
Electrical and Mechanical Instrument Makers Association, West Norwood, Surrey

2. Cutlery

* Sheffield Cutlery Manufacturers Association
* British Safety Razor and Blade Manufacturers Association, Sheffield
Cutlery Forgers and General Stampers Association, Sheffield
Sheffield Spoon and Fork Blank Manufacturers Association, Sheffield
Sheffield Stainless Steel Manufacturers Association, Sheffield (*also* 41.3 *and* .4)

91. BOLTS, NUTS, SCREWS, RIVETS, NAILS, ETC.

* British Bolt, Nut, Screw and Rivet Federation, Birmingham and Middlesbrough
includes
* Aircraft Bolt and Nut Manufacturers Association (*also* 83)
*** Black Bolt and Nut Manufacturers Association
* Bright Bolt and Nut Manufacturers Association
* Cold Headed Heat Treated Bolt Association
* Metal Thread Screw Association
* Small Rivet Association
all Birmingham
* British Rivet Association, Middlesborough
* Wood Screw Manufacturers Association, Birmingham
Cut Copper and Zinc Nail Manufacturers Association
Steel Nail Association
both Birmingham
Brass Shoe Rivet Association
* Shoe Rivet Association
both Birmingham
Cotter Pin Association
Steel Tack Association
both Birmingham
Door Bolt Manufacturers Association, Birmingham

Machinery Belt Fasteners Manufacturers Association, London
Screw Manufacturers Association, Birmingham
Staple Manufacturers Association, Birmingham (*also* 93)
Taper Pin Manufacturers Association, Birmingham
Cut Tip Nail, Cut Bill and Lino Bond Association
Washer Manufacturers Association of Great Britain, Birmingham

92. IRON AND STEEL FORGINGS NOT ELSEWHERE SPECIFIED

* National Forgemasters Association, Sheffield (*also* 41.2)

1. Drop forgings

* National Association of Drop Forgers and Stampers, Birmingham

2. Laminated springs

Laminated Railway Spring Manufacturers Association
Road Vehicle Laminated Spring Society
both Sheffield

3. Anchors and chains

Chain and Anchor Manufacturers Association
Machine Made Chain Manufacturers Association (*also* 69.11)
both Cradley Heath, Staffs.
* ** Chain Testers Association of Great Britain, London
Jack Chain Association, Birmingham

4. Other forging

Special Billet and Gun Forgings Association

93. WIRE AND WIRE MANUFACTURES

* Wire Rod Conference (*also* 41.3 *and* .4)
* British Wire Rod Rollers Association
Chain Link Fencing Association
* Federation of Wire Rope Manufacturers
Patented Steel Wire Association
* Woven Wire Manufacturers Association
all Sheffield
* ** British Steel Wire Industries Association
Mild Steel Wire Manufacturers Association
both Manchester
Wire Clip Manufacturers Association
* Brass Wire Association
both Birmingham

c* British Wire Netting Manufacturers Association, Birmingham
Fine Wire Staple Manufacturers Association, London
Paper Machine Wire Manufacturers Association, Glasgow
Scottish Wirework Manufacturers Association, Glasgow
Staple Manufacturers Association, Birmingham (*also* 91)
Wedge Wire Manufacturers Association, Manchester
** Wire Goods Manufacturers Association, Birmingham
Alloy and Special Steels Wire Rod Rollers Association
Locked Coil Ropemakers Association

94. HOLLOW-WARE

c National Hardware Alliance Ltd., London (*also* 90)

1. Domestic

Stainless Steel Fabricators Association of Great Britain (*also* 99.8)
British Aluminium Hollow-ware Manufacturers Association
Wrought Hollow-ware Trade Employers Association
all at Birmingham
Aluminium and Hardware Manufacturers Association
c British Pressure Cooker Manufacturers Association Ltd., London
Kitchen Equipment Manufacturers Association
Cast Iron Hollow-ware Makers Association, West Bromwich, Staffs.

2. Metal boxes and containers

British Tin Box Manufacturers Federation
British Closure Manufacturers Association (*also* 199.3)
Capsule Producers Association (*also* 199.1)
all London
Milk Can Manufacturers Association, Park Royal, Middlesex

3. Other industrial hollow-ware

Associated Tank Manufacturers, Rotherham
British Keg and Drum Manufacturers Federation
** Association of Steel Drum Manufacturers
both Liverpool
Flushing Cistern Makers Association, Dudley (*also* 42.3)
Galvanised Hollow-ware Association, Birmingham (*also* 99.7)
† Galvanised Tank Manufacturers Association, Birmingham (*also* 99.7)
* Tank and Industrial Plant Association, London
Wholesale Cabinet Hardware Manufacturers Association
Gasholder Manufacturers Association
Purifier Association
Gas Plant Manufacturers Development Council

95. BRASS MANUFACTURERS

Coffin Furniture Manufacturers Association, Birmingham

99. METAL INDUSTRIES NOT ELSEWHERE SPECIFIED

1. Metal furniture

* Metallic Bedstead Manufacturers Association, Birmingham
Bedding and Wire Mattress Manufacturers Association, Glasgow (*also* 171.1)
Hearth Furniture and Art Metal Manufacturers Association, Birmingham
Letter File Manufacturers Association, Birmingham (*also* 172)
Spring Mattress and Bedstead Fittings Association, Manchester (*also* 171.1)

2. Metal windows and door frames

c***† British Metal Window Association Ltd., London
c Steel Window Manufacturers Association Ltd.

3. Safes, locks, latches and keys

British Lock and Latch Manufacturers Association, Wolverhampton

4. Springs other than laminated

** Furnishing Spring Makers Federation, Manchester
Railway Coil Spring Association
Coil Spring Federation
both Sheffield

5. Needles, pins and fishhooks

* Federation of Needle, Fish Hook and Fishing Tackle Makers
Fish Hook Makers Association
Needle Makers Association
Sewing Machine Needle Manufacturers Association
all Redditch, Worcs.
RTU Hosiery Needle Makers and Allied Trades Association, Leicester
c Knitting Pin Association Ltd., London (*also* 199.1)
** Pin and Allied Trades Association, Birmingham
Safety Pin Association, Birmingham

6. Metal smallwares

British Fittings Manufacturers Association, Birmingham (*also* 131)
* Metallic Slide Fastener Association, Birmingham

7. Finishing of metal goods

Association of Metal Sprayers, Dudley
Electro-Platers and Enamellers Association
Galvanised Hollow-ware Association (*also* 94.3)
Galvanised Steel Gutter and Pipe Association, London (*also* 99.8)
Galvanised Tank Manufacturers Association, Birmingham (*also* 94.3)

Metal Finishing Association, London (*also* 102)
Metal Powder Sprayers Association, London
Schori Sprayers Association
Hot Dip Galvanizers Association, London (*also* 49.4)

8. Other

Aluminium Milk Bottle Cap Manufacturers Association, London
c Association of Nameplate Manufacturers Ltd., London
Back-up Rollmakers Association, Birmingham
British Mechanical Lighter Trade Association, Birmingham
British Metal Spectacle Manufacturers Association (*also* 100.3)
Bus Seat Frame Association, Birmingham
Cast Butt Hinge Manufacturers Association, West Bromwich, Staffs.
Expanded Curtain Rod Manufacturers Association
Curtain Rail Manufacturers Association, Birmingham
c Fire Extinguisher Trades Association, Ashford, Middlesex (*also* 31.4)
Galvanised Steel Gutter and Pipe Association, London (*also* 99.7)
Ground Thread Tap Association, Sheffield
Guild of Metal Perforators
Hair Clipper Manufacturers Association
† Hook and Band Association, Birmingham
Lead Trap Association, London
Metal Lathing Association, London
c† Reinforcement Manufacturers Association, London
Shoe Tip Association, Birmingham (*also* 148)
Stainless Steel Fabricators of Great Britain, Birmingham (*also* 94.1)
Steel Arch and Light Rail Association, London (*also* 41.3)
Steel Hinge Makers Association, Birmingham
Steel Rolling Shutter Association, London
* Steel Wool Manufacturers Association, London
Tensional Steel Strapping Association, London
**† Wall Tie Manufacturers Association, Birmingham

IX—PRECISION INSTRUMENTS, JEWELLERY

100. SCIENTIFIC, SURGICAL AND PHOTOGRAPHIC INSTRUMENTS

1. Photographic equipment

c British Photographic Manufacturers Association Ltd., London
c Incorporated Association of Kinematograph Manufacturers Ltd., London
CTU Joint Council of the Federated Photographic Manufacturers and Photographic Dealers Association

2. Optical instruments

* ** Glass Manufacturers Federation, London (*also* 22)
Specialist, Photographic, Cinematographic and Scientific Glassware Association

3. Ophthalmic optical instruments

Association of Wholesale and Manufacturing Opticians
British Ophthalmic Lens Association
both London
Ophthalmic Prescription Manufacturers Association
British Metal Spectacle Manufacturers Association (*also* 99.8)
British Plastic Spectacle Manufacturers Association (*also* 199.1)

4. Surgical, dental and veterinary instruments and appliances

c** Surgical Instrument Manufacturers Association Inc., London
includes
* British Surgical Support Suppliers Association, London
British Surgical Needle Manufacturers Association, Redditch
* Federation of Surgical Instrument Manufacturers, London
Surgical Appliance Manufacturers Association, Nottingham
Sterilised Catgut Manufacturers Association, Eastbourne
CTU Association of British Dental Traders, London

5. Measuring instruments, etc.

c* Scientific Instrument Manufacturers Association of Great Britain Ltd., London
c* British Industrial Measuring and Control Apparatus Manufacturers Association, London
British Nautical Instrument Trade Association, Glasgow
British Pressure Gauge Manufacturers Association, Birmingham

101. MANUFACTURE AND REPAIR OF WATCHES AND CLOCKS

1. Manufacture

c British Clock and Watch Manufacturers Association, London
British Watch and Clockmakers Guild, London
British Synchronous Clock Conference, London

102. JEWELLERY, PLATE, AND REFINING OF PRECIOUS METALS

c*** British Joint Association of Goldsmiths, Silversmiths, Horological and Kindred Trades (known as British Jewellers Association)

C Diamond Manufacturers Association Ltd.
Fancy Goods Association
C Gemmological Association of Great Britain
CTU Gold, Silver, Electro-Plate and Allied Trades Manufacturers Federation
Metal Finishing Association (*also* 99.7)
C National Association of Goldsmiths of Great Britain and Ireland
C National Jewellers Association
all London
Master Silversmiths Association, Sheffield
Diamond and Precious Stone Association, London

103. MUSICAL INSTRUMENTS

C Association of Musical Instrument Industries Ltd., East Finchley, Middlesex (*also* 73)
C Pianoforte Manufacturers Association Ltd.
Pianoforte Industrial and Export Group
all London
C Association of Manufacturers of, and Dealers in, Pianoforte Supplies Ltd.
Piano Trade Joint Committee
both London
Federation of Master Organ Builders, London
CTU Music Trades Association, Wimbledon (*also* 189)

X—TEXTILES

110. COTTON SPINNING, DOUBLING, ETC.

C* Federation of Master Cotton Spinners Associations Ltd., Manchester
* Cotton Spinners and Manufacturers Association, Manchester (*also* 111)
Cotton Twine Manufacturers Association, Heywood, Lancs.
Cotton Yarn Doublers Association, Manchester
* Condenser and Allied Spinners and Manufacturers Association, Manchester
Yarn Spinners Association, Manchester

111. COTTON WEAVING

* Cotton Spinners and Manufacturers Association, Manchester (*also* 110)
British Fustian Manufacturers, Bury, Lancs.
Cotton Velvet Council, Manchester (*also* 171.1)
Fine Cloth Manufacturers Association, Huddersfield
* Cotton Canvas Manufacturers Association, Manchester
Ventile Fabrics Association, Manchester
National Cotton Felt Manufacturers Association, Wakefield, Yorks.

112. WOOLLEN AND WORSTED

* Wool Textile Delegation, Bradford
includes

1. Woollen section

National Association of Scottish Woollen Manufacturers, Edinburgh
Association of Reclaimed Fibre Manufacturers (formerly Shoddy and Mungo Manufacturers Association), Batley, Yorks.
West of England Wool Textile Employers Association, Stroud, Glos.
Wool Carbonisers Federation, Bradford
* Woolcombing Employers Federation, Bradford
* Woollen and Worsted Trades Federation, Bradford

2 and 3. Worsted combing, topmaking, spinning and weaving

Woollen and Worsted Trades Federation, Bradford
includes
Textile Commission Manufacturers Association, Bradford
c* Worsted Spinners Federation Ltd., Bradford

Other wool associations:

1. Woollen section

Blanket Manufacturers Association, Leeds (*also* 122.2)
c Branded Knitting Wool Association Ltd., Bradford
Commission Woolcombers Association, Bradford
Hand Knitting Yarn Association, Bradford
c Harris Tweed Association Ltd., London and Stornoway

4. Wool felt

* British Paper Machine Felt Association, Bury, Lancs.
National Association of Woollen Felt Manufacturers, Leeds
* Pressed Felt Manufacturers Association, Rossendale, Lancs.

113. RAYON, NYLON, ETC., PRODUCTION

* British Man-made Fibres Federation, Manchester and London (*also* 114)
includes
Man-made Fibres Producers Committee, Manchester
* Rayon Staple Spinners and Doublers Association, Manchester
National Employers Association of Rayon Yarn Producers, Manchester
British Viscose Association, Manchester

114. RAYON, NYLON, ETC., WEAVING AND SILK

British Man-made Fibres Federation, Manchester and London (*also* 113)

1. Weaving

Rayon Weaving Association, Manchester

2. Other

c* Silk and Rayon Users Association (Inc.), London
British Rayon Crêpeists Association, Manchester
c British Silk Spinners Association Ltd., Bradford
British Silk Throwsters Association
Macclesfield Silk Trades Employers Association
both Macclesfield, Cheshire
Society of Silk Spinners and Merchants, Manchester
Corset Cloth Producers Association, Manchester

115. LINEN AND SOFT HEMP

* Central Council of the Irish Linen Industry
includes
c Flax Spinners Association Ltd.
both Belfast
* Flaxspinners and Manufacturers Association of Great Britain, Dundee (*also* 122)
c Association of Flax Processors of Great Britain Ltd., Billing, Northants.
Federation of Soft Fibre Associations, London
Fibre Trade Association, London
Irish Linen Guild, Belfast
Linen Sewing Thread Manufacturers of Great Britain and Northern Ireland, Glasgow
North Ireland Flax Millowners Association, Ballymena, Co. Antrim
Soft Hemp and Tow Spinners Association, London

116. JUTE

* British Jute Trade Federal Council, Dundee
includes
Association of Jute Spinners and Manufacturers, Dundee
c United Kingdom Jute Goods Association Ltd., London
Forfar and Kirriemuir Manufacturers Association, Forfar
Jute Carpets Manufacturers Association, Dundee
National Association of Jute and Jute Mixture Wadding Manufacturers, London (*also* 171.1)

117. ROPE, TWINE AND NET

** Hard Fibre Cordage Federation, London
Twine Manufacturers Association
Plaited Cordage Manufacturers Association
both London
British Hemp Rope Makers Association

English Net Manufacturers Association, Bridport, Dorset
Lancashire and District Cotton Rope and Cotton Twine Manufacturers Association, Heywood, Lancs.
Scottish Net Manufacturers Association, Glasgow

118. HOSIERY AND OTHER KNITTED GOODS

C* National Hosiery Manufacturers Federation, Leicester
British Hosiery Manufacturers Association, Leicester
Hand-Knitting Association, Bradford
Scottish Hosiery and Knitwear Manufacturers Association, Glasgow
Scottish Hosiery Manufacturers Federation, Glasgow
North of England Knitting Industries Association, Manchester
South of England Knitting Industries Association, London

119. LACE

RTU* Federation of Lace and Embroidery Employers Association
British Plain Net Manufacturers Association
Nottingham Lace Embroidery Manufacturers Association
Warp Lace and Net Manufacturers Association
all Nottingham
CTU Federation of British Lace Curtain and Curtain Net Manufacturers
Madras Manufacturers Association, Newmilns, Ayrshire
RTU Midland Counties Lace Manufacturers Association, Long Eaton, Notts.
National Council of the Scottish and Nottingham Lace Furnishing Manufacturers Association
Nottingham Lace Furnishing Manufacturers Association, Nottingham
Scottish Lace Furnishing Manufacturers Association, Newmilns, Ayrshire

120. CARPETS

* Federation of British Carpet Manufacturers, London
Association of Mohair and Pile Floor Rug and Matting Manufacturers, Huddersfield
* British Mat and Matting Manufacturers Association, London
Carpet Makers Alliance, Birmingham
Carpet Manufacturers Association, London

121. NARROW FABRICS

Textile Narrow Fabrics Council, Manchester

1. Elastic webs and cords

British Federation of Elastic Web Manufacturers
British Association of Elastic Webbing Manufacturers
British Association of Plastic Webbing Manufacturers (*also* 199.1)
all Leicester
British Elastic Braids Manufacturers Association, Leicester

2. Cotton smallwares

British Federation of Textile Smallware Manufacturers, Leek, Staffs.
Tape Manufacturers Association, Derby
Trimmings Manufacturers Association, London
Bias Binding Manufacturers Association, London

3. Other smallwares

** Adhesive Tape Manufacturers Association, Welwyn Garden City, Herts (*also* 39.4)
Adhesive Insulating Tape Manufacturers Committee, Manchester (*also* 39.4)
* Association of Solid Woven Belting Manufacturers
* Webbing Manufacturers Association
both Manchester
Wick Manufacturers Association, Manchester

122. MADE-UP TEXTILES

Flax Spinners and Manufacturers Association of Great Britain, Dundee (*also* 115)

1. Canvas goods and sacks

c Canvas Goods and Made-up Textiles Association Ltd., London
Canvas Hose Manufacturers Association, London
National Sail-Making Employers Association, Glasgow
Jute Sack and Bag Manufacturers Association, Dundee

2. Other made-up goods

Domestic Textiles Federation
includes
British Towel Manufacturers Association
Counterpane Manufacturers and Converters Association
Household Textiles Association
Ticking Group (*also* 171)
all Manchester
Condenser Sheeting Manufacturers Association, Manchester
Cotton Blanket and Raised Sheet Manufacturers Association, Manchester
Blanket Manufacturers Association, Leeds (*also* 112.1)
c National Federation of Bedding and Allied Trades, London (*also* 171.1)
* Surgical Dressings Manufacturers Association
* Surgical Textiles Conference
both Birmingham

* Association of Sanitary Towel Manufacturers, Chesterfield, Derby
* Medical and Surgical Plaster Makers Conference, Leicester (*also* 32.1)
Association of Embroiderers and Pleaters, London
British Cleaning Cloth Association, Manchester
** Cotton Bag Manufacturers Association, London
c* Lancashire Mechanical Cloth Manufacturers Association Ltd., Bury, Lancs.
Made-up Textiles Association, London
Mop Manufacturers Group, Manchester
Stitchers and Gold Blockers Association, Stockport
** Traced Art Needlework Manufacturers Association, London
Trade Hemstitchers Association, Belfast

123. TEXTILE FINISHING, ETC.

* Textile Finishing Trades Association, Manchester

1. Bleaching

Bleaching Trade Advisory Board
Employers Federation of Cotton Yarn Bleachers, Dyers and Sizers
Employers Federation of Bleachers
all Manchester
* Bleachers and Finishers Association, Belfast
Scottish Bleachers Association, Paisley

2. Printing

* Federation of Calico Printers, Manchester

3. Packing

Federation of Master Packers
* Master Packers Association, Manchester

4. Lace finishing

RTU Association of British Plain Net Finishers
Association of Lace and Net Finishers
RTU Hair-Net Finishers and Exporters Association
all Nottingham
RTU Lace and Net Dressers Association, Nottingham
c Lace Curtain Dyers and Finishers Association Ltd., Nottingham
c Gold Lace and Embroiderers Association Ltd., London

5. Other textile finishing

Confederation of Textile Dyers and Finishers
includes
Association of Dyers for Rubber Proofing
Association of Dyers for War Service Fabrics
Association of Flannelette Dyers

Association of Piece Dyers
Finishers Association
Striped Flannelette Association
Employers Federation of Dyers and Finishers
Wide Width Rayon and Cotton Menswear Lining Group
all Manchester
Flat Dyed Rayon Group
Spun Rayon Fabric Dyers Group
Rayon Crêpe Dyers Group
all Manchester
Association of Heavy Textile Proofers of Great Britain, Glasgow
Federation of Woollen Finishers and Dyers
includes
Flannel Finishers Association, Paisley, Scotland
Rubber Proofers Association, Manchester (*also* 190.2)
British United Shrinkers Association, Manchester
Colour Users Association, Manchester
Hydraulic Mangle Finishers Association
Irish Dyers and Finishers Association
both Belfast
Lining Association, Manchester
Midland Hosiery Dyers and Finishers Federation, Loughborough
National Federation of Hosiery Dyers and Finishers, Leicester
Scottish Federation of Dyers and Finishers, Paisley
Rayon Processers Association, Manchester

129. OTHER TEXTILE INDUSTRIES

1. Asbestos

c Asbestos Association Ltd.
British Brake Linings Manufacturers Association
both London

2. Flock and rag

c British Cotton Waste Association Ltd., Manchester
Cotton Flock and Cotton Millpuff Co-operation, Oldham
National Association of Washed Flock Manufacturers, Heckmondwike, Yorks. (*also* 171.1)
National Curled Woollen Flock Manufacturers Association, Gomersal, near Leeds (*also* 171.1)

3. Other

Association of British Kapok Manufacturers, London
c Glass Textile Association Ltd., Manchester (*also* 22)
Curled Hair Manufacturers Association, London (*also* 171.1)
Hair Manufacturers Association, Long Melford, Suffolk

XI—LEATHER, LEATHER GOODS AND FUR

130. LEATHER (TANNING AND DRESSING) AND FELL-MONGERY

1. Leather

* United Tanners Federation
Leather Producers Association for England, Scotland and Wales
c British Glacé Kid Tanners Association Ltd.
Sole Leather Tanners Association
all London
c British Leather Federation, London
c* Federation of Leather Belting Manufacturers of the United Kingdom
c Mechanical and Hydraulic Leather Manufacturers Association
c Roller Leather Incorporated Manufacturers Association
all Manchester
Master Tanners Association, Liverpool

2. Fellmongery

c United Kingdom Fellmongers Association, Menston, near Leeds

131. LEATHER GOODS

c National Leather Goods and Saddlery Manufacturers Association, London and Walsall
Belts and Accessories Manufacturers Association, London
British Fittings Manufacturers Association, Birmingham (*also* 99.6)
Buffalo Picker Manufacturers Association, Manchester
Hat Leather Manufacturers Association, Stockport

132. FUR

British Fur Trade Alliance, London
** British Hatters Fur Manufacturers Association, London
c Joint Board of the British Coney Fur Industry Ltd., London (formerly Joint Board of the Rabbit Skin Industry, Ltd.)

XII—CLOTHING

140. TAILORING

1. Proofed garments

c British Rainwear Manufacturers Federation, Manchester
Wholesale Clothing Manufacturers Federation of Great Britain, London (*also* 142.1)
c Oilskin Manufacturers Association of Great Britain Ltd., London
National Association of Clothing and Rainwear Manufacturers, Manchester
Waterproof and Rainproof Suppliers Association, Manchester

2. Other men's and boys' garments

* Wholesale Clothing Manufacturers Federation of Great Britain, London (*also* 142.1)
Association of London Master Tailors, London
Athletic Clothing Manufacturers Association, Manchester
Military Master Tailors Association, Bordon Camp, Hants.
Bespoke Tailors Guild, London
* Irish Wholesale Clothing Manufacturers Association, Belfast
C National Federation of Merchant Tailors (Inc.), London
Scottish Wholesale Clothing Manufacturers Association, Glasgow
Uniform Clothing Contractors Conference, Liverpool

3. Other women's, girls' and infants' garments

RTU Apparel and Fashion Industry's Association, London (*also* 142.3)
C Light Clothing Federation Ltd.
C Light Clothing and Allied Trades Association Ltd. (*also* 142.3)
both London
C Incorporated Society of London Fashion Designers, London
C Ladies' and Children's Clothing (Manchester) Manufacturers Association Ltd., Manchester
RTU Light Clothing Contractors Association, London
C London Model House Group Ltd., London
Scottish Light Clothing Manufacturers Association, Glasgow
C British Mantle Manufacturers Association, London
RTU Master Ladies' Tailors Organisation, London
Association of Makers of Nurses Uniform and Equipment, Stockport
National Children's Wear Association, London

142. OVERALLS, SHIRTS, UNDERWEAR, ETC.

1. Overalls

Overall Manufacturers Association of Great Britain, Liverpool
Wholesale Clothing Manufacturers Federation of Great Britain, London (*also* 140.1 and .2)
Factory Managers Clothing Association, London

2. Shirts, collars, etc.

Shirt, Collar and Tie Manufacturers Federation, London (*also* 147.3)
Belfast Shirt and Collar Manufacturers Association, Belfast
Scottish Shirt Manufacturers Association, Glasgow

3. Lingerie and baby linen

C Light Clothing and Allied Trades Association Ltd., London (*also* 140.3)
RTU Apparel and Fashion Industry's Association, London (*also* 140.3)
Blouse, Underclothing and Allied Trades Manufacturers Association, London

143. HATS, CAPS, AND MILLINERY

1. Millinery

Associated Millinery Designers of London
Direct Hat Manufacturers Association
both London
c London Millinery Manufacturers Association, London

2. Felt hats

** British Felt Hat Manufacturers Federation, Denton, near Manchester
Association of Hat and Helmet Manufacturers, London
c South of England Hat Manufacturers Federation, London

3. Cloth hats and caps

British Beret Manufacturers Association, London
Wholesale Cloth Cap and Hat Manufacturers Association, Manchester

4. Other

National Uniform Head-dress Manufacturers Association, London

147. DRESS INDUSTRIES NOT ELSEWHERE SPECIFIED

1. Corsets

* Corsetry Manufacturers Association London

2. Gloves

** National Association of Glove Manufacturers, London

3. Handkerchiefs, scarves and ties

Shirt, Collar and Tie Manufacturers Federation, London (*also* 142.2)
Handkerchief and Embroidery Association, Belfast
Tie Manufacturers Association, London

4. Umbrellas and walking sticks

** National Federation of Umbrella Manufacturers, London
National Federation of Umbrella Fabric Suppliers, Bradford
National Umbrella Handle and Stick Association, London
Umbrella Components Association, Sheffield

5. Other

c Artificial Flower Manufacturers Association of Great Britain Ltd., London (*also* 183.3)
National Association of Braces, Belts and Suspender Manufacturers, Leicester
** Ostrich and Fancy Feather Manufacturers Association, London
Shoulder Pad Manufacturers Association, London
Shroud Manufacturers Association, Birmingham
c Incorporated Guild of Hairdressers, Wigmakers and Perfumers, London

148. MANUFACTURE OF BOOTS, SHOES, SLIPPERS AND CLOGS (EXCLUDING RUBBER)

c* Incorporated Federated Associations of Boot and Shoe Manufacturers of Great Britain and Ireland, London
* Lancashire Boot, Shoe and Slipper Manufacturers Association, Rossendale, Lancs.
Boot and Shoe Stiffener Manufacturers Association, Leicester
Federated Association of Boot and Shoe Manufacturers in Scotland
National Association of Boot and Shoe Toe Puff Manufacturers, Leicester
** National Association of Cut Sole Manufacturers, London
National Association of Shoe Repair Factories, London
Shoe Tip Association, Birmingham (*also* 99.8)
Amalgamated Society of Master Cloggers, Burnley
Wholesale Clog Manufacturers Association, Halifax

XIII—FOOD, DRINK AND TOBACCO

General associations

c* Food Manufacturers Federation Inc., London
CTU Grocery Proprietary Articles Council, London

150. GRAIN MILLING

c*** Incorporated National Association of British and Irish Millers Ltd.
* Millers Mutual Association
both London
Association of Millers of Proprietary Brown Flours, Macclesfield
British Pearl Barley Millers Association, Edinburgh
National Association of Provender Millers of Great Britain and Northern Ireland (*also* 162.3)
Northern Ireland Millers Association, Belfast
Oatmeal Millers Association of England and Wales, London
Scottish Flour Millers Association, Glasgow
Scottish Oatmeal Millers Association, Edinburgh
Self-Raising Flour Association, London

151. BREAD AND FLOUR CONFECTIONERY

National Association of Master Bakers, Confectioners and Caterers, London
Federation of Wholesale and Multiple Bakers (Great Britain and Northern Ireland), London
Associated Oatcake Manufacturers
Bakery Allied Trades Association, London
Bakers Sundries Defence Committee, London

British Cake and Biscuit Association (*also* 152)
c* Cake and Biscuit Alliance Ltd. (*also* 152)
both London
Northern Ireland Bakery Employers Council
Irish Association of Master Bakers, Belfast
Scottish Association of Master Bakers, Edinburgh

152. BISCUITS

c* Cake and Biscuit Alliance Ltd. (*also* 151)
includes
British Cake and Biscuit Association, London (*also* 151)
* National Association of Biscuit Manufacturers, London
National Federation of Rusk Manufacturers, London
Wafer Biscuit Association, Birmingham

153. MEAT AND MEAT PRODUCTS

1. Wholesale slaughtering

Scottish Slaughtering Contractors Association, Glasgow

2. Bacon curing and sausages

National Small Registered Bacon Curers Association, Sherwood, Notts.
Sausage Manufacturers Association, London
Sausage and Cooked Meats Manufacturers Association
Scottish Association of Sausage and Cooked Meat Manufacturers

3. Other

Cooked Meats National Trade Association, London
Meat Paste Manufacturers Association, London

154. MILK PRODUCTS

1. Milk, butter and cheese

Association of British and Dominion Condensed Milk Manufacturers
Association of British Manufacturers of Roller Process Milk Powder
Association of British Manufacturers of Spray Process Milk Powder
English Butter Conference
all Trowbridge, Wiltshire
Association of Tinned Cream Manufacturers, Hayes, Middlesex
National Association of Creamery Proprietors and Wholesale Dairymen, London
Northern Ireland Association of Milk Product Manufacturers
Scottish Association of Milk Products Manufacturers, Glasgow
Butter Blenders and Packers Association, London

National Cheese Council
Cheshire Cheese Federation
both Whitchurch, Salop
Associated Cheese Processors, London
Association of Cheese Processors, Hayes, Middlesex
Cheddar and Caerphilly Cheesemakers Association, Axbridge, Somerset
Cheddar and Caerphilly Farmhouse Cheese Federation, Yeovil, Somerset
Cheshire Cheesemakers Association, London
Lancashire Cheese Association, New Longton, near Preston
Scottish Association of Farmhouse Cheesemakers, Ayr
Stilton and Leicester Cheesemakers Association, Melton Mowbray, Leics.
Wensleydale Cheese Makers Association, Darlington

2. Ice cream

c Ice Cream Alliance Ltd., London
c Wholesale Ice Cream Federation Ltd., London

155. SUGAR AND GLUCOSE

c British Sugar Refiners Association, London
British Glucose Manufacturers Association, London
Honey Producers Association, Iver, Bucks.
Invert Sugar Manufacturers Association
Caramel Manufacturers Association
both London
British Fondant Makers Association

156. COCOA, CHOCOLATE AND SUGAR CONFECTIONERY

c* Cocoa, Chocolate and Confectionery Alliance Ltd., London

157. PRESERVING OF FRUIT AND VEGETABLES

Canned Fruits Trades Standing Joint Committee, London
Fruit and Vegetable Canners Association of Great Britain, London
National Association of Quick Frozen Food Processors, London (*also* 162.6)

162. FOOD INDUSTRIES NOT ELSEWHERE SPECIFIED

1. Margarine

Margarine Manufacturers Association
Joint Executive Committee of Margarine and Compound Cooking Fat Manufacturers
both London

2. Fish curing

Association of British Salted Fish Curers and Exporters, Liverpool
c British Herring Trade Association Ltd., Aberdeen

Federation of British Kipperers, Aberdeen
Federation of British Salmon Smokers
Marinated Fish Products Association, London
Scottish Kipperers and Herring Freshers Association, Aberdeen

3. Cattle, dog and poultry foods

Association of Fish Meal Manufacturers, Toddington, Bedfordshire
Compound Animal Feeding Stuffs Manufacturers National Association, London
Joint Committee of Concentrate Manufacturers
National Association of Dog-biscuit Manufacturers
National Association of Provender Millers of Great Britain and Northern Ireland (*also* 150)
Scottish Compound Cake and Meal Manufacturers Association

4. Vinegar and other condiments

c Association of Non-brewed Condiment Manufacturers, London
Malt Vinegar Brewers Federation, London

5. Starch

** British Dextrine Manufacturers Association, London
British Maize Starch Manufacturers Association, Paisley
United Kingdom Starch Federation

6. Other

** Association of Gut Processors, London
Association of Manufacturers of Shortening and Compound, London
British Pilchard Canners Association, London
Coffee Essence Manufacturers Association, Leicester
Egg Breaking and Freezing Association
Federation of Edible Nuts Association, London
Isinglass Manufacturers Association, London
Edible Oil Association
National Association of Fish Cake Manufacturers
National Association of Quick Frozen Food Processors, London (*also* 157)
National Egg Association
National Egg Packers Association, London (*also* 182)
National Federation of Fish Quick Freezers
Beef Suet Manufacturers Association
c Raw Fat Melters Association of Great Britain (*also* 39.3)
both Manchester
Synthetic Cream Manufacturers Association, London

163. BREWING AND MALTING

* Brewers Society, London
** Allied Brewery Traders Association, London
Association of Malt Products Manufacturers, London
* Maltsters Association of Great Britain, London
Malt Roasters Association

168. OTHER DRINK INDUSTRIES

1. Spirit distilling, rectifying and compounding

* Scotch Whisky Association, Edinburgh
Pot Still Malt Distillers Association of Scotland, Elgin
Gin Rectifiers and Distillers Association, London
Northern Ireland Distillers and Wholesale Wine and Spirit Merchants Association, Belfast
British Compounders Association, London
Flaked Maize Manufacturers Association

2. Wine and cider

National Association of British Wine Producers, Kingston-on-Thames
* National Association of Cider Makers, Hereford

3. Soft drinks

Soft Drinks Industry Co-ordinating Advisory Council
C*** National Association of Soft Drinks Manufacturers Ltd.
both London
Apple Juice Producers Association of Great Britain
CTU British Colour Makers Association, London (*also* 31.1 *and* 34)
British Essence Manufacturers Association, London
Flavouring Compound Manufacturers Association of Great Britain, London
Scottish Federation of Aerated Water Manufacturers and Bottlers, Edinburgh
Belfast and Ulster Mineral Water Manufacturers Association, Belfast
National Rose Hip Producers Association, Putney

169. TOBACCO

CTU Tobacco Trade Association, London
C Federation of Home and Export Tobacco Manufacturers Ltd., London
Tobacco Federation of the British Empire, London

XIV—MANUFACTURERS OF WOOD AND CORK

170. TIMBER

1. Sawmilling, etc.

*† Timber Trade Federation of the United Kingdom, London
* Federated Home Timber Association, London
c Timber Development Association Ltd., London
** Association of British Plywood Manufacturers
c** Association of British Veneer Manufacturers Ltd., London
British Chipboard Manufacturers Association, London
Hardwood Flooring Manufacturers Association
National Sawmilling Association
Wood Floor Manufacturers Committee
all London
Pitwood Association of Scotland, Glasgow
Timber and General Fencing Contractors Association, London

2. Other woodwork for buildings

c*† English Joinery Manufacturers Association Inc., London
c† British Door Association Ltd., London
Door Association of Great Britain, London
c Flush Door Manufacturers Association Ltd., Trowell, Notts.
Hardwood Moulding Manufacturers Association, London
c* Timber Building Manufacturers Association of Great Britain Ltd., London
Scottish Joinery and Door Manufacturers Association, Glasgow

171. FURNITURE AND UPHOLSTERY

1. Soft furnishings

* Furnishing Fabrics Federation, Manchester
includes
Cotton Velvet Council, Manchester (*also* 111)
c Furnishing Fabrics Manufacturers Association Ltd., London
Moquette Manufacturers Association, Manchester
Moquette Weavers Association, Heckmondwike, Yorks.
Wholesale Furnishing Textile Association, London
c National Federation of Bedding and Allied Trades, London (*also* 122.2)
includes
Curled Hair Manufacturers Association (*also* 129.3)
National Association of Jute and Jute Mixture Wadding Manufacturers (*also* 116)
both London
National Association of Upholstery Felt Manufacturers
National Association of Upholstery Fibre Processers
both London

National Association of Washed Flock Manufacturers, Heckmondwike, Yorks (*also* 129.2)
National Curled Woollen Flock Manufacturers Association, Gomersal, Leeds (*also* 129.2)
National Feather Purifiers Association, London
Spring Mattress and Bedstead Fittings Association, Manchester (*also* 99.1)
Ticking Group, Manchester (*also* 122.2)
Bedding and Wire Mattress Manufacturers Association, Glasgow (*also* 99.1)
National Association of Down Quilt Manufacturers, London
National Association of Window Blind Manufacturers, London (*also* 172)
Ulster Bedding Manufacturers Association, Belfast

2. Other furniture and upholstery

British Furniture Trade Confederation
*** British Furniture Manufacturers Federated Associations
both London
Association of Folding Furniture Makers, London
Association of Master Upholsterers
Chair Frame Manufacturers Association
both London
British Radio Cabinet Manufacturers Association, London
British Association of Church Furnishers, London
Hospital Furniture and Domestic Equipment Group
National Federation of Manufacturers from Cane, Willow and Woven Fibre, Basford, Nottingham
C School Furniture Manufacturers Association Ltd., London
Scottish Furniture Manufacturers Association, Glasgow
Ulster Furnishing Federation, Belfast
Working Masters Association of the Furniture Trade, London

172. SHOP AND OFFICE FITTING

National Association of Shopfitters
National Display Equipment Association
Shopfront Moulding Manufacturers Association
all London
Letter File Manufacturers Association, Birmingham (*also* 99.1)
RTU Master Sign Makers Association, London (*also* 199.3)
National Association of Window Blind Manufacturers, London (*also* 171.1)

173. WOODEN CONTAINERS AND BASKETS

1. Coopering

National Association of Coopers, London
National Cooperage Federation, London

2. Boxes, crates, etc.

National Federation of Box and Packing Case Manufacturers
Fruit and Vegetable Wooden Box Association
both London
Federation of Veneer Package Manufacturers, Waltham Cross, Herts.

3. Baskets

c Employers Federation of Cane and Willow Workers Associations of Great Britain and Northern Ireland
National Basket and Willow Trades Advisory Committee
both London

179. MISCELLANEOUS WOOD AND CORK MANUFACTURES

1. Cork manufacturers

Cork Helmet Manufacturers Association, London
Crown Cork Manufacturers Association, London
Cork Trade Association, London
Corkboard Association, London

2. Wooden heels, lasts, etc.

British Wood Heel Processors Association
Last Manufacturers Association
National Association of Wood Heel Manufacturers
all Leicester
National Association of Built Heel Manufacturers, Kettering

3. Other wood manufactures

* Association of British Wood Wool Manufacturers, London
* Bobbin Manufacturers Association, Manchester (*also* 56)
Briar Pipe Trade Association, London
British Wood Pulp Association, London
Dowel Manufacturers Committee, London
c* Insulation Building and Hardboard Association Ltd., London (*also* 180.3)
Manufacturers of Undertakers Woodwork Association, Birmingham
** Truck and Ladder Manufacturers Association, London (*also* 89)
Underwood Products Association, Sevenoaks
Wood Wool Building Slab Manufacturers Association, London

XV—PAPER AND PRINTING

180. PAPER AND BOARD

1. Paper coating

Association of Waterproof Manufacturers, Bury, Lancs.
Coated Paper and Board Makers Association, London
Waterproof Paper Manufacturers Association, Manchester
Waxed Paper Makers Association, London

2. Transparent cellulose wrapping

Transparent Cellulose Wrappings Committee, Sheffield

3. Other

c* British Paper and Board Makers Association Inc., London
includes
Association of Makers of Banks, Bonds and Manifolds
Association of Board Makers
c Building Board Manufacturers Association of Great Britain, Limited
Association of Makers of Esparto Featherweight Papers
Filter Paper Makers Association
Association of Makers of Hand Made Papers
Association of Makers of Kraft Papers
Association of Makers of Imitation Kraft Papers
Association of Makers of Machine Coated Papers
Association of Makers of Manilla Papers
Association of Makers of M.G. Envelope Papers
Association of Makers of M.G. Poster Papers
Association of Makers of M.G. Sulphite Papers
Association of Makers of Middles and Ticket Pulp Boards
Association of Makers of Newsprint
National Associations of Packing and Wrapping Paper Makers
Association of Makers of Rag Tub Sized Papers
Royal Hands and Grocery Bags (1928) Association
Association of Makers of Strawpaper and Fourdrinier Chipboard
Association of Makers of Tissue Papers
Association of Makers of Tub Sized Papers
Association of Makers of Vegetable Parchment Paper
Association of Waxing, Bleached Imitation Parchment and Bleached Glazed Imitation Parchment
Association of Makers of Wood Free Papers
all London
Association of Makers of Esparto Papers, Edinburgh
** Association of Toilet Paper Manufacturers, London

Association of Corrugated Paper Makers
Society of Crêpe Paper Makers
both London
Paper Makers Allied Trades Association, Manchester
c Fibre Building Board Development Organisation Ltd., London
c† Insulation, Building and Hard Board Association Ltd., London (*also* 179.3)
RTU National Association of Manufacturers of Leather Board, Giltbrook, Notts.
Vulcanised Fibre and Leatheroid Association

181. WALLPAPER

* National Wallpaper Council, Dudley, Worcs.
* Wallpaper Manufacturers Employers Association, Manchester

182. CARDBOARD BOXES, CARTONS, AND FIBRE-BOARD PACKING CASES

Fibre Board Packing Case Manufacturers Association
*** British Paper Box Federation
British Carton Association
all London
Corrugated Fibre Case Manufacturers Association, London
* Federation of Paper Tube Manufacturers, Rochdale, Lancs.
* Master Packers Association, Manchester
National Egg Packers Association, London (*also* 162.6)

183. MANUFACTURES OF PAPER AND BOARD NOT ELSEWHERE SPECIFIED

1. Bags

* British Paper Bag Federation, London

2. Manufactured stationery

* Envelope Makers and Manufacturing Stationers Association
Stationers Association of Great Britain and Ireland (*also* 194.2)
both London
c** Greeting Card and Calendar Association, London

3. Other

c Artificial Flower Manufacturers Association of Great Britain Ltd. (*also* 147.5)
Association of Lace Paper Makers
Association of Makers of Paper Serviettes
Association of Photographic Mount Makers
Crimped Paper Food Cases Association
** Industrial Paper Towel Association
all London

** British Embroidery Transfer Manufacturers Association, London
Lampshade Manufacturers Association, London (*also* 22)

186. PRINTING AND PUBLISHING OF NEWSPAPERS AND PERIODICALS

* British Federation of Master Printers, London (*also* 189)
C Newspaper Proprietors Association Ltd., London
Newspaper Society, London
C Periodical Proprietors Association Ltd., London
Scottish Daily Newspaper Society, Glasgow
Scottish Newspaper Proprietors Association, Edinburgh

189. OTHER PRINTING AND PUBLISHING, BOOKBINDING, ENGRAVING, ETC.

* British Federation of Master Printers, London (*also* 186)
CTU Publishers Association, London
British Seal Printers Association, Walsall, Staffs.
RTU Electrotyping and Stereotyping Employers Federation, London
Federation of Engravers, Manchester
RTU* Federation of Master Process Engravers, London
Master Bookbinders Alliance of London, London
Monotype Users Associations, London
Association of Publishers and Wholesalers of Picture and Local View Postcards, London
C Music Publishers Association Ltd., London
CTU Music Trades Association, Wimbledon (*also* 103)
National Association of Engravers and Diestampers, London
Photo-Litho Reproducers Association, London
Scottish Alliance of Master Printers, Edinburgh

XVI—OTHER MANUFACTURING INDUSTRIES

190. RUBBER

1. Tyres and tubes

C* Tyre Manufacturers Conference Ltd.
Tyre Trade Joint Committee
both London
C National Association of Tyre Specialists Ltd., London
Retread Manufacturers Association, London

2. Other rubber goods

c* Federation of British Rubber and Allied Manufacturers Associations, London

includes

Association of British Ebonite Manufacturers
British All-Rubber Hose Manufacturers Association
British Association of Balata Belting Manufacturers
British Association of Latex Foam Manufacturers
British Cellular Rubber Manufacturers Association
British Mechanical Rubber Manufacturers Association
British Rubber and Plastic Belting Manufacturers Association (*also* 199.1)
British Rubber Flooring Manufacturers Association
British Rubber Hot Water Bottle Manufacturers Association
British Seamless Rubberware Manufacturers Association
British Wrapped Rubber Hose Manufacturers Association
Football Bladder Association
all Manchester
British Moulded Rubber Hose Manufacturers Association, London
British Rubber and Resin Adhesive Manufacturers Association, Leicester (*also* 39.4)
* English Rubber Thread Association, London
Food Jar Rings Association, Twickenham, Middlesex
Golf Ball Manufacturers Conference (*also* 193.2)
Lawn Tennis Ball Convention (*also* 193.2)
both London
Rubber Footwear Manufacturers Association, London
c Rubber Proofers Association, Manchester (*also* 123.5)
Rubber Surgical Equipment Manufacturers Association, Dalston
Screw Stopper Makers Association, London
Sole and Heel Manufacturers Association (Rubber, Synthetic Plastics), London

Association of British Reclaimed Rubber Manufacturers, Manchester
Crêpe Sole Rubber Association of London, London
British Rubber Sports Goods Manufacturers Association, London (*also* 193.2)
Washer Manufacturers Association of Great Britain, Birmingham

191. LINOLEUM, LEATHER CLOTH, ETC.

* Linoleum Manufacturers Association
Linoleum and Felt Base Employers Federation
both London
c* Association of British Roofing Felt Manufacturers Ltd., London
c Leather Cloth and Coated Fabrics Manufacturers Association, Manchester

192. BRUSHES AND BROOMS

* British Brush Manufacturers Association, London
British Brush Wood Turners Association, Worksop, Notts.
Broom Handle Manufacturers Association
National Society of Brushmakers, London

193. TOYS, GAMES AND SPORTS REQUISITES

1. Toys and games

c British Toy Manufacturers Association Ltd., London
Model Aircraft Trade Association, London
Model Engineering Trade Association (*also* 69.12)

2. Sports requisites

c Federation of British Manufacturers of Sports and Games Ltd.
includes
Association of Fishing Tackle Makers
British Skate Makers Association
Golf Ball Manufacturers Association (*also* 190.2)
Lawn Tennis Ball Convention (*also* 190.2)
all London
Gymnastic Equipment Manufacturers Association, Liverpool
British Rubber Sports Goods Manufacturers Association, London (*also* 190.2)

194. MISCELLANEOUS STATIONERS' GOODS

1. Pens and pencils of all kinds

* Association of British Steel Pen Makers, Birmingham
Association of British Ball Pen Manufacturers
** Fountain Pen Makers Association, London

2. Other stationers' goods

Stationers Association of Great Britain and Ireland, London (*also* 183.2)
** Carbon Paper, Inked Ribbon and Duplicating Material Manufacturers Association of Great Britain, London
* Drawing Office Material Manufacturers and Dealers Association, London
** Rubber Stamp Manufacturers Guild, London

195. PRODUCTION AND PRINTING OF CINEMATOGRAPH FILMS

1. Film studios

c Association of Specialised Film Producers, London
British Film Producers Association, London
Film Strip Producers Association
c Film Strip Publishers Association Ltd., London
c Scottish Film Council, Glasgow
c Display Producers and Screen Printers Association Ltd., London

2. Printing of films

Film Laboratory Association, London
c Film Strippers Association Ltd., London

199. MISCELLANEOUS MANUFACTURING INDUSTRIES

1. Plastics moulding, manipulating, etc.

c* British Plastics Federation, London (*also* 31.3)
Association of Plastic Line Manufacturers and Contractors, London
British Association of Plastic Webbing Manufacturers, Leicester (*also* 121.1)
** British Button Manufacturers Association, Birmingham
* British Comb Manufacturers Association, London
British Plastic Hardware Association, Birmingham
British Rubber and Plastic Belting Manufacturers Association, Manchester (*also* 190.2)
Capsule Producers Association, London (*also* 94.2)
** Casein Button Manufacturers Association, London
Casein Plastic Association, London (*also* 31.3)
Jointless Flooring (Oxychloride) Association, London
c Knitting Pin Association Ltd., London (*also* 99.5)
British Plastic Spectacle Manufacturers Association (*also* 100.3)

2. Photographic paper and films

Association of Cellulose Film Converters, London
Associated Manufacturers of Sensitised Materials
Federation of Engineers' Sensitised Material Manufacturers, London
Wholesale Photo-Finishers Association, London
X-Ray Film Manufacturers Association, Watford

3. Other

c Association of Manufacturing Builders Ltd., London
British Closure Manufacturers Association, London (*also* 94.2)
British Gas Mantle Association, London
Engine Waste Trade Group, Manchester
c Hairdressing Manufacturers and Wholesalers Association Ltd., London
Handle Manufacturers Association, Manchester
RTU Master Sign Makers Association, London (*also* 172)
** National Association of Firelighter Manufacturers, London
Oil Seal Manufacturers Association, Birmingham
Vacuum Flask Manufacturers Association
c Waste Trade Federation, London

Appendices

APPENDIX A

A CASE STUDY OF DEVELOPMENT: THE NATIONAL PAINT FEDERATION

Through the co-operation of the National Paint Federation it has been possible to build up an account of the main motives behind its growth and some of the stages of its development. This cannot, of course, be regarded as typical of all associations, but it gives a fair picture of the types of problem that stimulate collective action.

The initiative to form the Federation, which now unites a number of regional associations, came from one or two of the local associations—or rather from prominent members in them—and the first meeting was convened in November 1910 by one of the local associations. This body had previously invited manufacturers of the product outside its specified area to join it, and had gained sixteen members from this offer. Now it met with the representatives of four other local associations.

The chairman of the convening associations, in his address, advanced a number of reasons in support of the foundation of a national federation. He first showed that the local association had fostered co-operation and respect between members, and hoped that similar results would follow on a national scale. A national body would also stimulate the formation of local associations in areas where none yet existed.

Secondly, the industry was experiencing a number of economic difficulties. The prices of raw materials were rising, whereas the firms in the industry dared not increase the prices of their products commensurately or simultaneously with these rising costs. He hoped that the formation of a national federation would do much to improve this state of affairs. He was not in favour of price-fixing or regulations and fines to enforce it, but hoped that the existence of the federation would make for confidence between members, and such solidarity that all might increase their prices at the same time, and be confident that these would be observed. As will become evident, this was probably the decisive argument for federation.

Thirdly, a unified body would be able to influence the Government in matters concerning the industry. The chairman gave an instance of how his local association, supported by other representatives of the trade, had negotiated with the Home Office over laws regarding factory conditions, and as a result had limited their application to certain branches of the trade. He forecast that the federation would be of great assistance to the trade over tariff reform; its part would be to establish how far the materials used in the industry could take the status of raw materials. Again, in a representative capacity, it would be able to meet its opposite numbers in labour combinations.

At the end of this preliminary meeting the Articles of Association, which had been drawn up by the local chamber of commerce solicitor, were considered. A steering committee was appointed to deal with the question of legal formation, the Articles were signed, and the federation was incorporated towards the end of 1911, a year later. The inaugural meeting was held and the first council was elected in January 1912. The first secretary was the secretary of the local association, and the federation was managed from those offices until it moved to London a few years later. The costs of incorporation were £75 legal fees, 10s. stamps, and letters £1 2s. 6d. The first secretary's fee was £21.

Although the preliminary meeting was attended by more members of the convening local association than by those from other areas, at the end of its first year the membership of the new organisation was fairly evenly spread over the country, the four large local centres having between twenty and forty-nine members and one small one having only four. The total membership was one hundred and twenty-seven, although the Articles of Association allowed for two hundred. These firms produced a very large proportion of the national output of the product. There is no evidence to show how many firms were deemed necessary to form an association, but since the size of the smallest local association was four, size appeared to matter little.

The two early leaders of the movement for federation were the heads of two large firms in the local association. The other potential members were clearly known to each other before the formation of the federation, for there had been much correspondence between the local associations concerned. The number of members was probably increased gradually by personal contacts, as the mutual confidence engendered by the existence of the federation began to have its effect. There is no evidence of any opposition to the formation of the federation, nor of the attitude to it taken by non-members.

Membership of the federation was confined to manufacturers of the final products, although there was an attempt to include manufacturers of one of the materials used in production. This was defeated, for the federation wished to be in a position to negotiate with its members' suppliers. Probably for the same reason an affiliated group, the British Colour Makers Association, later left to form a separate association.

The council was constituted the governing body of the federation at the preliminary meeting. The local associations were represented on the committee by one member for every five subscribers to the federation.

The work of the federation in its first year was largely concerned with the supply of a raw material, lead. Sixteen out of twenty-one circulars issued during the first year were on this subject. By meetings with the international combine concerned, the relevant committee of the federation (appointed even before formal incorporation) was able to obtain more favourable terms for its members.

Other subjects mentioned in the first annual report which give some indication of the federation's activities included the limitation of extended credit in one section of the trade, minimum prices in others, packaging, carriage by passenger train (for which an *ad hoc* committee was appointed to approach the railways), and rebates. Perhaps the first contact with a government department was with the Director of the Census of Production Office. An early suggestion was the establishment of a Confidential Enquiry Bureau

> for the purpose of enabling manufacturers to communicate, through the medium of this department, with each other without names being mentioned.

Between 1912 and 1914 the federation grew in numbers and developed its activities. Particular subjects were dealt with by committees appointed as the need for them arose. The history of the federation is one of development and expansion not predetermined by theoretical precepts of organisation but shaped by the needs of the moment and conditioned by experience. As its activities extended, the federation became the recognised body which government departments, and other trade organisations, for instance those of users, would approach.

The federation continued to extend its activities between 1914 and 1919. It maintained its interest in prices, negotiating with raw material suppliers over their prices and terms of supply. The war caused it to assume additional duties in connection with the supply of other raw materials. Relations with the Government were strengthened. In 1916 the federation had more committees, three dealing with different types of product, one with raw materials, two with packaging and one finance. Attention was also being given to problems likely to arise after the war.

In 1917 the conditions created by the war made the federation negotiate labour problems with the Government, and in 1918 it participated in the National Joint Industrial Council for the industry, set up after the publication of the Whitley Report. At the same time the federation first became interested in research, in connection with the proposals for joint government and industrial aid for research.

After the war the activities of the federation extended gradually to cover most of the subjects dealt with today. Exports became of increasing interest; publicity campaigns were initiated. In 1922 contact with the B.S.I. was established and a representative appointed to a panel, whereas before only occasional consultation had taken place. Early in the 1920s representatives were appointed to serve on F.B.I. committees—a change in attitude from the refusal to join in 1919, when the federation felt that it was strong enough to look after its own interests on all fronts.

The different committees which appeared from time to time during this period show how the federation pursued its various interests and dealt with problems as they arose. During the whole period there were committees constantly concerned with the various kinds of product made, with the raw material used, with package and transport and with the internal affairs of the federation—financial and executive. Each period also had committees peculiar to it. Thus in 1917 there was a Trade After the War Committee, and an Emergency Committee In 1928 there was an Anti-Bribery Committee and a Status Enquiry Bureau. Two committees which reappear again in 1938 and show the extension of the federation's activities in the period were the Joint Industrial Council Committee and the Export Committee. The one significant new committee in 1938 is the Development Committee with its various sub-sections: the Costing Group, the Organisation of Federation Activity Group, the Organisation of Selling Group and the Wage Policy Group.

In 1940 the effect of World War II upon the federation resulted in much closer co-operation with the Government on matters such as the supply of raw materials, the wartime uses of the product, the conditions of contracts and the labour supply position.

The fluctuations in size and income of the federation can be seen from the following table showing the number of members and the income of the federation for every five years of its existence:

	Membership	*Total income*
1912	127	£250
1917	193	900
1922	244	2,000
1927	207	3,500
1932	163	4,000
1937	179	5,000
1942	316	9,000
1947	332	20,000
1952	268	23,500

The drop in membership in 1932 was caused by one of the groups, the British Colour Makers Association, splitting away from the federation. The doubling of income between 1942 and 1947 cannot be accounted for merely by the fall in the value of money: it argues that the federation's activities had greatly expanded during that period. Another association, the Society of British Paint Manufacturers, containing many large firms, was established in the industry in 1945.

APPENDIX B

INCORPORATED MANUFACTURERS' ASSOCIATIONS

A list of manufacturers' associations registered as Public Companies, and still active, in chronological order of registration. The date of incorporation is not, of course, necessarily the date of the foundation of the association.

Name	*Date*
Pianoforte Manufacturers Association Ltd.	1892
Incorporated Federated Associations of Boot and Shoe Manufacturers of Great Britain and Ireland	1898
Federation of Master Cotton Spinners Associations Ltd.	1900
Incorporated Guild of Hairdressers, Wigmakers and Perfumers	1900
British Joint Association of Goldsmiths, Horological and Kindred Trades	1901
British Acetylene Association	1901
Society of Motor Manufacturers and Traders Ltd.	1902
Machinery Users Association Inc.	1905
British Electrical and Allied Manufacturers Association (Inc.)	1905
National Traction Engine and Tractor Association	1905
Newspaper Proprietors Association Ltd.	1906
Association of British Glass Bottle Manufacturers Ltd.	1907
Association of Manufacturers and Dealers in Pianoforte Supplies	1908
Roller Leather Incorporated Manufacturers Association	1909
British Leather Federation	1909
Harris Tweed Association Ltd.	1909
Pressed Brick Makers Association Ltd.	1909
British Cycle and Motor Cycle Manufacturers and Traders	1910
London Oil and Tallow Trades Association Ltd.	1910
Incorporated Association of Kinematograph Manufacturers Ltd.	1911
National Paint Federation	1911
National Federation of Bedding and Allied Trades	1912
British Engineers Association Inc.	1912
British Paper and Board Makers Association Inc.	1912
Federation of Leather Belting Manufacturers of the United Kingdom	1912
Gunmakers Association Ltd.	1912
Periodical Proprietors Association Ltd.	1913
Music Publishers Association Ltd.	1915
Society of British Aircraft Constructors Ltd.	1916
Scientific Instrument Manufacturers Association of Great Britain	1916
British Chemical Ware Manufacturers Association Ltd.	1916

Name	Date
Association of British Chemical Manufacturers	1916
Incorporated National Association of British and Irish Millers Ltd.	1917
British Lampblown Scientific Glassware Manufacturers Association	1917
Lancashire Mechanical Cloth Manufacturers Association Ltd.	1917
British Photographic Manufacturers Association Ltd.	1918
Associated Brass and Copper Manufacturers of Great Britain Ltd.	1918
Asbestos Association Ltd.	1918
Ladies' and Children's Clothing (Manchester) Manufacturers Association Ltd.	1918
Worsted Spinners Federation Ltd.	1918
Canvas Goods and Made-up Textiles Association Ltd.	1919
Light Clothing and Allied Trades Association	1919
British Cotton Waste Association Ltd.	1919
Fire Extinguisher Trades Association	1919
Association of British Roofing Felt Manufacturers Ltd.	1919
Surgical Instrument Manufacturers Association Inc.	1919
Machine Tool Trades Association Inc.	1919
Electric Lamp Manufacturers Association of Great Britain Ltd.	1919
Fertilizer Manufacturers Association Ltd.	1919
National Sulphuric Acid Association Ltd.	1919
British Glacé Kid Tanners Association Ltd.	1919
Association of Musical Instrument Industries Ltd.	1919
Employers Federation of Cane and Willow Workers Associations	1919
Cocoa, Chocolate and Confectionery Alliance	1919
Federation of Bone Users and Allied Trades	1919
British Sugar Refiners Association	1919
British Electrical Development Association Inc.	1920
British Silk Spinners Association Ltd.	1920
British Sulphate of Ammonia Federation Ltd.	1920
London Association of Scale and Weighing Machine Manufacturers	1920
Federation of Gelatine and Glue Manufacturers Inc. Ltd.	1921
Waste Trade Federation	1921
National Federation of Merchant Tailors Inc.	1922
British Laboratory Ware Association Ltd.	1922
United Kingdom Glycerine Producers Association	1923
Asphalt Roads Association Ltd.	1924
National Leather Goods and Saddlery Manufacturers	1924
British Sulphate of Copper Association	1924
Foundry Trades Equipment and Supplies Association	1925
British Wire Netting Manufacturers Association	1925
Food Manufacturers Federation Inc.	1925
British Mantle Manufacturers Association Limited	1925

Name	Date
Federation of British Manufacturers of Sports and Games Ltd.	1926
Office Appliance and Business Equipment Trades Association	1927
National Jewellers Association	1927
Reinforcement Manufacturers Association Ltd.	1928
National Federation of Clay Industries	1928
Road Emulsion Association Ltd.	1928
National Lubricating Oil and Grease Federation	1928
Greeting Card and Calendar Association	1929
Low Temperature Coal Distillers Association of Great Britain Ltd.	1930
Furnishing Fabrics Manufacturers Association Ltd.	1932
British China Clay Producers Federation Ltd.	1932
National Association of Goldsmiths of Great Britain and Ireland	1932
British Metal Window Association Ltd.	1933
Copper Development Association	1933
National Association of Master Asphalters Ltd.	1933
British Plastics Federation	1933
Association of Nameplate Manufacturers Ltd.	1934
British Oil Burner Manufacturers Association	1934
Timber Development Association Ltd.	1934
Bakery Equipment Manufacturers Society	1934
Electric Vehicle Association of Great Britain	1934
Patent Glazing Manufacturers Association Ltd.	1934
Association of British Manufacturers of Printer's Machinery Ltd.	1935
Cement and Concrete Association	1935
Creosote Producers Association Ltd.	1936
Sand Lime Brick Manufacturers Association	1936
Electro-Medical Trade Association Ltd.	1936
Insulation Building and Hardboard Association	1937
Knitting Pin Association Ltd.	1937
Lace Curtain Dyers and Finishers Association Ltd.	1937
Steel Window Manufacturers Association Ltd.	1938
British Chemical Plant Manufacturers Association	1938
South of England Hat Manufacturers Federation Ltd.	1938
Film Strippers Association Ltd.	1938
Oilskin Manufacturers Association of Great Britain Ltd.	1938
Silk and Rayon Users Association Inc.	1939
Association of Animal Gut Cleaners	1940
Association of British Organic Fertilizers Ltd.	1940
Branded Knitting Wool Association Ltd.	1940
Association of Manufacturing Builders Ltd.	1940
Timber Building Manufacturers Association of Great Britain Ltd.	1940
Diamond Manufacturers Association Ltd.	1941

Name	Date
British Ball Clay Producers Federation Ltd.	1941
Cake and Biscuit Alliance Ltd.	1941
English Joinery Manufacturers Association Inc.	1941
Mechanical and Hydraulic Leather Manufacturers Association	1941
Cast Iron Heating Boiler and Radiator Manufacturers Association Ltd.	1941
Incorporated Society of London Fashion Designers	1942
British Tarpaviers Federation	1942
Proprietary Association of Great Britain	1942
Gauge and Toolmakers Association Ltd.	1942
National Hosiery Manufacturers Federation	1942
Range Boilermakers Association Ltd.	1943
Joint Board of British Coney Fur Industries Ltd.	1943
Mica Trade Association	1943
Horticultural Fertilizer Association Ltd.	1943
British Rainwear Manufacturers Federation	1943
Telecommunication Engineering and Manufacturing Association	1943
School Furniture Manufacturers Association Ltd.	1943
Paint Manufacturers and Allied Trades Association	1943
Artificial Flower Manufacturers Association of Great Britain Ltd.	1944
Fan Manufacturers Association Ltd.	1944
Ice Cream Alliance Ltd.	1944
British Toy Manufacturers Association Ltd.	1944
Gold Lace and Embroiderers Association Ltd.	1944
Association of British Veneer Manufacturers Ltd.	1944
Building Board Manufacturers Association of Great Britain	1945
Wholesale Ice Cream Federation	1945
Hearing Aid Manufacturers Association	1945
Radio Industry Council	1945
British Internal Combustion Engine Manufacturers Association	1945
Toilet Preparations Federation Ltd.	1945
Society of British Paint Manufacturers Ltd.	1945
Aluminium Development Association	1945
Dairy Engineers Association	1945
Dairy Appliance Manufacturers and Distributors Association	1945
Association of Flax Processors of Great Britain Ltd.	1946
United Kingdom Fellmongers Association	1946
Lead Development Association	1946
British Clock and Watch Manufacturers Association	1946
Federation of British Rubber and Allied Manufacturers Association	1946
Hairdressing Manufacturers and Wholesalers Association Ltd.	1946
Federation of Home and Export Tobacco Manufacturers Ltd.	1947
Reinforced Concrete Association	1947

Name	*Date*
Sheet Metal Industries Association Ltd.	1947
Tyre Manufacturers Conference Ltd.	1947
Gemmological Association of Great Britain	1947
National Association of Tyre Specialists Ltd.	1947
Association of Specialised Film Producers	1947
Foamed Slag Producers Federation Ltd.	1947
Flush Door Manufacturers Association Ltd.	1947
Superphosphate Manufacturers Association	1948
Raw Fat Melters Association of Great Britain	1948
British Door Association Ltd.	1948
United Kingdom Jute Goods Association Ltd.	1948
Light Clothing Federation Ltd.	1948
London Millinery Manufacturers Association Ltd.	1949
British Power Press Manufacturers Association	1949
London Model House Group Ltd.	1949
Glass Textile Association Ltd.	1950
Food Machinery Association	1950
Film Strip Publishers Association Ltd.	1950
British Pressure Cooker Manufacturers Association	1951
Association of Non-brewed Condiment Manufacturers	1951
Council of British Manufacturers of Petroleum Equipment	1951
National Association of Soft Drinks Manufacturers Ltd.	1951
Leather Cloth and Coated Fabrics Manufacturers Association	1952
National Hardware Alliance	1953
National Caravan Council Ltd.	1953
Fibre Building Board Development Organisation Ltd.	1953
Association of Vermiculite Exfoliators Ltd.	1954
Motor Accessories Manufacturers Association Ltd.	1955

APPENDIX C

MANUFACTURERS' ASSOCIATIONS REGISTERED AS TRADE UNIONS

Register No.		*Date of registration*
1200 T	Notts Lace and Net Dressers Association	1900
1435 T	Master Ladies' Tailors Organisation	1909
1483 T	Electrotyping and Stereotyping Employers Federation	1911
1618 T	Midland Counties Lace Manufacturers Association	1915
1624 T	Lace Machine Builders and Allied Trade Association	1916
1639 T	Federation of Master Process Engravers	1916
1642 T	Federation of Lace and Embroidery Employers Association	1916
1718 T	Hosiery Needle Makers and Allied Trades Association	1919
1766 T	National Association of Master Monumental Masons	1920
1907 T	British Typewriter Manufacturers Association	1926
1947 T	National Brassfoundry Association	1928
1993 T	Typewriter (and Allied) Trades Federation of Great Britain and Ireland	1933
1994 T	Radio and Electronic Component Manufacturers Federation	1933
1996 T	Apparel and Fashion Industry's Association	1933
2016 T	National Association of Restaurant Engineers	1935
2033 T	Master Sign Makers Association	1937
2059 T	British Cast Concrete Federation	1939
2065 T	National Association of Crankshaft and Cylinder Grinders	1940
2077 T	Light Clothing Contractors Association	1942
2083 T	National Association of Manufacturers of Leather Board	1942
2090 T	Hair Net Finishers and Exporters Association	1943
2101 T	Chemists Federation of Manufacturers, Wholesalers and Retailers of Medical and Pharmaceutical Products	1945
2105 T	Association of British Plain Net Finishers	1945

(A number of local associations, e.g. of packing case makers, have been excluded.)

APPENDIX D

MANUFACTURERS' ASSOCIATIONS WHICH APPEAR IN THE REGISTER OF FRIENDLY SOCIETIES AS CERTIFICATED TRADE UNIONS

	Date of certificate
British Motor Trade Association	1914
Cable Makers Association	1916
Wagon Repairing Association	1917
National Federated Electrical Association	1918
Gold, Silver, Electro-Plate and Allied Trades Manufacturers Federation	1919
Carrier Tricycle Association	1919
Association of British Dental Traders	1924
British Radio Valve Manufacturers Association	1926
Tobacco Trade Association	1931
United Kingdom White Lead Convention	1932
British Colour Makers Association	1932
Joint Council of the Federated Photographic Manufacturers and the Photographic Dealers Association	1932
Cement Makers Federation	1935
Music Trades Association	1935
Paint Materials Trade Association	1936
Stock Brick Manufacturers Association	1938
Publishers Association	1938
Electrical Fair Trading Council	1939
Federation of British Lace Curtain and Curtain Net Manufacturers	1939
Associated Paving Manufacturers	1939
Cycle Trade Union	1942
National Association of Putty Manufacturers	1945
Electrical Sign Manufacturers Association	1946
Ship and Boat Builders National Federation	1947
Grocery Proprietary Articles Council	1947
Wholesale Memorial Manufacturers Association	1948
Electric Light Fittings Association	1948
Association of Manufacturers of Electric Wiring Accessories	1951
Association of Manufacturers of Small Switch and Fuse Gear	1952

APPENDIX E

THE ACTIVITIES OF A SMALL ASSOCIATION

Six month's diary of main activities of a small industrial association (1953). Most of the examples mentioned in the report are taken from the work of large associations. The diary illustrates the contribution made by associations serving smaller industries. This association shares the services of its secretary with a larger organisation.

January

i. Discussions between Secretary and F.B.I. on arrangements by which the association would write the text of a monograph to be published by the F.B.I.

ii. The Secretary attended a meeting of five related associations to discuss German competition. It was decided to conduct an investigation into German wages and costs in the industry on the basis of information which it was hoped could be obtained from the Control Commission in Germany.

iii. A meeting was held of interested members to make arrangements for a display to be held at the Heriot-Watt College in Edinburgh in conjunction with a course of lectures on industrial efficiency.

iv. Members were consulted by letter about criticisms of alleged shortages and excessive delivery periods which the Chairman of the South Western Regional Board of Industry had made to the F.B.I. The F.B.I. was subsequently briefed and answered the criticisms.

v. The Ministry of Supply requested the association to provide quarterly information on price changes. Members were consulted by letter as a result of which it was agreed that the association could not comply with the Ministry's request. The Ministry was advised accordingly but given the names of individual members who might be prepared to supply such information.

February

i. Meeting of committee at which the above points were reported or discussed. Also discussed were the report of the Productivity Team on Heavy Chemicals and the future of the B.I.F. The latter had been raised at a meeting of the F.B.I.'s Grand Council, which a representative of the association attends every month.

ii. At the association's suggestion, the Ministry of Fuel and Power in Glasgow convened a meeting of the Scottish representatives of members to finalise arrangements for the exhibition of machinery to be held in Edinburgh.

iii. At the request of the President of the Midlands Section of the Institute of Fuel arrangements were made by post for a number of members to co-operate in a display of the industry's products to be held at the Technical College, Stoke-on-Trent.

iv. The president wrote to the presidents of four other associations giving the association's views on the B.I.F. in relation to this industry's exhibition.

v. Representations were made to the organisers of the industry's exhibition in relation to a publicity handout.

vi. Final details were worked out in conjunction with other interested associations for a visit to this country of an O.E.E.C. team representing the European oil industry.

vii. The secretary had discussions with the F.B.I. on the financing of the proposed monograph.

viii. An article was written for a special Canadian edition of *Machinery Lloyd*. Photographs were collected from a number of members to illustrate this.

ix. Information about the industry was supplied to an American publication.

March

i. A general meeting of members was held at which a number of the above subjects were discussed. Also discussed were the possibility of a joint stand at the exhibition, export incentive schemes, an application for membership, the publicity which had been given to the annual luncheon, an exhibition to be held in Paris, the million-pound loan to industry for fuel economy apparatus and the balloting of Coronation seats.

ii. The Handbook Drafting Committee met. Following this the Secretary was engaged in many telephone conversations and much correspondence with all members and also in discussions with the agents who had been made responsible for the layout of the handbook. This activity went on until the publication of the handbook.

iii. The chairman and secretary had an interview with a technical writer in relation to the monograph.

iv. The association co-operated with *Scope* on a long illustrated article.

v. The secretary had an interview with a member of the staff of the *Financial Times* in relation to an article.

vi. The display of the industry's machinery in Edinburgh was held. The views of participating members on this display were exchanged.

vii. The association nominated new representatives to three B.S.I. committees.

April

i. A meeting of the committee was held at which a number of the above topics were discussed. Also discussed were a recent correspondence in *The Times*, the possibility of further representations to the Ministry of Fuel and Power on a matter affecting the industry, the desirable period between successive exhibitions and participation in an exhibition at Manchester.

ii. The president wrote a letter on behalf of the association to the Editor of *The Times* in connection with the correspondence. Information on this subject was also supplied to a technical journal.

iii. The chairman and secretary of the association attended a meeting of the Organising Committee of the exhibition.

iv. The display of certain products of the industry was held at Stoke-on-Trent.

v. The organisers of the exhibition at Manchester were approached on behalf of the association.

vi. A special meeting of a section of the association was held mainly in order to discuss the recent correspondence.

May

i. A general meeting of members was held at which a number of the above subjects were discussed. Also discussed were policies governing future exhibitions, the future of the British Industries Fair, various applications for membership and duty-free imports of machinery.

ii. The secretary made representations to the F.B.I. to ensure that the association's views were taken account of in the comments which the F.B.I. were submitting to the government committee considering the duty-free import of machinery.

iii. A distribution list for the 1953 Handbook was agreed upon and worked out.

iv. The chairman of the association wrote a short message to appear in the *Financial Times*.

v. A lunch was held with representatives of the B.B.C. to discuss the possibilities of members providing suitable news for use in the overseas departments of the B.B.C. Members were subsequently informed of the kind of information which the B.B.C. representatives agreed they could use.

vi. A working party of three was appointed to make a critical examination of all aspects of the next exhibition.

vii. Discussions were held with the large users with a view to seeing in what additional ways the association could support the Research Association.

June

i. A committee meeting was held at which a number of the above subjects were discussed. Also discussed was the government million-pound loan for certain types of machinery.

ii. A letter was sent to the Minister of Fuel and Power on the question of the inclusion of the industry's products within the terms of the loan.

iii. An illustrated article on the industry was written for the *F.B.I. Review*.

iv. The Ministry of Fuel and Power extended the terms of the million-pound loan to include products of the industry among other equipment.

v. The association supplied information to two technical journals.

vi. The industry's exhibition opened at Olympia.

INDEX

Major references are given in bold type

Z